Cassell's
Businessman's Travel Guide

Cassell's Businessman's Travel Guide

to the world's top trading countries

Dan Hillman

CASSELL
LONDON

CASSELL LTD.
35 Red Lion Square, London WC1R 4SG
and at Sydney, Auckland, Toronto, Johannesburg,
an affiliate of
Macmillan Publishing Co., Inc.,
New York.

First published 1978

Maps prepared by Gemini News Service Ltd.

ISBN 0 304 29906 5

Filmset in Great Britain by
Northumberland Press Ltd.,
Gateshead, Tyne and Wear.
Printed by The Camelot Press Ltd.,
Southampton

Preface

Facts should not need explanation but in a book of this nature a few notes about the way they have been set out might prove helpful. In this expanded version, even fewer explanations are necessary.

The general pattern of the book is:

Area and population
Area is given in both square kilometres and square miles. The airports named in this section are the country's main international arrival points and the ones most likely to be used by arriving businessmen.

Climate
Temperatures are given in both Centigrade and Fahrenheit. Clothing for various seasons of the year is recommended.

People
This comprises the population's basic ethnic background, plus the main religions and the distribution of population.

Language
I have included a rating indicating to what degree local businessmen and hotel staff speak English, the language that continues to gain ground as the travellers' universal tongue.

Economic background
This is a brief analysis of the country's economy.

Trade
Gross National Product figures are the latest available from the International Monetary Fund just before publication of this book. Other trade information, such as exports, imports and chief trading partners, has been culled from a number of official sources.

Currency
Rates of exchange are those prevailing at mid-1978.

Travel, Vaccination
In planning this book, I considered dispensing with these sections on the grounds that visa and health requirements change frequently. I decided on inclusion because a rough guide was better than none. I urge readers to check current regulations with an airline or travel agent before departure.

Airlines
The Airlines given in this section are the principal carriers flying to the main destination of each country. Since airlines discontinue and add routes, check before booking your ticket. The fares listed are for *one-way* first class (F) and economy (Y) tickets to the main destination (or destinations) of each country that prevailed as from 1 April, 1978. Since many cheaper fares are becoming available, it is best to consult a reputable travel agent.

Duty-free allowances
This is another section in which regulations are subject to change. Latest information is always available from airlines.

Embassies
This section includes High Commissions and Consulates where appropriate.

Hotels
For each country I have tried to list the main five- and four-star hotels of the kind that businessmen tend to use. This is not to say there are not other, equally good hotels. I have included, too, a rough indication of the price of a room per night.

National holidays
Perhaps the most common trap for even experienced travellers, national holidays are extremely difficult to pinpoint for many countries of the world. Moslem holidays, particularly, vary each year, depending often on the sighting of the moon. The traveller's rule is simple: check before departure.

Communications
I have given the cost of a telephone and telex call, as well as a cable, and the length of time it takes for an airmail letter to travel to London. While I realise that many users of this book will not be British, the information provided should give a rough guide to the costs involved in communicating with other countries.

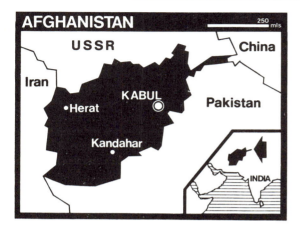

AFGHANISTAN

USSR China

Iran

•Herat

KABUL

Pakistan

Kandahar

INDIA

Area and population
657,500 sq kms (250,000 sq mls). Pop. 17 million.
Capital: Kabul (500,000).
Chief cities: Kandahar (116,000), Herat (62,000),
Jalalabad (45,000). *Airport:* Khwaja Rawash (Kabul).

Climate
Varies with altitude. Temperatures in Kabul range from
−31°C (−24°F) in Jan to 36°C (97°F) in July. Average
is −3°C (26°F) in Jan and 24°C (76°F) in July.
Clothing: As the above indicates, dress for the time of
year. A raincoat and overshoes are needed in the
spring.

People
50% Pathans, with Tadzhik, Uzbek, Hazorah and
nomadic minorities. *Religion:* Moslem.
Distribution: 15% urban.

Languages
Pushtu and Dari. *English rating:* Good.

Economic background
By far the most important economic factors are
agriculture and animal husbandry. The chief crop is
wheat (the Afghans' staple food), followed by barley,
rice, maize, vegetables, cotton, tobacco, sugar, fruits
and nuts. Natural gas is exported to the USSR, and coal
is mined. Industry is also just beginning; chiefly cotton
textiles, cement, vegetable oil, woollen and artificial silk
textiles, and fertilisers.

Trade
Gross National Product: 77,831 million afghanis.
Exports: 10,000 million afghanis, chiefly fresh fruit,
hides and skins, wool, carpets, cotton, oil seeds.
Imports: 12,000 million afghanis, chiefly tea, petroleum,
woollen fabrics, vehicles, medicines, pharmaceuticals,
cotton fabrics, machinery. *Chief trading partners:* USSR,
Japan, China, USA, W. Germany, UK.
Inflation rate: Not available.

Prospects
Development is continuing under a seven-year plan
ending Apr 1983. The government encourages overseas
investment.

Currency
Afghani = 100 puls. £ = 73 afghanis; $ = 45 afghanis

Travel
Visas required.

Vaccinations
Smallpox, cholera.

Airlines
Iran Air, Ariana, Aeroflot.
Flying times: Copenhagen $12\frac{1}{2}$ hrs; London 15 hrs;
New York 24 hrs; Sydney 12 hrs. *Fares:* Copenhagen
F Dkr5,730 Y Dkr3,595; London F £441.50 Y £277;
New York F $1,347 Y $826; Sydney F A$1,073 Y A$760.
Airport to city: 16 kms (10 mls). *Taxi fare:* 180 afghanis.

Duty-free allowances
Reasonable quantities of tobacco products and alcoholic
beverages for personal use.

Local time
GMT $+4\frac{1}{2}$ hrs.

Embassy phone numbers
Kabul: UK 30511.

Hotels
Kabul: Kabul, Metropole, Spinzar, Inter-Continental.
Prices up to about 2,000 afghanis per night.

International banks
None.

Credit cards
American Express, Diners Club.

Afghanistan

Office hours
08.00–12.00 and 13.00–16.00 Sat–Wed,
08.00–13.00 Thurs.

National holidays
All Moslem holidays, plus 27 May, 17–19 July,
31 Aug, 9 Sept, 15, 24 Oct.

Voltage
220 volts 50 cycles single phase.

Communications
Tel: 930 afghanis per 3 mins. *Telex:* Has only just
been introduced. *Airmail:* 7 days. *Cable:* 36 afghanis
per word.

Social customs
Afghani businessmen have become Westernised in
recent years, but Moslem susceptibilities should be
respected. The visitor will meet a great deal of
courtesy and kindness, and there is much exchanging
of business cards.

Algeria

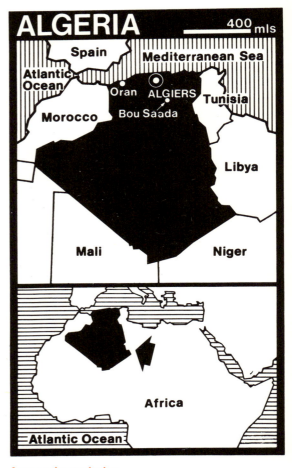

Area and population
2,293,100 sq kms (922,000 sq mls). Pop. 17 million.
Capital: Algiers (2 million).
Chief cities: Oran (440,000), Constantine (280,000),
Annaba (formerly Bône) (180,000),
Sidi-Bel-Abbès (105,000). *Ports:* Algiers, Oran.
Airport: Dar-el-Beida (Algiers).

Climate
Temperate. Algiers temperatures rise to 32°C (90°F),
with average 72% humidity. Summer (June–Sept)
very hot. Sahara temperatures reach 43°C (110°F).
Clothing: Lightweight suits in summer, European-weight
clothes in winter.

People
Arab-Berber stock, with a European population now
reduced to 60,000. *Religion:* Moslem.
Distribution: 38% urban.

Language
Arabic, but French still used commercially.
English rating: Poor.

Economic background
Algeria's economy is now dominated by Saharan oil and natural gas, which is paying for the country's industrialisation, with particular emphasis on iron and steel, chemicals and fertilisers. With the departure of 1 million Europeans when Algeria became independent in 1962, the government established a socialist economy. Mines and farms were nationalised, but some industrial companies were allowed to continue in partnership with Algerian state enterprises.

Trade
Gross National Product: 48,335 million dinars.
Exports: 17,803 million dinars, chiefly oil and gas, food, beverages and tobacco, raw materials, semi-finished goods, finished goods.
Imports: 16,821 million dinars, chiefly finished goods, semi-finished goods, machinery, food, chemicals, iron and steel, textiles, transport equipment, electrical machinery. *Chief trading partners:* France, W. Germany, USA, Italy, Spain, Belgium/Luxembourg, UK, Brazil.
Inflation rate: Not available.

Prospects
At the end of its second four-year development plan, Algeria planned continued industrialisation, putting more emphasis on infrastructure. Future projects include plans to produce tractors, diesel engines, agricultural tools and machinery, public works equipment, machine tools, motor cycles, cars and trucks.

Currency
Dinar = 100 centimes. £ = 7.59 dinars; $ = 3.94 dinars.

Travel
Visas not required by visitors from most of Europe, Africa or Arab countries. Visitors should ensure that their passport bears no evidence of visits to Israel.

Vaccinations
None, but smallpox vaccination recommended. Yellow fever and cholera certificates required if arriving from Asia.

Airlines
British Caledonian, Air Algérie, Air France, Sabena.
Flying times: Copenhagen 6¼ hrs; London 3 hrs; New York 11 hrs; Sydney 24 hrs. *Fares:* Copenhagen F Dkr2,590 Y Dkr1,960; London F £135 Y £100; New York F $787 Y $389; Sydney F A$1,425 Y A$912.
Airport to city: 24 kms (15 mls). *Taxi fare:* 50 dinars.

Duty-free allowances
200 cigarettes *or* 50 cigars *or* tobacco equivalent; 1 bottle of spirits and 2 bottles of wine.

Local time
GMT +1 hr (+2 hrs in summer).

Embassy phone numbers
Algiers: UK 60.56.01.

Hotels
Algiers: Expensive—prices up to 350 dinars per night. They include El-Aurassi, Alotti, Suisse, St George, Albert, Ziri.

International banks
None.

Credit cards
None.

Office hours
Variable. State enterprises 08.00–12.00 and 14.30–18.00 Sat–Wed, 08.00–12.00 Thurs.

National holidays
All Moslem holidays, plus 1 Jan, 1 May, 19 June, 5 July, 1 Nov.

Voltage
127 volts AC.

Communications
Tel: 15.30 dinars per 3 mins. *Telex:* 5.40 dinars per 3 mins.
Airmail: 4 days. *Cable:* 1.20 dinars per word.

Social customs
Most entertaining is done in hotels and restaurants; wives usually stay at home. Drinking alcohol is not forbidden.

Language
Spanish. *English rating:* Good.

Economic background
One of the most highly developed countries in Latin America, Argentina acknowledges that political instability has resulted in lack of full economic progress. Political discontent continues and there is still no clear economic policy. While goods for industrial purposes are allowed to be imported, Argentina prohibits the import of cars and luxury items.

Trade
Gross National Product: 364,600 million pesos.
Exports: US$3,000 million, chiefly vegetable products, live animals and skins, animal and vegetable oils, chemicals, machinery. *Imports:* US$4,000 million, chiefly machinery, base metals, chemicals, minerals, paper, transport equipment, vegetable products. *Chief trading partners:* USA, Japan, W. Germany, Brazil, Italy, Chile, France, UK, Bolivia, USSR, Netherlands, Mexico. *Inflation rate:* 172.9%.

Prospects
Not dazzling, largely because of political uncertainty and general lack of business confidence exacerbated by kidnappings of foreign businessmen, which have led to the withdrawal of some overseas companies.

Currency
Peso = 100 centavos. £ = 1,500 pesos; $ = 797.87 pesos.

Travel
No visas required if stay lasts no longer than 90 days.

Vaccinations
Smallpox.

Airlines
Aerolineas Argentinas, Air France, Braniff, British Caledonian, El Al, Iberia, KLM, Lufthansa, Pan Am, Sabena, Swissair, TWA.
Flying times: Copenhagen 18½ hrs; London 18 hrs; New York 12 hrs; Sydney 24 hrs. *Fares:* Copenhagen F Dkr9,320 Y Dkr6,210; London F £721.50 Y £424.50; New York F $876 Y $565; Sydney F A$1,368 Y A$915. *Airport to city:* 50 kms (31.5 mls). *Taxi fare:* 125 pesos (seat in shared limousine).

Area and population
2,777,815 sq kms (1,072,000 sq mls). Pop. 25 million.
Capital: Buenos Aires (10 million).
Chief cities: Rosario (800,000), Cordoba (800,000), Bahia Blanca (192,000), Comodoro Rivadavia (100,000), Corrientes (138,000), La Plata (480,000), Mar del Plata (350,000), Mendoza (120,000). *Ports:* Buenos Aires, Bahia Blanca, Rosario. *Airport:* Ezeiza (Buenos Aires).

Climate
Sub-tropical to sub-Antarctic. Maximum summer temperatures in Buenos Aires reach 39°C (95°F), with average 70% humidity. *Clothing:* Lightweight Dec–Mar; overcoats needed June–Aug.

People
97% European stock. *Religion:* 95% Roman Catholic.
Distribution: 75% urban.

Argentina

Duty-free allowances
400 cigarettes; two bottles of alcoholic beverages; personal effects.

Local time
GMT −3 hrs.

Embassy phone numbers
Buenos Aires:

Australia 32.68.41	Sweden 38.30.01
Canada 32.90.81	Switzerland 31.64.91
Denmark 32.69.01	W. Germany 32.94.24
Japan 83.10.31	UK 80.70.70
Netherlands 33.60.66	USA 46.32.11
Norway 32.19.04	

Hotels
Buenos Aires: Sheraton, Plata, Presidente, Claridge, Alvear Palace, Lancaster, Nogaro. Prices from 4,000 to 13,000 pesos per night.

International banks
Bank of London and South America (Lloyds), Royal Bank of Canada, First National City Bank of New York, First National City Bank of Boston.

Credit cards
American Express, Diners Club.

Office hours
09.00–19.00 Mon–Fri. In summer some offices close for a month.

National holidays
1, 6 Jan, Maundy Thursday, Good Friday, 1, 25 May, 20 June, 9 July, 17 Aug, 1 Nov, 8, 25 Dec.

Voltage
220 volts AC.

Communications
Tel: 4,986 pesos per 3 mins. *Telex:* 3,741 pesos per 3 mins. *Airmail:* 3–5 days. *Cable:* 305 pesos per word.

Social customs
Rather more formality in business dealings than is common in Europe. If you are dining with Argentinians expect to eat late (21.00–22.00).

Australia

Area and population
7,686,854 sq kms (2,967,909 sq mls). Pop. 13.9 million.
Capital: Canberra (200,000).
Chief cities: Sydney (3 million), Melbourne (2.6 m), Brisbane (950,000), Adelaide (852,000), Perth (725,000), Hobart (131,000), Darwin (50,000 before the evacuation that followed the 1974 cyclone).
Ports: Adelaide, Brisbane, Fremantle, Hobart, Melbourne, Newcastle, Perth, Sydney.
Airports: Brisbane, Darwin, Perth, Kingsford Smith (Sydney), International (Melbourne).

Climate
Considerable variation. Summer temperatures (Nov–Mar) often rise above 38°C (100°F) in the main cities. Winter temperatures (June–Aug) are about 12°C (53°F) in Sydney and 10°C (50°F) in Melbourne. Very high humidity in Sydney. *Clothing:* Lightweight, but overcoats in winter.

People
99% European. *Religion:* 35% Anglican, 25% Roman Catholic, 10% Methodist, 9% Presbyterian, 1.5% Baptist. *Distribution:* 84% urban.

Language
English.

Economic background
Behind Australia's prosperity lie vast mineral resources (every major mineral is found on the continent), extensive agriculture, based on cereals, cattle and sheep, and manufacturing industry that is particularly strong in engineering, vehicle construction, chemicals and construction. Badly hit by world recession of 1974,

Australia is recovering slowly and the government is battling against inflation, which in the year to Mar 1975 reached 17.6%. Wood and wheat are the major agricultural contributors to the economy, although there are important amounts of beef, sugar, dairy products, lamb and fruit. Industry has grown substantially since 1945, and there are more than 27,000 manufacturing establishments, employing more than 1.2 million people. New capital expenditure by the manufacturing industry has doubled in the past 10 years. While local industries are protected by tariffs, about 50% of imports enter duty-free. Australia has substantial deposits of iron ore, bauxite, nickel and other non-ferrous metals, coal, natural gas, oil and uranium. Most of the iron ore and coal is exported to Japan. Australia is 70% self-sufficient in oil and is developing its supplies of natural gas.

Trade
Gross National Product: A$53,386 million.
Exports: A$9,555.8 million, chiefly ores, cereals, textile fibres, meat, wool, coal and coke, sugar, machinery, chemicals. *Imports:* A$8,240.3 million, chiefly machinery, transport equipment, textiles, mineral fuels, chemicals. *Chief trading partners:* USA, Japan, UK, W. Germany, New Zealand, Saudi Arabia, Hong Kong, Canada, USSR, China. *Inflation rate:* 8.2%.

Prospects
The government is pursuing policies aimed at restoring consumer and business confidence following the recession.

Currency
Dollar (A$) = 100 cents. £ = A$1.64; $ = A$0.87.

Travel
Visas required.

Vaccinations
Smallpox. Cholera inoculation required by visitors entering via India, Pakistan and South East Asia.

Airlines
Qantas, British Airways, Alitalia, KLM, Thai, Malaysian, Olympic, Singapore, JAT, JAL, UTA, Pan Am, Philippine, Air New Zealand, Garuda, Lufthansa, Canadian Pacific, Air India, Cathay Pacific.
Flying times (to Sydney): Copenhagen $24\frac{1}{2}$ hrs; London 27 hrs; New York 24 hrs.
Fares (to Sydney): Copenhagen F Dkr10,460 Y Dkr6,670; London F £806 Y £514; New York F $2,348 Y $1,446.

Airport to city: Brisbane 6.5 kms (4 mls); Darwin 8 kms (5 mls); Perth 10 kms (6 mls); Sydney 11 kms (6.8 mls); Melbourne 21 kms (13.5 mls).
Taxi fares: Brisbane A$3.50; Melbourne A$8.50; Perth A$4; Sydney A$4.50.

Duty-free allowances
200 cigarettes *or* 50 cigars *or* $\frac{1}{2}$ lb tobacco; 1 litre of spirits *or* 1 litre of wine.

Local time
New South Wales, Victoria, Australian Capital Territory and Tasmania: GMT+11 hrs (+10 hrs Mar–Oct). *South Australia:* GMT+$10\frac{1}{2}$ hrs (+$9\frac{1}{2}$ hrs Mar–Oct). *Queensland:* GMT+10 hrs. *Northern Territory:* GMT+$9\frac{1}{2}$ hrs. *Western Australia:* GMT+8 hrs.

Embassy phone numbers
Sydney:

Canada 27.7565	Sweden 27.3710
Denmark 27.2224	Switzerland 328.7511
Japan 29.6636	W. Germany 338.7733
Netherlands 27.8951	UK 27.7521
Norway 92.6915	USA 241.1031

Melbourne:

Canada 63.8431	Sweden 63.6643
Denmark 62.2593	Switzerland 267.2266
Japan 267.3244	W. Germany 26.1261
Netherlands 26.2511	UK 602.1877
Norway 61.2093	USA 699.2244

Hotels
Adelaide: Australia, Park Royal Motor Inn.
Brisbane: Ansett Gateway Inn, Crest International, Gazebo Terrace, Lennons Plaza. *Canberra:* City Travel Lodge, Rex, Noahs Lakeside International. *Hobart:* Four Seasons Town House Motor, Hadley's, Wrest Point. *Melbourne:* Australia, Beverly Crest, Chateau Commodore, Hilton, Sheraton, Southern Cross, St Kilda, Zebra Motor. *Perth:* Gateway Inn, Highways Town House, Parmelia, Riverside Explorer, Sheraton-Perth, Town House, Transit Inn. *Sydney:* Boulevard, Hilton, Hyde Park Plaza, Menzies, Wentworth.
Outside Sydney centre: Chevron, Hyatt, Sebel Town House.

International banks
Most major banks are represented in Australia. In addition the principal Australian banks are: Australia and New Zealand Banking Group, Bank of Adelaide,

Australia

Bank of New South Wales, Commercial Bank of Australia, Commercial Banking Company of Sydney, Commonwealth Trading Bank of Australia, National Bank of Australasia.

Credit cards
All major credit cards.

Office hours
09.00–17.00 Mon–Fri.

National holidays
1, 2, 30 Jan, Good Friday, Easter Monday, 25 Apr, 25–27 Dec. In addition, state holidays include:
Australian Capital Territory and New South Wales: Canberra Day (set each year), Queen's Birthday (June), Bank Holiday (Aug), Eight Hour Day (Oct).
Victoria: Labour Day (Mar), Queen's Birthday (June), Show Day (Sept), Melbourne Cup Day (Nov).
Queensland: Labour Day (May), Queen's Birthday (June), People's Day RNA Show (Aug).
South Australia: Adelaide Cup Day (May), Queen's Birthday (June), Labour Day (Oct), 28 Dec.
Western Australia: Public Service Holiday (Jan), Labour Day (Mar), Public Service Holiday (Mar *or* Apr), Foundation Day (June), Show Day (Sept), Queen's Birthday (Oct).
Tasmania: Eight Hour Day (Mar), Bank Holiday (Mar), Queen's Birthday (June), Launceston Show (set each year), Hobart Show (set each year), Bank Holiday (Nov).

Voltage
220–250 volts AC 50 cycles.

Communications
Tel: A$9.00 per 3 mins person-to-person.
Telex: A$2.25 per min. *Airmail:* 5–7 days.
Cable: 17 cents per word (7-word minimum).

Social customs
Informality, with much use of Christian names soon after meeting. But for all their ease, Australian businessmen expect punctuality in keeping appointments. There is a great deal of hospitality and friendliness towards visitors. Australian wine and beer are excellent.

Austria

Area and population
83,850 sq kms (32,366 sq mls). Pop. 7.5 million.
Capital: Vienna (Wien) (1.6 million).
Chief cities: Graz (248,000), Linz (208,000), Salzburg (137,000), Innsbruck (121,000), Klagenfurt (84,000), Bregenz (25,700), Wels (47,000).
Airport: Schwechat (Vienna).

Climate
Temperate. Temperatures in Vienna range from 0°C (32°F) in Dec and Jan to 19°C (66.2°F) in July. Snow usually stays from Jan to Mar. *Clothing:* Warm overcoat and heavy footwear needed in winter. Lightweight clothes in summer.

People
South Germanic with Slavic admixtures. *Religion:* Predominantly Roman Catholic.
Distribution: 43% urban.

Language
German. *English rating:* Good.

Economic background
Though only half of its mountainous land is arable, agriculture and a highly developed industry form the base of Austria's economy. Minerals are important, particularly magnesite, of which Austria is the world's largest producer, and iron ore. Industry has grown significantly since the war, particularly iron and steel and aluminium, together with paper production, chemicals and plastics. Considerable government investment in industry has helped.

Trade

Gross National Product: ASch654,500 million.
Exports: ASch130,884 million, chiefly machinery, iron and steel, textiles, chemicals, wood, paper.
Imports: ASch163,376 million, chiefly machinery, transport equipment, textiles, mineral fuels, chemicals.
Chief trading partners: W. Germany, Italy, Switzerland, France, UK, USSR, Netherlands, USA, Iraq, Poland, Sweden, Hungary. *Inflation rate:* 3.8%.

Prospects

Austria's standard of living is rising steadily, and government help for industry and the modernisation of agriculture continues.

Currency

Schilling (ASch) = 100 groschen. £ = ASch28.05;
$ = ASch14.92.

Travel

Visas not required.

Vaccinations

Not required.

Airlines

Austrian, British Airways, El Al, Lufthansa, South African, Air Canada, Qantas, Swissair, SAS, KLM, Air France, Alitalia, Iberia, TWA.
Flying times: Copenhagen $1\frac{3}{4}$ hrs; London 2 hrs; New York $8\frac{1}{2}$ hrs; Sydney 23 hrs. *Fares:* Copenhagen F Dkr1,920 Y Dkr1,300; London F £148.50 Y £99; New York F $765 Y $381; Sydney F A$1,466 Y A$937.
Airport to city: 18 kms (11 mls). *Taxi fare:* ASch250–300.

Duty-free allowances

200 cigarettes *or* 50 cigars *or* 250 grammes of tobacco; 1 litre of spirits, 2 litres of wine.

Local time

GMT+1 hr.

Embassy phone numbers

Vienna:

Australia 52.84.63	Sweden 33.45.43
Canada 63.36.91	Switzerland 72.51.11
Denmark 52.79.04	W. Germany 73.65.11
Japan 63.46.96	UK 73.15.75
Netherlands 24.85.87	USA 34.75.11
Norway 72.58.23	

Hotels

Vienna: Ambassador, Bristol Vienna, Hilton, Imperial, Inter-Continental, Sacher. *Innsbruck:* Europa, Tyrol. *Graz:* Steirerhof. A good-class Vienna hotel charges up to ASch1,050 per night from 1 Jan to 30 Apr and ASch1,250 per night for the rest of the year.

International banks

Apart from international banks, Austrian banks include Creditanstalt-Bankverein, Oesterreichische Länderbank and Schoeller & Co.

Credit cards

All major credit cards.

Office hours

08.00–16.00 or 17.00 Mon–Fri.

National holidays

1, 6 Jan, Easter Monday, 1 May, Ascension Day (May), Whit Monday (May *or* June), Corpus Christi (May *or* June), 15 Aug, 26 Oct, 1 Nov, 8, 25, 26 Dec.

Voltage

220 volts AC.

Communications

Tel: ASch15 per min. *Telex:* Available at hotels.
Airmail: 2–3 days. *Cable:* ASch28.30 for 7-word minimum.

Social customs

Business meetings are likely to be more formal than elsewhere in Europe. The old-world courtesies are given and expected in Austria, including the correct form of address, such as Herr Doktor and Herr Direktor. Hand-shaking at business meetings is frequently performed in order of the importance of those present. If invited home, take flowers or chocolate for the host's wife. *Best buys:* Knitwear, petit-point, leather goods, silverware, jewellery and gaily coloured woollens.

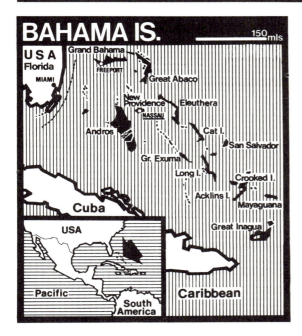

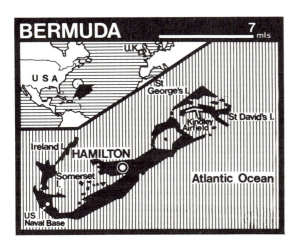

Area and population

Bahamas:
11,406 sq kms (4,404 sq mls). Pop. 168,800.
Capital: Nassau (101,000). *Chief city:* Freeport.
Ports: Freeport, Nassau. *Airports:* International (Nassau),
Freeport.
Bermuda:
53 sq kms (21 sq mls). Pop. 53,000.
Capital: Hamilton (2,000). *Chief city:* St George (1,600).
Port: Hamilton. *Airport:* Kindley Field.

Climate

Bahamas: Winter temperatures (Nov–May) average
21°C (70°F), rising to 29°C (85°F) in summer.
Humidity up to 80%. *Bermuda:* Sub-tropical, with
temperatures ranging from 10°C (50°F) Nov–Apr to
27°C (80°F) Apr–mid Nov. High humidity.
Clothing: Lightweight; warmer clothes for winter in
Bermuda.

People

Bahamas: 85% West Indian, with British and American
minorities. *Religion:* Christian, chiefly Baptist,
Roman Catholic and Anglican.
Bermuda: European and West Indian stock.
Religion: Chiefly Anglican.

Language

English.

Economic background

In both groups of islands—Bahamas comprises
700 islands, of which 22 are inhabited, and Bermuda
comprises 150 islands, of which 20 are inhabited—the
economy is based almost entirely on tourism, although
Bahamas is trying to develop industries such as rum,
cement, oil refining, mining, pharmaceuticals, fishing
and salt. In addition, Nassau has been expanding as
a banking centre. Bermuda, too, is trying to diversify
but because of the islands' size, there are only small
factories.

Trade

Gross National Product: Not available.
Bahamas:
Exports: B$122.7 million, chiefly alcoholic beverages,
building materials, fuel wood, perfumery.
Imports: B$414.6 million, chiefly food, cars, machinery,
electrical appliances, iron and steel, petroleum.
Bermuda:
Exports: BD$718,000, chiefly concentrated essences,
beauty preparations, drugs, medicines.
Imports: BD$154.6 million, chiefly food, clothing,
building materials, transport equipment, fuels, alcoholic
beverages, furniture. *Chief trading partners:* USA, UK,
Canada, France, W. Germany, Japan. *Inflation rate:* 5%.

Prospects

Tourism is likely to be the mainstay of both economies
for some time to come, although Bahamas offers some
prospect of small-scale industry.

Currency

Bahamas: Bahamas dollar (B$) = 100 cents. £ = B$1.88.
Bermuda: Bermuda dollar (BD$) = 100 cents.
£ = BD$1.88. Both dollars on par with US dollar.

Travel

Visas not required.

Vaccinations

Bahamas: Not required unless travelling from an infected area. *Bermuda:* Smallpox.

Airlines

British Airways, Air Canada, Delta, American, Eastern, Lufthansa.
Flying times (to Nassau): Copenhagen $12\frac{1}{4}$ hrs; London $10\frac{1}{2}$ hrs; New York $2\frac{1}{2}$ hrs; Sydney $26\frac{1}{2}$ hrs.
Fares: Copenhagen F Dkr5,080 Y Dkr3,155; London F £380 Y £233.50; New York F $181 Y $121; Sydney F A$1,536 Y A$997.
Airport to city: 16 kms (10 mls). *Taxi fare:* B$7.
Flying times (to Bermuda): Copenhagen $10\frac{3}{4}$ hrs; London $8\frac{1}{2}$ hrs; New York 1 hr; Sydney 25 hrs.
Fares: Copenhagen F Dkr4,665 Y Dkr2,760; London F £340.50 Y £192.50; New York F $143 Y $98; Sydney F A$1,836 Y A$1,168.
Airport to city: 19 kms (12 mls). *Taxi fare:* US$5.

Duty-free allowance

Bahamas: 200 cigarettes *or* 50 cigars *or* 1 lb tobacco; 1 bottle of spirits *or* 1 quart of wine.
Bermuda: 200 cigarettes *or* 100 cigars *or* 1 lb tobacco; 1 quart of spirits and 1 quart of wine.

Local time

Bahamas: GMT−5 hrs. *Bermuda:* GMT−4 hrs.
(Both 1 hr earlier end Apr–end Oct.)

Embassy phone numbers

Bahamas:

Denmark 322.8681	Switzerland 322.8349
Netherlands 2.8210	W. Germany 4.2016
Norway 2.8681	UK 5.7471
Sweden 7.7785	USA 332.1181

Hotels

Bahamas:
Freeport: Bahamas Princess, Princess Tower, Holiday Inn, Oceanus Bay, Oceanus Beach, Xanadu Princess.
Nassau: Anchorage, Sheraton, British Colonial, Ambassador, Balmoral, Beach Inn, Britannia Beach, Holiday Inn, Loews Paradise, Nassau Beach, Ocean Club, South Ocean Beach Hotel.
Bermuda:
Elbow Beach Surf Club, Inverurie, Bermudiana, Princess, Holiday Inn, Sonesta Beach, Southampton Princess, Castle Harbour, Belmont.
Prices vary according to season but in tourist (winter) season US$60–100 per night.

International banks

Local banks plus (in Bahamas) Barclays Bank International, Royal Bank of Canada, Canadian Imperial Bank of Commerce, Chase Manhattan, First National City Bank of New York, Bank of Montreal, Bank of Nova Scotia.

Credit cards

All major credit cards.

Office hours

09.00–17.00 Mon–Fri.

National holidays

Bahamas: 1 Jan, Good Friday, Easter Monday, Whit Monday (May *or* June), Labour Day (June), 10 July, Emancipation Day (Aug), 12 Oct, 25, 26 Dec.
Bermuda: 1 Jan, Good Friday, 24 May, Queen's Birthday (June), Cricket Cup Match (Thursday and Friday before the First Monday in Aug), 11 Nov, 25, 26 Dec.

Voltage

Bahamas: 120–208 volts 3 phase, 4 wire, 60 cycles or 120–240 volts single phase, 3 wire, 60 cycles.
Bermuda: 115 volts for lighting and 115–230 volts for power.

Communications

Bahamas:
Tel: B$15 per mins. *Telex:* B$12 per 3 mins.
Airmail: 3–4 days. *Cables:* 26 cents per word.
Bermuda:
Tel: BD$7.20 per 3 mins. *Airmail:* 3 days.
Cable: 24 cents per word.

Social customs

The constant warm weather makes for a great deal of informality, although it is usual to wear a lightweight suit to business appointments. A conservative and low-key approach to business is recommended.

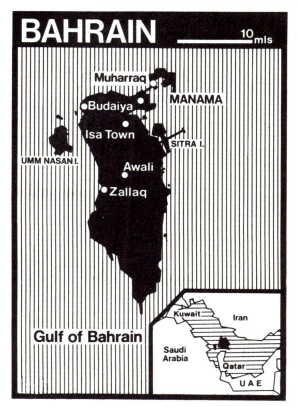

BAHRAIN
10 mls

Muharraq
Budaiya
MANAMA
Isa Town
SITRA I.
UMM NASAN I.
Awali
Zallaq
Gulf of Bahrain

Kuwait
Iran
Saudi Arabia
Qatar
U A E

Area and population
598 sq kms (231 sq mls). Pop. 265,000.
Capital: Manama (97,000).
Chief cities: Muharraq (51,000), Isa Town (35,000), Awali (5,000), Rifaa (10,500). *Port:* Manama.
Airport: Muharraq (Manama).

Climate
With high humidity throughout the year, summer temperatures often exceed 29°C (85°F). Winters are cooler with an average of 21°C (70°F). Only 7.6 cms (3 ins) of rain per year. *Clothing:* Lightweight suits or cotton trousers and shirts for summer, medium-weight for winter.

People
Arabs, with Persian, Indian, Pakistani, Saudi Arabian and Omani minorities, plus 3,000 Europeans.
Religion: Moslem. *Distribution:* Mainly urban.

Language
Arabic. *English rating:* Excellent.

Economic background
Though its economy is based on oil, Bahrain has prepared for the time when oil runs out by encouraging industrial diversification. Agriculture, fishing, shipbuilding and repairing and aluminium smelting are being developed with a great deal of government assistance. Much of Bahrain's income is spent on building up industry and on social services.

Trade
Gross National Product: Not available.
Exports: BD240 million, chiefly crude petroleum and refined oil products, prawns. *Imports:* BD232.9 million, chiefly machinery, electrical machinery, construction equipment, consumer goods. *Chief trading partners:* UK, USA, Japan, China, Australia, Italy, W. Germany, Netherlands, France, Saudi Arabia, Iran, Dubai, Argentina, Qatar. *Inflation rate:* 15.4%.

Prospects
Bahrain's future depends on the success of its industry and the extent to which it becomes a financial centre.

Currency
Bahraini dinar (BD) = 1,000 fils. £ = BD0.731; $ = BD0.387.

Travel
Visas required except by UK citizens.

Vaccinations
Smallpox. Inoculations against yellow fever and cholera required if visitor is arriving from an infected area.

Airlines
British Airways, Gulf Air, Kuwait, Qantas, Singapore, MEA, KLM, UTA, Pan Am, Iraqi, Alia, Saudia.
Flying times: Copenhagen 10 hrs; London $4\frac{1}{4}$ hrs by Concorde, 8 hrs by conventional jet; New York $12\frac{1}{4}$ hrs; Sydney 16 hrs. *Fares:* Copenhagen F Dkr8,130 Y Dkr3,710; London (Concorde) £437.50, (jet) F £380.50 Y £267.50; New York F $1,178 Y $716; Sydney F A$1,003 Y A$664.
Airport to city: 6.5 kms (4 mls). *Taxi Fare:* BD2.500.

Duty-free allowance
400 cigarettes and $\frac{1}{2}$ lb of cigars and tobacco; 2 bottles alcohol for non-Moslems.

Local time
GMT+3 hrs.

Embassy phone numbers
Manama: UK 54002.

Hotels
Hilton, Ramada, Delmon, Moon Plaza, Tylos, Gulf, Middle East, Sahara, Omar Khayyam, Capital, Bristol, Park. Prices up to BD30 per night.

International banks
British Bank of the Middle East, Chartered, Grindlays, Arab Bank, City Bank, Chase Manhattan, Algemene Nederland.

Credit cards
All major credit cards.

Office hours
07.00–13.00 and 14.30–17.00 Sat–Thurs.

National holidays
All Moslem holidays plus 1 Jan, National Day (Dec).

Voltage
230 volts AC.

Communications
Tel: BD3.600 per 3 mins. *Telex:* BD1.430 per min.
Airmail: 3–4 days. *Cable:* 150 fils per word.

Social customs
Moslem customs prevail, although it is possible to drink spirits in the leading international hotels. Most Bahraini businessmen speak English.

Bangladesh

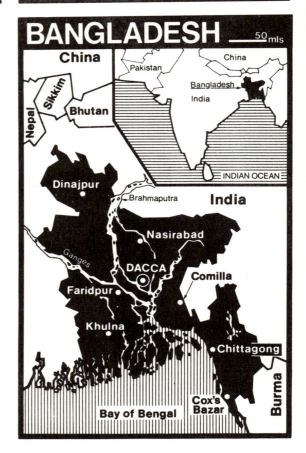

Area and population
142,776 sq kms (55,126 sq mls). Pop. 72 million.
Capital: Dacca (1.3 million).
Chief cities: Chittagong (417,000), Khulna (80,000).
Ports: Chittagong, Chalna. *Airport:* Tezgaon (Dacca).

Climate
Tropical and monsoonal. Temperatures range from 10°C (50°F) in Jan to 40°C (104°F) in Apr.
254 cms (100 ins) rain falls Apr–Oct. Best time to visit is Nov–Mar. *Clothing:* Lightweight throughout the year, but in Nov–Mar woollens are needed. Take an umbrella in the monsoon season (Apr–Oct).

People
Chiefly Bengali. *Religion:* 85% Moslem, 15% Hindu.
Distribution: 10% urban.

Language
Bengali. *English rating:* Excellent.

Economic background

Bangladesh is an agricultural country with a low *per capita* income, depending largely upon sugar-cane, jute, wheat, tea and rice. The manufacturing industry employs only 1% of the labour force. The government is committed to raising living standards and activating the economy through annual development plans, placing emphasis on quick-yielding projects in agriculture and industry.

Trade

Gross National Product: 50,300 million taka (estimated). *Exports:* US$1,096 million, chiefly jute, rice, sugar, wheat, tea, cotton textiles. *Imports:* US$346 million, chiefly machinery and equipment.
Chief trading partners: USA, UK, India, Australia, France, Italy, Japan, W. Germany, Argentina, Belgium. *Inflation rate:* Not available.

Prospects

Dependent upon overseas aid, Bangladesh can only hope to flourish as industry develops; but this is a long-term undertaking.

Currency

Taka = 100 poisha. £ = 27.94 takas; $ = 14.86 takas.

Travel

No visas required.

Vaccinations

Smallpox, typhoid, cholera, yellow fever. Anti-malarial tablets recommended.

Airlines

Air France, British Airways, Bangladesh Biman, Air India, Thai, Aeroflot, Interflug.
Flying times: Copenhagen $15\frac{1}{4}$ hrs; London 12 hrs; New York 14 hrs; Sydney (no direct flights) 16 hrs.
Fares: Copenhagen F Dkr6,775 Y Dkr4,460; London F £522 Y £343.50; New York F $1,502 Y $939; Sydney F A$870 Y A$618.
Airport to city: 7 kms ($4\frac{1}{2}$ mls). *Taxi fare:* 15 takas.

Duty-free allowances

200 cigarettes *or* 50 cigars. 1 bottle of alcoholic beverage.

Local time

GMT+6 hrs.

Embassy phone numbers

Dacca: UK 243251.

Hotels

Dacca: Inter-Continental, Purban. Prices about US$35 per night.

International banks

Grindlays, Chartered, American Express.

Credit cards

American Express, Diners Club.

Office hours

08.00–17.00 Mon–Fri, but times may vary. Shops are open 09.00–21.00 Mon–Wed, 09.00–14.00 Thurs–Sat.

National holidays

All the important Moslem holidays, plus 26 Mar, 7 Nov, 16 Dec.

Voltage

220–240 volts AC.

Communications

Tel: 50 takas per min. *Telex:* 75 takas per 3 mins. *Airmail:* 4 days. *Cable:* 1.36 takas per word (22-word minimum).

Social customs

An intensely religious country, Bangladesh observes all the strict rules of Islam. During the month of Ramadan, people do not eat, drink or smoke in the daylight hours. At other times orthodox Moslems do not eat pork or drink alcohol.

Barbados: see West Indies

them both an importance far beyond their size. Belgium's economic success is also due to two other important factors: diamond cutting and transport services; two-thirds of the world's diamonds are polished and cut in Antwerp. The port is one of the biggest and busiest in the world as well as being one of Europe's main entrepôt ports.

Area and population
30,513 sq kms (11,778 sq mls). Pop. 9.8 million.
Capital: Brussels (Bruxelles) (1 million).
Chief cities: Antwerp (Anvers) (929,000),
Liège (621,000), Charleroi (456,000),
Ghent (Gand, Gent) (478,000), Mons (264,000),
Bruges (Brugge) (251,000),
Ostend (Oostende) (56,000),
Mechelen (Malines) (65,000). *Ports:* Antwerp, Ghent,
Ostend, Zeebrugge. *Airport:* National (Brussels).

Climate
Pleasant with no extremes. Average temperature in summer is 16°C (60°F) and in winter about 5°C (41°F).
Clothing: Lightweight in summer, medium-weight in winter, with overcoat.

People
55% Flemings, 44% Walloons, 1% German.
Religion: Predominantly Roman Catholic.
Distribution: 84% urban.

Languages
French and Flemish. *English rating:* Excellent.

Economic background
With coal as its only major mineral resource, Belgium has developed into one of the most industrialised nations of Europe, relying on manufacturing and trading rather than agriculture for its revenue. Manufacturing, particularly steel, metal-working and chemicals, is the backbone of the economy. The refining of oil has become important, too, in the post-war years. Belgium formed an economic union with Luxembourg which gives

Trade
Gross National Product: BFrs2,320,000 million.
Exports (together with Luxembourg): BFrs1,264,814 million, chiefly chemicals, textiles, diamonds, iron and steel products, machinery, vehicles, glass, non-ferrous metals. *Imports:* BFrs1,363,470 million, chiefly grains, ores, oil, chemicals, textiles, diamonds, metals, machinery, electrical equipment, vehicles.
Chief trading partners: W. Germany, Netherlands, France, UK, USA, Saudi Arabia, Italy, Zaire, Japan, Sweden, Switzerland, Denmark, Spain. *Inflation rate:* 5.2%.

Prospects
While sensitive to any movement in world trade, the Belgium–Luxembourg Union is confident about future industrial expansion.

Currency
Belgian franc = 100 centimes. £ = BFrs61.20;
$ = BFrs32.55.

Travel
Visas not required.

Vaccinations
Not required.

Airlines
All major international airlines.
Flying times: Copenhagen 2½ hrs; London 1 hr;
New York 8¾ hrs; Sydney 27 hrs. *Fares:* Copenhagen
F Dkr1,520 Y Dkr1,085; London F £62 Y £41.50;
New York F $684 Y $325; Sydney F A$1,466 Y A$937.
Airport to city: 12 kms (7.5 mls). *Taxi fare:* BFrs450.

Duty-free allowances
Visitors living in Europe: 300 cigarettes *or* 75 cigars *or* 400 grammes of tobacco; 1.5 litres of spirits, 3 litres of wine. *Visitors living outside Europe:* 400 cigarettes *or* 100 cigars *or* 500 grammes of tobacco; 1.5 litres of spirits, 3 litres of wine.

Local time
GMT+1 hr (+2 hrs Apr–Sept).

Belgium

Embassy phone numbers
Brussels:

Australia 13.41.46	Sweden 649.21.58
Canada 513.79.40	Switzerland 511.80.11
Denmark 684.25.25	W. Germany 770.58.30
Japan 513.63.68	UK 219.11.65
Netherlands 511.39.60	USA 513.38.30
Norway 736.20.45	

Hotels
Brussels: Astoria, Atlanta, Bedford, Diplomat, Hilton, Lendi, Macdonald, Metropole, Plaza, President Centre, Ramada, Royal Windsor, Sheraton. *Antwerp:* De Keyser, Empire, Theater, Waldorf. Prices up to BFrs2,000 per night.

International banks
Most international banks are represented.

Credit cards
All major credit cards.

Office hours
08.30 or 09.00–12.00 or 12.30 and 14.00 or 14.30–17.30 or 18.00 Mon–Fri.

National holidays
1 Jan, Easter Monday, 1 May, Ascension Day (May), Whit Monday (May *or* June), 21 July, 15 Aug, 1, 11, 15 Nov, 25, 26 Dec.

Voltage
220 volts AC.

Communications
Tel: BFrs5 per 48-sec unit. *Telex:* BFrs14 per min. *Airmail:* 1–2 days. *Cable:* BFrs150 plus BFrs6 per word.

Social customs
A conservative, bustling atmosphere prevails in Belgian business, but relationships are usually easy to make and maintain. Business lunches rather than dinners are favoured, and invitations home are common. Always send flowers to the hostess, preferably prior to arrival. Although it has become the unofficial capital of Europe as headquarters of the European Economic Community, Brussels has maintained its provincial atmosphere. Its restaurants, however, are among the finest in the world and, taking into account the quality of their food, among the cheapest. *Best buy:* Lace.

Bermuda: see Bahamas and Bermuda

Bolivia

Area and population
1,098,851 sq kms (424,165 sq mls). Pop. 5.6 million. *Capitals:* La Paz (800,000) and Sucre (85,000). *Chief cities:* Cochabamba (150,000), Santa Cruz (131,000), Oruro (120,000), Potosi (97,000), Trinidad (23,000). *Airport:* El Alto (La Paz).

Climate
Tropical. Average temperature 25°C (77°F), with little variation. Wet season in La Paz lasts Dec–Feb, with rain every day. *Clothing:* Medium-weight clothes; overcoat needed in winter (May–Aug), raincoat and umbrella for summer visit.

People
63% Amerindian, 22% mixed origin, 15% European. *Religion:* Roman Catholic. *Distribution:* 35% urban.

Language
Spanish. *English rating:* Fair.

Economic background
Tin and other minerals, and now oil and gas, are Bolivia's main sources of revenue, although the government is pushing ahead with limited industrialisation. Tin is particularly significant, providing half of Bolivia's exports. Agriculture is based on

cotton, coffee, sugar, rice, beef cattle and sheep. Bolivia has immense forest reserves, but its poor communications preclude the development of a big export business. In manufacturing, Bolivia's main sectors are textiles, drinks and food processing.

Trade
Gross National Product: 37,317 million pesos.
Exports: US$338.3 million, chiefly tin, petroleum, tungsten, silver, antimony, copper, lead, zinc, coffee.
Imports: US$203.8 million, chiefly machinery, vehicles, iron and steel, food.
Chief trading partners: USA, Argentina, Japan, W. Germany, Brazil, UK, Chile.
Inflation rate: Not available.

Prospects
As a member of the Latin American Free Trade Association and the Andean Pact, Bolivia is pursuing its development through ambitious schemes involving, among other things, hydro-electricity, cement and sugar.

Currency
Peso ($b) = 100 centavos. £ = $b37.60; $ = $b20.00.

Travel
Visas not required. Most visitors enter on a 90-day tourist card.

Vaccinations
Smallpox. TAB injection recommended.

Airlines
Iberia, Lufthansa, Braniff, LAB, Aerolineas Argentinas.
Flying times: Copenhagen 28 hrs; London 22 hrs; New York 8 hrs; Sydney 24 hrs. *Fares:* Copenhagen F Dkr8,715 Y Dkr5,835; London F £601.50 Y £392.50; New York F $739 Y $477; Sydney F A$1,673 Y A$1,073.
Airport to city: 14 kms (8.5 mls).
Taxi fare: $b20.

Duty-free allowances
200 cigarettes and 50 cigars and 1 lb tobacco; 1 opened bottle of alcoholic beverage.

Local time
GMT−4 hrs.

Embassy phone numbers
La Paz: UK 29404.

Hotels
La Paz: Copacabana, Crillon, Libertador, La Paz, Sucre Palace. Prices range up to $b570 per night.

International banks
Banco do Brasil, Banco de la Nacion Argentina, Banco Popular del Peru, First National City Bank, Bank of America, Bank of Boston.

Credit cards
All major credit cards.

Office hours
09.00–12.00 and 14.00–18.00 Mon–Fri; some firms open 09.00–12.00 Sat.

National holidays
1 Jan, Good Friday, 1 May, Corpus Christi (May *or* June), 16 July (La Paz only), 6 Aug, 12 Oct, 2 Nov, 25 Dec plus other public holidays declared at short notice.

Voltage
110 volts AC and 220 volts.

Communications
Tel: $b437.52 per 3 mins. *Telex:* $b376.25 per 3 mins.
Airmail: 5–7 days. *Cable:* $b22 per word.

Social customs
Mainly European business customs prevail, with a formal exchange of cards and hand-shaking on arrival and departure. Since La Paz is the highest capital in the world, newly arrived visitors are advised to rest for at least half a day; after that, walk slowly. *Best buys:* Llama and alpaca woollen clothes, ponchos, gold and silver.

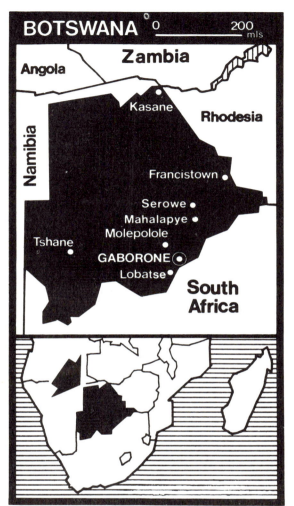

Area and population
575,000 sq kms (222,000 sq mls). Pop. 700,000.
Capital: Gaborone (35,000).
Chief cities: None, but largest towns are Lobatse,
Francistown, Serowe (35,000), Kanye (11,000),
Molepolole (10,000). *Airport:* Gaborone.

Climate
Sub-tropical. Winter (May–Sept) temperatures range
from 21° to 27°C (70° to 80°F), with cold mornings and
evenings. In summer (Oct–Apr) temperatures reach
38°C (100°F) and this is also the rainy season.
Clothing: Lightweight but slightly heavier clothing for
winter mornings and evenings.

People
Tswana, with a minority of Bushmen.
Religion: Christian. *Distribution:* 84% urban.

Language
Setswana. *English rating:* Excellent.

Economic background
A successful beef and diamonds economy has helped
Botswana to develop since it attained independence
from Britain in 1966. Cattle provides a good living for
rural people. Minerals are also a source of wealth, and
diamonds provide much of Botswana's export revenue.
There is little industry and most consumer goods are
imported from South Africa.

Trade
Gross National Product: 100.4 million rand.
Exports and Imports: No figures available.
Inflation rate: Not available.

Currency
Pula = 100 thebes. £ = P1.55; $ = P0.82.

Travel
Visas not required for UK, Commonwealth, European,
South African or US visitors.

Vaccinations
Smallpox.

Airlines
South African Airways, Air Botswana.
Flying times (no direct flights): Copenhagen 20 hrs;
London 13 hrs; New York 19$\frac{1}{4}$ hrs; Sydney 19 hrs.
Fares: Copenhagen F Dkr8,080 Y Dkr5,065; London
F £579.50 Y £356.50; New York F $1,213 Y $802;
Sydney F A$1,030 Y A$788.
Airport to city: 2.5 kms (1.5 mls). *Taxi fare:* P2.

Duty-free allowances
There are no customs barriers between South Africa
and Botswana.

Local time
GMT+2 hrs.

Embassy phone numbers
Gaborone: UK 2483.

Botswana

Hotels
Gaborone: President, Gaborone, Holiday Inn. Prices up to P15 per night.

International banks
Barclays Bank International, Standard Bank.

Credit cards
All major credit cards.

Office hours
Oct–Apr: 07.30–12.45 and 14.00–16.30.
Apr–Oct: 08.00–13.00 and 14.15–17.00.

National holidays
1 Jan, Good Friday, Easter Monday, Ascension Day (May), Whit Monday (May *or* June), 31 May, 10, 11 July, 30 Sept, 24 Oct, 25, 26 Dec.

Voltage
240 volts.

Communications
Tel: 2.40 rand per min. *Telex:* 2.38 rand per min.
Airmail: 4–7 days. *Cable:* 18 cents per word (7-word minimum).

Social customs
None of significance. Water outside the main towns should be boiled, and in the northern wildlife parks malaria is prevalent.

Brazil

Area and population
8,511,960 sq kms (3,286,000 sq mls). Pop. 110 million.
Capital: Brasilia (800,000).
Chief cities: Rio de Janeiro (4 million),
São Paulo (5.5 m), Pôrto Alegre (1.5 m), Recife (2 m),
Belem (600,000), Salvador (1.2 m),
Belo Horizonte (1.5 m). *Ports:* Rio de Janeiro, Santos,
Recife. *Airports:* Galeo (Rio), Viracopos (São Paulo),
Guararapes (Recife).

Climate
Varies from the humidity of the Amazon to the temperate conditions in the south. Rio temperatures range from 13°C (56°F) to 36°C (96°F). Average humidity 85%. *Clothing:* Tropical to lightweight; avoid nylon. Sunglasses essential.

People
62% European, mainly Portuguese stock, 11% Negro, 26% mixed origin. *Religion:* 90% Roman Catholic. *Distribution:* 57% urban.

Language
Portuguese. *English rating:* Fair.

Economic background
Biggest and industrially most advanced nation in Latin America, Brazil is plagued by inflation in spite of government efforts to combat it. Economic growth has been phenomenal, culminating in 11% growth in 1973. Motor, cement, electrical energy and steel industries registering fastest growth in Latin America, and

Brazil

Brazil

Brazil

Brazil

expansion in all sectors continuing. Even so, Brazil still restricts imports of all but essential items.

Trade
Gross National Product: 477,200 million cruzeiros.
Exports: US$8,655 million, chiefly coffee beans, raw cotton, iron ore, cane-sugar, pine wood, vehicles.
Imports: US$12,169 million, chiefly wheat, crude petroleum, machinery, chemicals, metals.
Chief trading partners: USA, W. Germany, Japan, Saudi Arabia, Iraq, Italy, France, UK, Argentina, Belgium/Luxembourg, Canada. *Inflation rate:* 39.2%.

Prospects
Economy will depend upon Brazil's continuing efforts to hold down inflation. Government is still committed to growth rate of 10% per year.

Currency
Cruzeiro = 100 centavos. £ = 33.94 cruzeiros; $ = 18.05 cruzeiros.

Travel
Visas not usually required provided the visitor holds a valid smallpox vaccination certificate. Special visa required if business activities involve payment in Brazilian currency.

Vaccinations
Smallpox.

Airlines
Air Canada, Air France, El Al, Iberia, British Caledonian, KLM, Pan Am, Sabena, TWA, Varig, Viasa.
Flying times: Copenhagen 14½ hrs; London 12 hrs; New York 9½ hrs; Sydney 24 hrs. *Fares:* Copenhagen F Dkr8,945 Y Dkr5,840; London F £688.50 Y £445; New York F $858 Y $547; Sydney F A$1,849 Y A$1,331.
Airport to city: Rio 20 kms (12.5 mls); São Paulo 96 kms (60 mls). *Taxi fares:* Rio 30 cruzeiros; São Paulo 160 cruzeiros. *Airport tax:* 62 cruzeiros payable on departure.

Duty-free allowances
400 cigarettes *or* 50 cigars *or* ½ lb tobacco; 2 litres spirits, 3 litres wine.

Local time
East Zone (incl. Rio, São Paulo, Brasilia): GMT−3 hrs.
West Zone: GMT−4 hrs.
Far West (Acre): GMT−5 hrs.

Embassy phone numbers
Rio:

Australia 245.3030	Sweden 225.7527
Canada 242.4140	Switzerland 222.1896
Denmark 225.1303	W. Germany 225.7220
Japan 225.7311	UK 225.7252
Netherlands 246.4050	USA 252.8055
Norway 242.9742	

Hotels
Numerous in both Rio de Janeiro and São Paulo. Expect to pay about US$40 per night.

International banks
Bank of London and South America (Lloyds), Royal Bank of Canada, First National City Bank of New York, First National Bank of Boston, Banco Holandes Unido SA.

Credit cards
American Express, Barclaycard, Diners Club.

Office hours
Varied but usually 09.00–18.00 Mon–Fri, with up to 2 hours lunch from 12.00.

National holidays
1 Jan, 20 (Rio only), 25 Jan (São Paulo only), Carnival (usually Feb; can last ten days), Good Friday, 21 Apr, 1 May, Corpus Christi (May *or* June), 7 Sept, 2, 15 Nov, 25, 26 Dec.

Voltage
110 volts AC (Rio and São Paulo); 220-240 volts (Brasilia).

Communications
Tel: 100.28 cruzeiros per 3 mins.
Telex: 200 cruzeiros per 3 mins. *Airmail:* 4–6 days.
Cable: 61.95 cruzeiros per 7 words.

Social customs
Friendly but dynamic society; personal relationships essential in business. Allow plenty of time for appointments and be prepared for much hand-shaking. Everything comes to a halt at Carnival, so avoid this time. Safety excellent. *Best buys:* Wooden ornaments, diamonds.

Area and population

110,912 sq kms (42,818 sq mls). Pop. 8.7 million.
Capital: Sofia (965,000).
Chief cities: Plovdiv (309,000), Varna (251,000),
Bourgas (144,000), Stara Zagora (122,000),
Pleven (107,000), Pernik (87,000). *Ports:* Varna,
Bourgas. *Airport:* Vrajdebna (Sofia).

Climate

Variable. Sofia's winter can be hard, with temperatures
well below freezing in winter and in summer rising to
scorching heat, although a typical summer temperature
is 18°C (65°F).
Clothing: European-weight for most of the year, but
warm clothing, including heavy overcoat and overshoes,
required in winter.

People

80% ethnic Bulgarians, 9% Turks, with other minorities.
Religion: 70% Bulgarian Orthodox, 9% Moslems.
Distribution: 51% urban.

Language Bulgarian. *English rating:* Fair.

Economic background

Industrialisation since the war, backed by rising
agricultural and mining sectors, has led to a good
rate of growth in Bulgaria. Its economy is tied in with
Comecon, the Eastern European trading bloc, so that
industries are developed according to integrated plans.

Trade

Gross National Product: 13,093 million leva.
Exports: 3,200 million leva, chiefly sugar, hoisting and
hauling equipment, clothing, rolling stock, tobacco.
Imports: 3,171 million leva, chiefly ferrous metals,
equipment and material for complete factories, textile raw
material. *Chief trading partners:* USSR, E. Germany,
Poland, Czechoslovakia, Italy, W. Germany, Romania,
Yugoslavia, Switzerland, Hungary, France, UK.
Inflation rate: Not available.

Prospects

With one of the world's highest growth rates, Bulgaria's
development is expected to continue.

Currency

Lev = 100 stotinki. £ = 1.65 leva; $ = 0.87 leva.

Travel

Visas not required.

Vaccinations

Not required unless travelling from an infected area.

Airlines

Balkan, British Airways, Air Algérie, Lufthansa,
Aeroflot, Malev, Austrian, JAT, Swissair, Interflug,
Iraqi, CSA.
Flying times: Copenhagen 4 hrs; London $3\frac{1}{4}$ hrs;
New York $12\frac{1}{2}$ hrs; Sydney 37 hrs. *Fares:* Copenhagen
F Dkr2,840 Y Dkr1,800; London F £239 Y £159;
New York F $900 Y $483; Sydney F A$1,395
Y A$891.
Airport to city: 10 kms (6 mls). *Taxi fare:* 1.40 leva.

Duty-free allowances

200 cigarettes *or* 250 grammes of cigars *or* tobacco;
2 litres of spirits, 3 litres of wine.

Local time

GMT+2 hrs.

Embassy phone numbers

Sofia: UK 885361.

Hotels

Sofia: Balkan, Bulgaria, Hemus, Riga, Sofia,
Moskva Park. Prices up to 27 leva per night.

International banks

None.

Credit cards

All major credit cards.

Bulgaria

Office hours
08.45 or 09.00–12.30 or 13.00 Mon–Fri.

National holidays
1 Jan, 1, 2, 24 May, 9, 10 Sept, 7 Nov.

Voltage
220 volts AC.

Communications
Tel: 3.01 leva per min. *Telex:* 2.91 leva per 3 mins.
Airmail: 4–7 days. *Cable:* 37 stotinki per word.

Social customs
This is a country where a nod means 'NO' and a shake
means 'YES'. There is a fair exchange of hospitality with
officials of the state trading organisations. Bulgarian
wine is excellent.

Burma

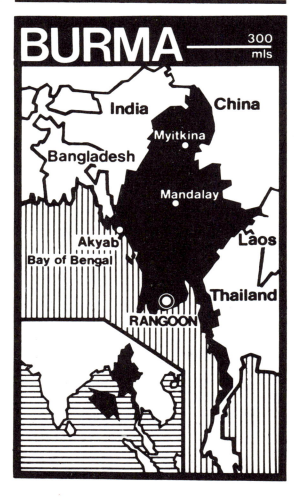

Area and population
678,000 sq kms (261,789 sq mls). Pop. 30.2 million.
Capital: Rangoon (3.2 million).
Chief cities: Mandalay (3.7 m), Moulmein (834,000),
Bassein (822,000), Akyab (1.7 m). *Ports:* Rangoon,
Moulmein, Bassein, Akyab.
Airport: Mingaladon (Rangoon).

Climate
Monsoonal. Rangoon temperatures range from
21°C (70°F) in dry season to 32°C (90°F) in hot season,
with an average humidity of 80%. In Rangoon, expect
heat from mid-Feb to mid-May, rain from mid-May to
mid-Oct, and dry, cooler season from mid-Oct to
mid-Feb. *Clothing:* Tropical-weight clothing throughout
the year.

People
75% Burmese, 11% Karen, 0.6% Shans.
Religion: 85% Buddhist. *Distribution:* 19% urban.

Language
Burmese. *English rating:* Excellent.

Economic background
Burma is a one-party socialist republic in which all
economic activity, including exports and imports,
is controlled by the government. All trade is channelled
through one central organisation, the Myanma
Export/Import Corporation. One of the poorest countries
in South East Asia, Burma has one important crop—rice
—although there are important tonnages of oil seeds,
sugar-cane, cotton, jute and rubber. Foreign investment
is banned and Burma has low foreign-exchange
reserves.

Trade
Gross National Product: 14,852 million kyats.
Exports: US$223,948,000, chiefly rice, teak, metals,
ores, oil cakes. *Imports:* US$293,641,000, chiefly
machinery, transport equipment, base metals,
cotton yarns, cotton fabrics, paper.
Chief trading partners: Japan, China, Indonesia,
W. Germany, Singapore, Bangladesh, France, UK,
Sri Lanka, Malaysia, Hong Kong.
Inflation rate: Not available.

Prospects
Burma is still very dependent upon outside aid, and,
though there are long-term development plans, little
improvement is expected in the economy in the
foreseeable future.

Currency
Kyat = 100 pyas. £ = 12.86 kyats; $ = 6.84 kyats.

Travel
Even tourists need a visa. Business visas are valid
for seven days, and are obtainable from Burmese
embassies and consulates, provided the applicant can
show evidence of business connections with Burma.

Vaccinations
Cholera and smallpox. Occasionally certificates of
vaccination against plague, yellow fever, typhus or
typhoid are required. Best to check before departure.

Airlines
British Airways, Air France, KLM, Aeroflot, Thai.
Flying times: Copenhagen 17 hrs; London 15 hrs;
New York 19 hrs; Sydney 10 hrs. *Fares:* Copenhagen
F Dkr8,000 Y Dkr4,830; London F £616.50 Y £375.50;
New York F $1,612 Y $996; Sydney F A$194
Y A$139.
Airport to city: 19 kms (12 mls). *Taxi fare:* 20–30 kyats.
Bus fare: 7 kyats.

Duty-free allowances
200 cigarettes *or* 50 cigars; 1 quart spirits,
1 quart wine; 1 pint perfume.

Local time
GMT+6½ hrs.

Embassy phone numbers
Rangoon: UK 15700

Hotels
Rangoon: Inya Lake Hotel, Strand, Thamada. Prices
about 50 kyats per night.

International banks
None.

Credit cards
None.

Office hours
09.30–16.00 Mon–Fri, 09.30–12.30 Sat.

National holidays
Movable Buddhist holidays, plus 4 Jan, 12 Feb,
2, 27 Mar, 1 May, 19 July, 25 Dec.

Voltage
230 volts AC 50 cycles.

Communications
Tel: 30 kyats per 3 mins. *Telex:* None. *Airmail:* 7 days.
Cable: 1.50 kyats per word.

Social customs
Shoes should be removed before entering a religious
building. These days Burma seems to mistrust foreigners,
although its people remain cheerful and friendly. All
foreign currency must be declared on an entry form,
which must be handed back on departure.

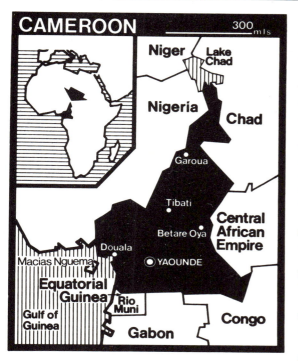

processing of aluminium. The manufacture of consumer goods is based at Douala and Edea. The country is a union of the former East (French) Cameroon and West (British) Cameroon.

Trade
Gross National Product: CFAfrancs 313,800 million. *Exports:* 2,000.7 million French francs (estimated), chiefly coffee, cocoa beans, aluminium, wood, cotton, rubber. *Imports:* 2,000 million French francs (estimated), chiefly vehicles and transport equipment, industrial machinery and other capital goods. *Chief trading partners:* France, USA, W. Germany, Italy, Gabon, UK, Netherlands. *Inflation rate:* 14.4%.

Currency
CFAfranc. £ = CFAfrs421; $ = CFAfrs223.

Travel
Visas required.

Vaccinations
Smallpox, yellow fever, cholera.

Airlines
Air Afrique, Pan Am, Ethiopian, UTA, Swissair, Sabena, Air Zaire.
Flying times: Copenhagen (no direct flights) $10\frac{1}{4}$ hrs; London (no direct flights) $9\frac{1}{4}$ hrs; New York 18 hrs; Sydney 36 hrs. *Fares:* Copenhagen F Dkr6,635 Y Dkr4,690; London F £491.50 Y £342.50; New York F $1,045 Y $653; Sydney F A$1,400 Y A$915.
Airport to city: 4.0 kms (2.5 mls). *Taxi fare:* Approx. CFAfrs500 (some hotels collect passengers at the airport).

Duty-free allowances
200 cigarettes; 1 bottle of spirits.

Local time
GMT+1 hr.

Embassy phone number
Douala: UK 422177.

Hotels
Douala: Akwa Palace, Hotel des Cocotiers. *Yaoundé:* Mont Fébé Palace, Hotel Central. Prices about CFAfrs9,000 per night.

Area and population
470,000 sq kms (183,000 sq mls). Pop. 5.8 million (estimated). *Capital:* Yaoundé (180,000). *Chief cities:* Douala (380,000), Garoua (32,000). *Ports:* Douala, Kribi, Victoria. *Airport:* Douala.

Climate
Tropical. Temperatures in Douala range from 19° to 32°C (67° to 93°F), and in Yaoundé from 17° to 29°C (63° to 88°F). Coolest part of the year is July–Sept. *Clothing:* Lightweight cotton clothes (no nylon), light shoes, sunglasses and raincoat.

People
200 tribal groups, chiefly Bantus, Kirdis, Peuhls. *Religion:* 33% Christian, 15% Moslem, remainder animist. *Distribution:* 13% urban.

Languages
French and English, depending on area.

Economic background
While 80% of the people work in agriculture, Cameroon has fairly extensive industry, based chiefly on the

Cameroon

International banks
Banque Internationale pour l'Afrique Occidentale.

Credit cards
American Express, Diners Club.

Office hours
East Cameroon: 08.00–12.00 and 14.30–17.30 Mon–Fri.
West Cameroon: 08.00–12.00 and 14.00–16.30 Mon–Fri,
08.00–12.00 Sat.

National holidays
Together with some Moslem holidays, 1 Jan, 11 Feb,
Good Friday, Ascension Day (May), 1, 20 May.
1 Oct, 10, 25 Dec.

Voltage
East Cameroon: 110 volts and 220 volts.
West Cameroon: 220 volts.

Communications
Tel: CFAfrs2615 per 3 mins. *Telex:* Limited availability.
Airmail: 4–8 days. *Cable:* CFAfrs164.801 per word.

Social customs
A lot of hand-shaking in the business community,
but no special customs. Since Cameroon is in the
malarial zone, a supply of anti-malarial drugs is
necessary, taking them two weeks before arrival and
continuing two weeks afterwards. Water should be
boiled before drinking, but there is plenty of bottled
water available. Restaurants are good, but expensive.

Canada

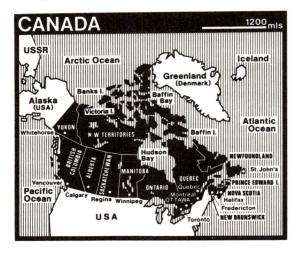

Area and population
9,976,139 sq kms (3,851,809 sq mls). Pop. 23.1 million.
Capital: Ottawa (613,000).
Chief cities: Montreal (2.8 million), Toronto (2.7 m),
Vancouver (1.1 m).
Other cities:
Alberta: Edmonton (543,000) Calgary (457,000).
British Columbia: Victoria (208,000). *Manitoba:*
Winnipeg (590,000). *New Brunswick:* Saint John
(109,000), Fredericton (22,000). *Newfoundland:*
St. John's (133,000). *Nova Scotia:* Halifax (271,000).
Ontario: Hamilton (505,000), Kitchener (232,000),
London (223,000), Sudbury (157,000),
Windsor (262,000). *Prince Edward Island:*
Charlottetown (19,000). *Quebec:* Quebec
City (487,000). *Saskatchewan:* Regina (152,000),
Saskatoon (142,000). *Yukon:* Whitehorse (11,500),
Yellowknife (9,000).
Ports: Churchill, Halifax, Hamilton, Montreal,
New Westminster, Quebec, St John's, Saint John,
Toronto, Vancouver, Victoria, Windsor.
Airports: Municipal (Charlottetown), International
(Edmonton), International (Halifax), Dorval and Mirabel
(Montreal), Quebec City, Municipal (Regina), Saint
John, Tor Bay (St John's), International (Toronto),
International (Winnipeg), International (Vancouver).

Climate
Varied but marked by very cold winters and hot
summers. Areas farthest from open water are the
coldest. Toronto temperatures range from −4°C (24°F)
in Jan to about 22°C (71.6°F) in July, while
Regina temperatures range from −17°C (2°F) to
19°C (67°F). Vancouver experiences a British-type

climate. The lowest temperature ever recorded in Canada was −63°C (−81°F) at Snag, in the Yukon.
Clothing: Lightweight to medium-weight suits, but very warm clothing in winter, including hat and overshoes.

People
44% British, 30% French, 23% other Europeans, 1% Asian, 1% Indian and Eskimo, 1% others.
Religion: 46% Roman Catholic, 20% Church of Canada, 13% Anglicans, 21% Jewish, Greek Orthodox and other faiths. *Distribution:* 76.1% urban.

Languages
English and French.

Economic background
With a *per capita* income of more than $4,000 a year, Canada is the fourth wealthiest nation, after Switzerland, Sweden and the United States, although, like many countries in the West, it has suffered from high inflation. The base of its economy lies in three main sectors: agriculture and forestry, minerals and energy, and manufacturing. Farm income exceeds $5,000 million a year, and Canada exports a similar figure of wood, wood products and paper. As one of the world's largest producers of minerals (crude petroleum, copper, nickel, zinc, iron ore, natural gas and its by-products, asbestos, cement, coal and potash), Canada's exports in these sectors exceeds $7,000 million a year. Manufacturing, to the chagrin of most Canadians, is dominated by the United States, and includes vehicles, pulp and paper production, meat processing, refining, iron and steel, dairy products, machinery, smelting and chemical production.
Up to 70% of Canada's trade is with the United States.

Trade
Gross National Product: $155,000 million.
Exports: $133,103 million, chiefly vehicles, newsprint, ores, pulp, cereals, crude petroleum, iron and steel, dairy products, chemicals. *Imports:* $34,636 million, chiefly vehicles, machinery, steel, crude oil, aircraft, textiles, chemicals. *Chief trading partners:* USA, Japan, UK, Venezuela, W. Germany, Iran, Saudi Arabia, France, Italy, Australia, Netherlands, USSR, Belgium/Luxembourg, China. *Inflation rate:* 8.7%.

Prospects
If inflation and wage demands can be curbed, Canada's prospects are among the brightest in the Western world.

Currency
Dollar = 100 cents. £ = $2.11; $ = $1.12.

Travel
Visas not required.

Vaccinations
Smallpox.

Airlines
All major international airlines. Canada's chief airlines, Air Canada and Canadian Pacific, maintain an excellent internal network, and Canada's cities are also served by USA domestic airlines.
Flying times:
Toronto: Copenhagen 8¼ hrs; London 7¾ hrs; New York 1 hr; Sydney 23 hrs. *Fares:* Copenhagen F Dkr5,105 Y Dkr2,545; London F £394.50 Y £195; New York F $86 Y $54; Sydney F A$2,050 Y A$1,274;
Vancouver: Copenhagen 14 hrs; London 12½ hrs; New York 6 hrs; Sydney 18¼ hrs. *Fares:* Copenhagen F Dkr6,435 Y Dkr3,240; London F £535 Y £253; New York F $314 Y $196; Sydney F A$1,063 Y A$748.
Airport to city: Charlottetown 8 kms (5 mls); Edmonton 28 kms (17.5 mls); Halifax 37 kms (23 mls); Montreal: Dorval 23.3 kms (14.5 mls), Mirabel 53 kms (33 mls); Quebec City 14.5 kms (9 mls); Regina 5 kms (3 mls); Saint John 16 kms (10 mls); St John's 9.5 kms (6 mls); Toronto 29 kms (18 mls); Winnipeg, 6.5 kms (4 mls); Vancouver 15 kms (9 mls).
Taxi fare: Toronto $10–15; Montreal $20–30 (but bus from Mirabel is $5); Vancouver $10–15.

Duty-free allowances
200 cigarettes *or* 50 cigars *or* 2 lb tobacco; 1 quart of spirits *or* 1 quart of wine.

Local time
Six time zones. *Newfoundland:* GMT−3½ hrs. *Atlantic Standard Time:* GMT−4 hrs. *Eastern Standard Time* (incl. Toronto and Montreal): GMT−5 hrs. *Central Standard Time:* GMT−6 hrs. *Mountain Standard Time:* GMT−7 hrs. *Pacific Standard Time* (incl. Vancouver): GMT−8 hrs. (All zones (except Yukon) 1 hr earlier end Apr–end Oct.)

Embassy phone numbers
Toronto:

Australia 367.6783	Sweden 967.7172
Denmark 962.5661	Switzerland 364.3371

Japan 363.7038
Netherlands 364.5443
Norway 487.3635
Vancouver:
Australia 684.1177
Denmark 684.5171
Japan 684.5868
Netherlands 684.6448
Norway 682.2281

W. Germany 925.2813
UK 864.1290
USA 595.1700

Sweden 684.5971
Switzerland 684.2231
W. Germany 684.8377
UK 683.4421
USA 685.4311

Hotels
Calgary: Calgary Inn, Four Seasons, Holiday Inn,
International, Palliser, Sheraton-Summit.
Edmonton: Holiday Inn, Macdonald, Plaza, Château
Lacombe, Edmonton Inn, Riviera Motor.
Halifax: Château Halifax, Nova Scotian.
Montreal: Bonaventure, Holiday Inn, Four Seasons,
Le Château Champlain, Laurentian, Queen Elizabeth,
Ramada, Ritz Carlton, Sheraton Mount Royal, Windsor,
Skyline. *Ottawa:* Château Laurier, Sheraton-El Mirador,
Skyline. *Regina:* Saskatchewan. *Toronto:* Four Seasons,
Sheraton, Inn on the Park, King Edward, Lord Simcoe,
Park Plaza, Prince, Royal York, Sutton Place, Toronto,
Westbury, Hilton Airport, Holiday Inn Airport, Howard
Johnson's Airport, Skyline. *Vancouver:* Ritz
International, Sheraton Landmark, Vancouver, Bayshore
Inn, Holiday Inn. *Winnipeg:* Fort Garry,
Sheraton-Carlton, Winnipeg Inn. Prices for first class
hotels now range from $45 to $50 per night.

International banks
Most major international banks and in addition:
Bank of Montreal, Canadian Imperial Bank of Commerce,
Royal Bank of Canada, Toronto-Dominion Bank,
Banque Canadienne Nationale.

Credit cards
All major credit cards.

Office hours
09.00–17.00, but 08.30–16.30 in British Columbia.

National holidays
1 Jan, Good Friday, Easter Monday, Monday
immediately preceding 24 May, 1 July, First Monday
in Sept, 9 Oct, 11 Nov, 25, 26 Dec. In addition:
Alberta, Manitoba, Saskatchewan, British Columbia:
First Monday in Aug. *Newfoundland:* 13 Mar, 24 Apr,
16 May, 19, 27 June, 10 July. *Nova Scotia:* Natal
Day (July *or* Aug). *New Brunswick:* 1 Aug.
Ontario: First Monday in Aug. *Quebec:* 24 June.

Voltage
110–220, 220, 120–208, 440 and 550 volts, all
60 cycles.

Communications
Tel: From $4.50 per 3 mins. *Telex:* $2.25 per min.
Airmail: 2–3 days. *Cable:* 31 cents per word
(7-word minimum).

Social customs
While there is informality, Canadian businessmen strike
a hard bargain and observe strict compliance with
agreed delivery dates. In general, Canadian society is
pleasant and sociable, and few overseas businessmen
dislike visiting Canada. Hotels and restaurants can be
superb.

Canary Islands

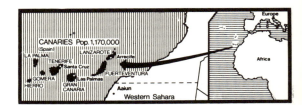

Area and population
7,270 sq kms (2,807 sq mls), comprising 7 islands,
the chief of which are Grand Canary (Gran Canaria)
and Tenerife. Pop. 1.1 million.
Capital: Las Palmas (355,000), on Grand Canary.
Chief city: Santa Cruz (250,000), on Tenerife.
Ports: Las Palmas, Santa Cruz.
Airports: Gando (Grand Canary), Los Rodeos (Tenerife).

Climate
Warm and dry. Annual mean temperature between
19° and 24°C (66° to 76°F) the year round.
Clothing: Lightweight.

People
Mostly European (Spanish stock).
Religion: Roman Catholic.

Language
Spanish. *English rating:* Excellent.

Economic background

As sources of revenue, the Canary Islands depend on tomatoes, potatoes and other agricultural produce, the diminishing trade in ship provisions, and (increasingly important) tourism. Recently times have been hard. The islands report an unemployment rate of 12%, a population growth rate of 2.5% and a *per capita* income 20% less than mainland Spain. Their prospects depend very much on the policies that have yet to emerge from Madrid.

Trade

No figures available separate from those of Spain.

Currency

Spanish peseta (Pta) = 100 centimos. £ = Ptas145.80; $ = Ptas77.55.

Travel

Visas not required.

Vaccinations

Not required.

Airlines

Iberia, British Caledonian, Lufthansa, Royal Air Maroc, TAP, Air France, South African Airways.
Flying times: Copenhagen $8\frac{1}{2}$ hrs; London 6 hrs; New York $12\frac{1}{2}$ hrs; Sydney 27 hrs. *Fares:* Copenhagen F Dkr3,080 Y Dkr2,440; London F £195 Y £148; New York F $684 Y $325; Sydney F A$1,473 Y A$940.
Airport to city: Las Palmas 20 kms (12.5 mls); Santa Cruz 13 kms (8 mls). *Bus fares:* Las Palmas Ptas30; Santa Cruz Ptas25.

Duty-free allowances

Reasonable amounts. Passengers' baggage is not usually subjected to Customs inspection. Spirits and tobacco are cheap in the Canaries.

Local time

GMT(+1 hr Apr–Sept).

Embassy phone numbers

Las Palmas: UK 26.25.08.

Hotels

Las Palmas: Cristina, Reina Isabel, Santa Catalina.
Tenerife: San Felipe, Semiramis Tenerife. About Ptas1300 per night.

International banks

Spanish banks.

Credit cards

All major credit cards.

Office hours

Nov–Apr: 08.30–13.30 and 14.30–16.30 Mon–Fri, 09.30–12.30 Sat. *May–Oct:* 08.30–13.30 Mon–Fri, 09.30–12.30 Sat.

National holidays

1, 6 Jan, 7–8 Feb (Tenerife only), 19 Mar, Maundy Thursday, Good Friday, 29 Apr (Las Palmas only), 1, 3 May (Tenerife only), Ascension Day (May), Corpus Christi (May *or* June), 29 June, 18, 25 July, 15 Aug, 8 Sept (Las Palmas only), 14 Sept (Tenerife only), 12 Oct, 1 Nov, 8, 25 Dec.

Voltage

110–125 volts AC but in modern hotels 220 volts AC.

Communications

Same as Spain.

Social customs

Much the same as in Spain. Canary businessmen usually take their holidays in the summer months. Business visitors to the Canaries in winter should take into account that most hotels are packed with holiday-makers.

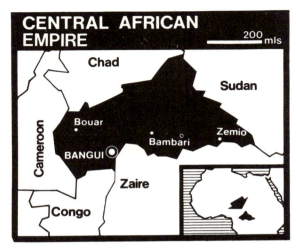

CENTRAL AFRICAN EMPIRE

200 mls

Chad

Sudan

Cameroon

Bouar

Zemio

Bambari

BANGUI

Zaire

Congo

Trade

Gross National Product: 57,100 million CFAfrancs (1971).
Exports: 180 million French francs (estimated), chiefly cotton and coffee. *Imports:* 182 million French francs (estimated), chiefly machinery and electrical equipment, textiles, mineral products, vehicles, industrial chemicals, pharmaceuticals, metals. *Chief trading partners:* France, W. Germany, USA, Italy, Netherlands, UK, Israel. *Inflation rate:* Not available.

Prospects

One of the poorest countries in the world, with little hope at present for development.

Currency

CFAfranc. £ = CFAfrs421; $ = CFAfrs223.

Travel

Visas required.

Vaccinations

Smallpox, yellow fever, cholera.

Airlines

UTA, Air Afrique, Aeroflot.
Flying times (no direct flights): Copenhagen 14½ hrs; London 11 hrs; New York 20 hrs; Sydney 36 hrs.
Fares: Copenhagen F Dkr6,510 Y Dkr4,960; London F £488.50 Y £363.50; New York F $1,080 Y $684; Sydney F A$1,368 Y A$915.
Airport to city: 4 kms (2.5 mls).
Taxi fare: Approx CFAfrs500.

Duty-free allowances

1,000 cigarettes or 250 cigars or 2 kilos tobacco.

Local time

GMT+1 hr.

Hotels

Bangui: Safari, Rock, Minerva, Palace, St Sylvestre. Prices about CFAfr4,000 per night.

International banks

Banque Nationale de Paris,
Banque Internationale pour l'Afrique Occidentale.

Credit cards

American Express, Diners Club.

Area and population

606,000 sq kms (234,000 sq mls). Pop. 1.6 million.
Capital: Bangui (240,000).
Chief cities: Berberati (38,000), Bossangoa (35,000).
Airport: Bangui.

Climate

Hot, with dry and wet seasons. Mean temperature of 25°C (77°F) in Bangui, rising to 40°C (104°F). Rain falls May–Oct: 1636 mm (64 ins) in Bangui. Average humidity 93%. *Clothing:* Bush shirts and shorts, light cotton dresses.

People

80 ethnic groups, chiefly Banda, Baya, Mandjia plus 6,600 Europeans, mostly French. *Religion:* 60% animist, 35% Christian, 5% Moslem.

Languages

French and Sango.
English rating: Hardly anyone speaks English.

Economic background

Subsistence agriculture maintains most of the Central African Empire's people. Cassava is the staple crop, Europeans grow coffee, providing the country with its meagre foreign earnings, and a few peasants cultivate cotton. Some timber is exported, but there is little industry. A brewery is said to be the largest concern.

Central African Empire

Chile

Office hours

08.00–12.00 and 16.00–19.00 Mon–Sat.

National holidays

1 Jan, 29 Mar, Easter Monday, 1, 14, 25 May,
Ascension Day (May), Whit Monday (May *or* June),
13, 15 Aug, 1, 10 Nov, 1, 25 Dec.

Voltage

220–380 volts 50 cycles.

Communications

Tel: CFAfr2,625 per 3 mins. *Telex:* CFAfr1,215
per 3 mins. *Airmail:* 4–7 days. *Cable:* CFAfr160
per word.

Social customs

While the Central African Empire is one of the poorest
nations of the world, its cost of living for foreigners
is one of the highest. All food, except fruit and
vegetables, is imported. Businesses are run by
expatriate French and Portuguese. Anti-malarial
precautions are essential and the water should be boiled.

Area and population

741,768 sq kms (286,377 sq mls). Pop. 10.5 million.
Capital: Santiago (4 million).
Chief cities: Valparaiso and Vina del Mar
(combined pop. of 500,000), Concepcion (700,000),
Antofagasta (200,000), Arica (100,000),
Iquique (50,000), Temuco (110,000),
Ports: Antofagasta, Arica, Iquique, Valparaiso.
Airport: Pudahuel (Santiago).

Climate

Every climate and landscape. Santiago and
Valparaiso temperatures average 28°C (82°F) in Jan
and 10°C (50°F) in July. Days are hot, nights cool.
Rainy season in Santiago: May–Aug.
Clothing: Lightweight (Dec–Mar). Businessmen should
be conservatively dressed. Warm top clothes are needed
for rest of the year.

People

70% Spanish-Indian, 30% European, chiefly Spanish.
Religion: Roman Catholic. *Distribution:* 74% urban.

Language

Spanish. *English rating:* Good.

Economic background

Chile is a developing country, traditionally relying on outside sources, mostly from the USA, for economic support. An unhappy political and economic situation followed the overthrow and death of the left-wing President Allende in 1973, but the military government has reduced customs duties and liberalised import lists. Chile, whose prosperity relies on the world price of copper (up to 80% of the country's earnings), plans to develop industry and encourage foreign investment. One of the government's main aims is to fight inflation, which reached 340% in 1975.

Trade

Gross National Product: US$8,751.1 million.
Exports: US$2,480 million, chiefly copper, industrial products, iron ore, nitrates, agricultural and fishing products. *Imports:* US$2,000 million, chiefly raw materials, transport equipment, plant and machinery, consumer goods. *Chief trading partners:* USA, Argentina, W. Germany, Australia, Brazil, Ecuador, UK, France, Japan, Netherlands, Canada, Belgium/Luxembourg, Italy. *Inflation rate:* 47.5%.

Prospects

The government is making efforts to stabilise Chile's economic situation. Political uncertainties, however, prevail.

Currency

Peso ($) = 100 centavos. £ = $60.51; $ = $32.18. (rate fluctuates daily).

Travel

No visas required but visitors need tourist cards, available on landing.

Vaccinations

Smallpox.

Airlines

British Caledonian, Braniff, Iberia, SAS, Lufthansa, KLM, Sabena, Swissair, Air France, LAN.
Flying times: Copenhagen 24¾ hrs; London 17 hrs; New York 12 hrs; Sydney 36 hrs.

Fares: Copenhagen F Dkr9,975 Y Dkr6,900; London F £776 Y £531.50; New York: F $825 Y $532; Sydney F A$1,968 Y A$1,456.
Airport to city: 21 kms (13 mls). *Taxi fare:* US$10.

Duty-free allowances

400 cigarettes and 25 large cigars and 500 grammes tobacco; 2.5 litres of spirits.

Local time

GMT−4 hrs (−3 hrs mid-Oct–mid-Mar).

Embassy phone numbers

Santiago: UK 239166.

Hotels

Santiago: Carrera-Sheraton, El Conquistador, Crillon, Panamericano, Sheraton San Cristobal, Tupahue. Rates change because of fluctuating value of the peso: best hotels the equivalent of about US$20 per night.

International banks

None.

Credit cards

All major credit cards.

Office hours

08.30–12.30 and 14.00–18.00 Mon–Fri, 08.30–12.30 Sat.

National holidays

1 Jan, Good Friday, Easter Monday, 1, 21 May, 15 Aug, 18, 19 Sept, 12 Oct, 1 Nov, 8, 25 Dec.

Voltage

220–380 volts AC.

Communications

Tel: $149.50 per min. *Telex:* $37.20 per min. *Airmail:* 3–4 days. *Cable:* $10.20 per word (7-word minimum).

Social customs

Chile retains Spanish business customs. Visitors will find that lunch is now taken at 13.00 since the government has banned the two- to three-hour lunch break, and dinner is also late—never earlier than 20.30 and sometimes as late as 22.30. All imported goods are expensive. Imported spirits are prohibitively expensive, but the local gin is good.

CHINA

500 mls

USSR

Mongolia

PEKING

N. Korea
S. Korea

Japan

Tientsin

Nanking

Shanghai

Chungking

Foochow

Nepal Bhutan

Canton

India Pakistan

Burma

Pacific Ocean

Laos

Thailand

Philippines

Kampuchea

Vietnam

Indian Ocean

Area and population
9,759,000 sq kms (3,768,000 sq mls). Pop. 800 million.
Capital: Peking (7 million).
Chief cities: Shanghai (11 m), Tientsin (4 m),
Shenyang (3.5 m), Nanking (2.5 m), Wuhan (3.5 m),
Chungking (3 m), Canton (3.5 m), Harbin (2.5 m).
Ports: Hsinkang, Shanghai, Tsingtao.
Airports: Capital (Peking), Hung-chiao (Shanghai),
Paiyun (Canton).

Climate
Varies according to area. Peking has a mean Jan
temperature of −4°C (24.8°F) but this rises in
midsummer to 26°C (78.8°F). South China,
including Canton, has temperatures of above
15.6°C (60°F) the year round. *Clothing:* Lightweight
for summer, but warm clothing needed for winter in
Peking. Locally-made hats with ear flaps are cheap.

People
94% Han, 6% Uigur, Hui, Yi, Tibetan and other
minorities. *Religion:* Confucianism,
Buddhism, Taosim. *Distribution:* 20% urban.

Language
Chinese (most common is the Northern Chinese
dialect). *English rating:* Fair.

Economic background
Even though it has been growing rapidly since 1950,
China is still in the early stages of industrial

development. Agriculture is still by far the most
important sector, providing a livelihood for the majority
of its people. Crops include rice, tung, oil, wheat,
tobacco, soya beans, peanuts and cotton. Industry is
developing quickly in some sectors, such as engineering
and nuclear science—and China aims to achieve an
independent and relatively complete industrial and
economic system by 1980 and a modern economy by
the year 2000. Its mineral resources are among the
richest in the world but are still not fully developed.

Trade
Gross National Product: US$223,000 million.
Exports: US$6,750 million, chiefly manufactured goods,
such as textile yarn, oil seeds, nuts, hides and
minerals. *Imports:* US$7,130 million, chiefly
manufactured goods, iron and steel, machinery and
equipment, chemicals and fertilisers.
Chief trading partners: Japan, W. Germany, France,
Canada, Australia, USA, UK, Italy, Netherlands, USSR,
Hong Kong, Malaysia. *Inflation rate:* Not available.

Prospects
China is committed to agricultural improvements and,
in industry, to oil exploration, port development, mining,
power generation, iron and steel, telecommunications,
electronics, and land and air communications.

Currency
Renminbi (yuan) = 100 fen (cents). £ = RMB3.22;
$ = RMB1.71.

Travel
Visas required.

Vaccinations
Smallpox, cholera.

Airlines
Air France (to Peking), Swissair (to Peking and
Shanghai), CAAC (the Chinese airline), PIA, Iran Air,
Aeroflot, JAL, Ethiopian. Visitors can also fly to
Hong Kong and go by train to Canton.
Flying times: Copenhagen 16 hrs; London (via Geneva)
20 hrs; New York 28 hrs; Sydney 12 hrs.
Fares: Copenhagen F Dkr9,365 Y Dkr5,210;
London F £722 Y £423.50; New York F $1,626
Y $957; Sydney F A$1,404 Y A$988.
Airport to city: Peking 26 kms (16 mls); Shanghai
12 kms (7.5 mls). Travel between the airport and hotel
is usually arranged by the visitor's hosts.

China

Duty-free allowances
600 cigarettes; 4 bottles of spirits.

Local time
GMT+8 hrs.

Embassy phone numbers
Peking:

Australia 522381	Norway 521329
Canada 521475	Sweden 521770
Denmark 522431	Switzerland 551914
Japan 522361	W. Germany 522161
Netherlands 521731	UK 521961

Hotels
Peking: Hsin Chiao, Nationalities, Friendship, Peking.
Shanghai: Ching Chiang, International, Peace.
Prices range from RMB50 to 150 per night.

International banks
Bank of China. There are branches of the Hong Kong and
Shanghai Bank and the Chartered Bank in Shanghai.

Credit cards
None.

Office hours
08.00–12.00 and 14.00–18.00 Mon–Sat.

National holidays
1 Jan, Chinese New Year (3 days in Jan *or* Feb),
1 May, 1 Aug, 1 Oct.

Voltage
220 volts AC 50 cycles.

Communications
Tel: RMB9.60 per 3 mins. *Airmail:* 3–6 days.
Cable: RMB1.30 per word (7-word minimum).

Social customs
Western visitors are treated very hospitably and while
business negotiations are long and taxing, the Chinese
are invariably courteous and helpful. Dinners, which start
at about 19.00, are frequent. The Chinese will appreciate
your business card being printed in your own language
and Chinese. *Best buys:* Jade, porcelain.

Colombia

Area and population
1,138,618 sq kms (438,000 sq mls). Pop. 25 million.
Capital: Bogota (3 million).
Major cities: Medellin (1.2 m), Cali (1 m),
Barranquilla (800,000), Bucaramanga (350,000),
Cartagena (375,000). *Ports:* Cartagena,
Barranquilla, Santa Marta, Buenaventura.
Airports: El Dorado (Bogota), Ernesto Cortisso
(Barranquilla), Palmaseca (Cali).

Climate
Bogota's temperatures range from −1°C (30°F) in Jan
to 26°C (79°F) in July.   *Clothing:* Winter clothing is
needed all the year round because of night frosts due to
the city's high altitude. Best time to visit is Dec–Feb.

People
60% mestizos, 20% Europeans, 14% mulattos,
4% Negroes, 2% Amerindians.
Religion: 96% Roman Catholic. *Distribution:* 64% urban.

Language
Spanish. *English rating:* Good.

Economic background

Colombia has the fourth largest population in Latin America, and is a coffee republic whose fortunes rely on current world prices and trends. The country has made efforts in recent years to encourage other industries, notably textiles and mining, and the government has invested heavily in roads, railways, ports, telecommunications and electric power. Trade with neighbouring countries in the so-called Andean Group has boomed, particularly in the export of emeralds, meat, chemical products, metal products, wood and wood products. Nevertheless, economic crises, and their resultant stop-go policies, have prevented the steady growth that Colombian industrialists desire.

Trade

Gross National Product: US$10,000 million.
Exports: $1,500 million, chiefly coffee, cotton, emeralds, petroleum, chemical products, metals, wood.
Imports: $2,000 million, chiefly plant and machinery, electric plant and equipment, metals, foodstuffs, raw materials, plastics and rubber, paper, paperboard. *Chief trading partners:* USA, W. Germany, Japan, Peru, Ecuador, Venezuela, Argentina, France, Canada, Sweden, Mexico, *Inflation rate:* 23.3%.

Prospects

While its burgeoning oil industry will help to insulate Colombia against the world oil crisis, the key to prosperity is the government's success in holding down inflation and pursuing a policy to stimulate the economy.

Currency

Peso = 100 centavos. £ = 73.27 pesos; $ = 38.97 pesos.

Travel

No visas necessary if staying for not more than 30 days.

Vaccinations

Smallpox (yellow fever and cholera if coming from an infected area).

Airlines

British Caledonian, Air France, Braniff, Viasa, Iberia, Avianca, Lufthansa, Pan Am.
Flying times: Copenhagen 17 hrs; London 12 hrs; New York 6 hrs; Sydney 24 hrs.
Fares: Copenhagen F Dkr6,935 Y Dkr4,490; London F £481.50 Y £312.50; New York F $419

Y $297; Sydney F A$2,077 Y A$1,367.
Airport to city: 12 kms (7½ mls). *Taxi fare:* 70 pesos.

Duty-free allowances

200 cigarettes and 50 cigars; 2 bottles of spirits.

Local time

GMT−5 hrs.

Embassy phone numbers

Bogota:

Canada 35.5066	Sweden 55.3777
Denmark 32.6753	Switzerland 45.2933
Japan 32.6918	W. Germany 45.1020
Netherlands 55.5666	UK 69.8100
Norway 81.0580	USA 32.9100

Hotels

Bogota: Bacata, Hilton, Continental, Cordillera, Dann, B I Presidente, Tequendam. Prices are $10–30 per night.

International banks

Bank of London and Montreal, Royal Bank of Canada, First National City, Banque Nationale de Paris.

Credit cards

American Express, Diners Club.

Office hours

Government offices: 08.00–15.00 Mon–Fri.
Banks: 09.00–15.00 Mon–Fri.
Commercial offices: 08.00–12.00 and 14.00–17.30 or 18.00 Mon–Fri. *Shops:* 09.00–12.30 and 14.30–18.30 Mon–Sat.

National holidays

1, 6 Jan, 19 Mar, Maundy Thursday, Good Friday, 1 May, Ascension Day (May), Corpus Christi (May *or* June), 2, 29 June, 20 July, 7, 15 Aug, 12 Oct, 1, 11 Nov, 8, 25 Dec.

Voltage

160 volts AC 60 cycles and, increasingly, 110–160 volts AC.

Communications

Tel: US$14 per 3 mins. *Telex:* Available.
Airmail: 5–6 days. *Cable:* 65 US cents per word.

Social customs

Firstly, beware of pickpockets and thieves. Rest on first day in Bogota—the high altitude can be debilitating. In business, Colombians tend to be conservative and prior appointments are necessary. Dark suits are favoured. *Best buys:* Emeralds and hand-marked silver, plus pottery and textiles.

People's Republic of Congo

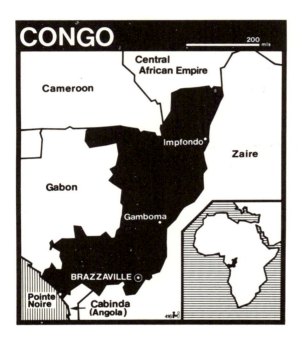

Area and population

342,000 sq kms (132,000 sq mls). Pop. 1,250,000. *Capital:* Brazzaville (310,000). *Chief cities:* Pointe Noire (142,000), Dolisie. *Port:* Pointe Noire. *Airport:* Maya Maya (Brazzaville).

Climate

Hot, humid, equatorial climate. Average temperatures range from 21° to 27°C (70° to 80°F). Humidity up to 96%. Two dry seasons, Jan–Mar and June–Sept. Average 142 cms (56 ins) rain a year. *Clothing:* Lightweight cottons and linens. Jackets and ties not needed for business calls unless calling at government offices.

People

Predominantly Bantus, chiefly Kongos, Tekes, Boutanguis, Gabonais, 10,000 Europeans. *Religion:* 50% animist, 49% Christian, mostly Roman Catholic, 1% Moslem. *Distribution:* 34% urban.

Language

French. *English rating:* Poor.

Economic background

Congo, a former French colony, earns much of its revenue from forest products, which are mostly in the hands of French expatriates. Industry has developed, mainly in Brazzaville and Pointe Noire, but is based primarily on the processing of forestry and agricultural products. For all its problems, Congo maintains a liberal trade policy.

Trade

Gross National Product: US$180 million (estimate). *Exports:* No recent figures available, but chiefly timber, diamonds, copper, fertilisers, textile fibres, metal ores. *Imports:* No recent figures available, but chiefly machinery and transport equipment, iron and steel, beverages, textiles, essential oils. *Chief trading partners:* France, W. Germany, Netherlands, UK. *Inflation rate:* Not available.

Prospects

Outlook remains poor.

Currency

CFAfranc. £ = CFAfrs421; $ = CFAfrs223.

Travel

Visas required.

Vaccinations

Smallpox, yellow fever, cholera.

Airlines

Air Afrique, UTA, Air Algérie. *Flying times:* Copenhagen 17¼ hrs; London 11 hrs; New York 23 hrs; Sydney 36 hrs. *Fares:* Copenhagen F Dkr6,635 Y Dkr4,920; London F £494 Y £363.50; New York F $1,080 Y $684; Sydney F A$1,232 Y A$857. *Airport to city:* 4 kms (2 mls). *Taxi fares:* Approx CFAfrs300.

Congo

Duty-free allowances
50 cigarettes *or* 25 cigars.

Local time
GMT+1 hr.

Embassy phone numbers
None.

Hotels
Relais, Olympic Palace, Petit Logis, Cosmos, Mfoa.
Price at Relais, which is regarded as the best, is about
CFAfrs7,000 per night.

International banks
None.

Credit cards
Diners Club.

Office hours
Variable but generally 08.00–13.00 Mon and Tues,
08.00–12.00 and 14.30–17.30 Wed and Thurs,
08.00–12.00 Sat.

National holidays
1 Jan, Easter Monday, 1 May, Ascension Day (May),
Whit Monday (May *or* June), 22 June, 15 Aug, 1 Nov,
25, 31 Dec.

Voltage
220 volts AC.

Communications
None.

Social customs
French manners prevail in most business circles.
Visitors to Brazzaville should take care not to walk alone
at night. Malaria is still prevalent in Congo and
anti-malarial drugs should be taken a fortnight before
arrival. Avoid uncooked fruit and vegetables, and drink
only boiled water.

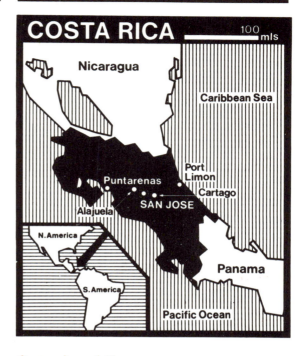

Area and population
50,901 sq kms (19,653 sq mls). Pop. 1.86 million
(estimated).
Capital: San Jose (92,000).
Chief cities: Alajuela (33,600), Puntarenas (30,000),
Cartago. *Ports:* Port Limon, Puntarenas.
Airport: Santamaria International (San Jose).

Climate
Tropical on the coast, temperate in the interior.
Coastal temperatures rise to 35°C (95°F), and to
26°C (79°F) in the interior. San Jose's temperatures
range from 15° to 26°C (59° to 79°F).
Clothing: Lightweight. Raincoat and umbrella are
essential in the rainy season (June–Nov).

People
Predominantly European, largely Spanish stock, with a
European–Indian minority. *Religion:* Roman Catholic.
Distribution: 34% urban.

Language
Spanish. *English rating:* Poor.

Economic background
With a *per capita* income of US$480, the highest in
Central America, Costa Rica lives chiefly on its coffee,

bananas, sugar, rice and beans. With such a small population there is little industry; industry and mining account for only 20% of the gross national product. There is some production of chemicals, including fertilisers, plastics and tyres. Considerable bauxite deposits have been found, and an aluminium smelter is planned.

Trade
Gross National Product: US$1,169.6 million.
Exports: US$344.4 million, chiefly coffee, bananas, meat, chemical products, sugar, manufactured goods and cocoa. *Imports:* US$455.3 million, chiefly chemicals, textiles, yarns, machinery, paper, transport equipment, iron and steel. *Chief trading partners:* USA, Japan, Guatemala, W. Germany, El Salvador, Nicaragua, Venezuela, UK, Italy. *Inflation rate:* Not available.

Currency
Colon = 100 centimés. £ = C16.16; $ = C8.59.

Travel
Visas required.

Vaccinations
Smallpox.

Airlines
Pan Am, LACSA, Iberia. *Flying times:* Copenhagen (no direct flights) $22\frac{1}{4}$ hrs; London (no direct flights) 15 hrs; New York 8 hrs; Sydney 24 hrs.
Fares: Copenhagen F Dkr6,520 Y Dkr4,175; London F £465.50 Y £310; New York F $393 Y $273; Sydney F A$2,063 Y A$1,344.
Airport to city: 18 kms (11 mls). *Taxi fare:* US$5.

Duty-free allowances
$\frac{1}{2}$ kilo of tobacco products; 3 litres of spirits.

Local time
GMT−6 hrs.

Embassy phone numbers
San Jose: UK 21.56.88.

Hotels
San Jose: Europa, Royal Dutch, President, Gran Hotel de Costa Rica, Balmoral, Amstel, Pays Bas. Prices about US$20 per night.

International banks
Bank of America.

Credit cards
American Express, Diners Club.

Office hours
08.00–11.30 and 13.30–17.30 Mon–Fri, 08.00–12.00 Sat.

National holidays
1 Jan, 19 Mar, Maundy Thursday, Good Friday, 1 May, Corpus Christi (May *or* June), 29 June, 25 July, 2, 15 Aug, 15 Sept, 10 Oct, 8, 25, 29–31 Dec.

Voltage
110 volts AC.

Communications
Tel: US$18 per 3 mins. *Telex:* US$4.80 per min. *Airmail:* 4–5 days. *Cable:* US$0.55 per word (7-word minimum).

Social customs
European customs prevail among businessmen in San Jose. Outside the city drinking water should be boiled, and in any event do not eat uncooked food, since intestinal disorders are prevalent.

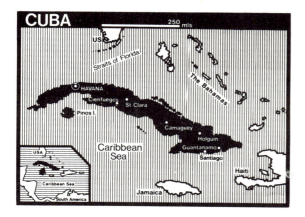

Area and population
114,493 sq kms (44,206 sq mls). Pop. 9.1 million.
Capital: Havana (2 million).
Chief cities: Santiago de Cuba (310,000),
Santa Clara (143,000), Cienfuegos (88,000),
Camaguey (216,000), Matanzas (94,000),
Pinar del Rio (83,000). *Port:* Havana.
Airport: Jose Marti (Havana).

Climate
Sub-tropical. Havana temperatures range from
17°C (63°F) in winter to 30°C (86°F) in summer.
Rainfall in autumn and summer may be 177 cms (70 ins)
in Havana. Humidity up to 95%. *Clothing:* Lightweight.

People
73% European stock, 15% mixed, 12% Negro.
Religion: Roman Catholic. *Distribution:* 60% urban.

Language
Spanish. *English rating:* Fair.

Economic background
Under Fidel Castro, Cuba has developed a communist
economy. All means of production, including farms of
over 67 hectares (160 acres), have been taken over by
the state. The USSR has extended big credits since
1960 and while few statistics have been issued, sugar
still dominates the economy. Other revenue is derived
from sugar by-products, tobacco, meat, nickel and fish.

Trade
Gross National Product: No recent figure available.
Exports: 2,222.2 million pesos, chiefly sugar, ores and
concentrates, molasses, tobacco, cigarettes, cigars.

Imports: 2,225.9 million pesos, chiefly food, chemicals,
pharmaceuticals, iron and steel, machinery, tractors,
fuels, crude petroleum. *Chief trading partners:* USSR,
Japan, W. Germany, Canada, UK, Spain, France,
E. Germany, Bulgaria, Italy, Czechoslovakia.
Inflation rate: Not available.

Prospects
Industrial development has been given a high priority
by the government.

Currency
Peso = 100 centavos. £ = 1.41 pesos; $ = 0.75 pesos.

Travel
Visas required.

Vaccinations
Not required.

Airlines
Iberia, Aeroflot, Air Canada, Interflug.
Flying times (no direct flights): Copenhagen 13 hrs;
London 13 hrs; New York 4 hrs; Sydney 24 hrs.
Fares: Copenhagen F Dkr4,805 Y Dkr3,145;
London F £336.50 Y £210; New York
(via Kingston) Y $248; Sydney F A$1,821 Y A$1,174.
Airport to city: 18 kms (11 mls). *Taxi fare:* 5 pesos.

Duty-free allowances
Articles for personal use are admitted free of duty.

Local time
GMT−5 hrs (−4 hrs end Apr–end Sept).

Embassy phone numbers
Havana: UK 61.5681.

Hotels
Havana: Capri, Riviera, Havana Libre, Nacional.
Prices up to 30 pesos per night.

International banks
None.

Credit cards
None.

Office hours
08.30–12.30 and 13.30–17.30 Mon–Fri,
08.30–12.00 Sat.

Cyprus

National holidays
1 Jan, 1 May, 25–27 July, 10 Oct.

Voltage
110–120 volts or 220–240 volts AC.

Communications
Tel: 5 pesos per min (3-min minimum).
Telex: Not available. *Airmail:* Several weeks.

Social customs
Many goods are scarce or unobtainable in Cuba, so a
visitor should take everything he needs, such as razor
blades, medicine, books and film. On entry visitors are
obliged to convert their foreign currency into pesos and
the transaction is recorded on a yellow form. On
departure, remaining pesos will be reconverted back to
other currencies on production of the form.
Gifts to individuals involved in business transactions are
forbidden and hospitality should not be lavish. Tipping is
prohibited.

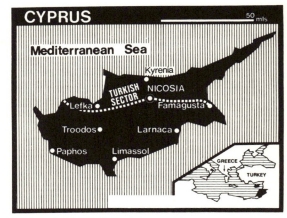

Area and population
9,251 sq kms (3,572 sq mls); 40% of island now under
Turkish control. Pop: 659,000 (estimated).
Capital: Nicosia (110,000).
Chief cities: Limassol (50,000), Larnaca (21,000),
Paphos (11,000); Famagusta (formerly 40,000)
and Kyrenia (4,000) under Turkish control.
Ports: Limassol, Larnaca, Famagusta, Kyrenia.
Airports: Larnaca (for Greek Cyprus),
Ercan (for Turkish Cyprus).

Climate
Mediterranean. Dry and sunny. Average temperatures
18°C (65°F) in winter to 37°C (100°F) or more in
summer. Average humidity 67%.
Clothing: Tropical-weight in summer, lightweight in
winter.

People
78% Greek, 18% Turkish. *Religion:* Greeks practise
Eastern Orthodoxy, Turks Islam. *Distribution:* 40% urban.

Languages
Greek and Turkish. *English rating:* Excellent.

Economic background
Until 1974, when Turkey invaded Cyprus, the economy
was progressing vigorously, and the island was
developing as an industrial and distribution base for the
Middle East. For two years Cyprus's economy suffered
badly but now, thanks to tourism and the resilience
of its people, a much brighter future is forecast.

Trade
Gross National Product: £C298.9 million.
Exports: £C55.8 million, chiefly fruit, vegetables, ores,

wines, iron pyrites, asbestos. *Imports:* £C113.7 million, chiefly manufactured goods, machinery and transport equipment, food, chemicals, fuels, crude materials. *Chief trading partners:* UK, Greece, Turkey, France, W. Germany, Italy, Japan, USA, Syria, Libya, USSR. *Inflation rate:* Not available.

Prospects

While much depends on a political settlement between Greek and Turkish Cypriots, Greek Cyprus is prospering as a result of tourism and industrial entrepreneurism. Turkish Cyprus, heavily subsidised by Turkey, is less fortunate in its recovery, although Turkey is striving to make its area economically viable.

Currency

£C = 1,000 mils. £ = £C0.707; $ = £C0.376. In Turkish Cyprus, the Turkish lira is in circulation at TL36 = £C1.

Travel

No visas required for Greek Cyprus. Entry to Turkish Cyprus by air via Istanbul or, for businessmen and tourists, through UN lines in Nicosia. Applications for entry made in Nicosia are generally granted.

Vaccinations

None, but passengers coming from areas in which smallpox, cholera or yellow fever are prevalent need international certificates. Typhoid vaccination, while not compulsory, is advised.

Airlines

Cyprus Airways, British Airways, Olympic Airways, MEA. The Turkish Airlines fly into Ercan from Istanbul and Ankara.
Flying times: Copenhagen $6\frac{1}{2}$ hrs; London 4 hrs; New York 12 hrs; Sydney 28 hrs.
Fares: Copenhagen F Dkr3,195 Y Dkr2,280; London F £254.50 Y £170; New York F $917 Y $554; Sydney F A$1,162 Y A$768.
Airport to city (Nicosia): 37 kms (23 mls).
Taxi fare: £C5.

Duty-free allowances

200 cigarettes *or* 50 cigars *or* $\frac{1}{2}$ lb tobacco; $\frac{1}{8}$ gallon of spirits and $\frac{1}{8}$ gallon of wine.

Local time

GMT+2 hrs. Local summer time of GMT+3 hrs applied in Turkish Cyprus mid-Mar to mid-Oct, and in Greek Cyprus mid-May to mid-Sept.

Embassy phone numbers

Nicosia: UK 73131–5.

Hotels

Hilton in Nicosia, Amathus Beach or Apollonia Beach in Limassol recommended. All under £C10 per day.

International banks

Barclays Bank International, Chartered, Grindlay Brandts.

Credit cards

All major credit cards.

Office hours

Winter: 08.30–13.00 and 14.30–17.30 Mon–Fri, 08.00–13.00 Sat. *Summer:* 08.00–13.00 and 16.00–18.30 Mon–Fri, 08.00–13.00 Sat.

National holidays

1, 6, 19 Jan, 25 Feb, 25 Mar, Greek Orthodox Easter, 1, 28, 29 Oct, 25, 26 Dec in Greek Cyprus. Turkish Cyprus observes all Moslem holidays.

Voltage

240 volts AC (domestic); 415 volts 3-phase (industrial).

Communications

Tel: 487 mils per mins. *Telex:* 1,125 mils per 3 mins. *Airmail:* 2–3 days. *Cable:* 80 mils per word.

Social customs

Hospitable people, friendly and outgoing, much given to drinking Turkish coffee, now renamed Cyprus coffee in Greek Cyprus. In summer, heat can be tremendous.

Area and population
127,840 sq kms (49,359 sq mls). Pop. 15 million.
Capital: Prague (Praha) (1.1 million).
Chief cities: Brno (360,000), Bratislava (341,000),
Ostrava (301,000), Pilsen (Plzen) (156,000),
Kosice (174,000),
Airport: Ruzyne (Prague).

Climate
Varied. Winter temperatures in Prague range from
0° to 4°C (32° to 39°F), and summer temperatures rise to
19°C (66°F). Rain is frequent. *Clothing:* European, but
warm overcoat and heavy shoes needed in winter.

People
65% Czechs, 30% Slovaks, with Germans, Ukrainian and
Hungarian minorities. *Religion:* 75% Roman Catholic.
Distribution: 60% urban.

Languages
Czech and Slovak. *English rating:* Fair.

Economic background
With one of the most developed economies in Eastern
Europe, Czechoslovakia has advanced agriculture and
industry. Its agriculture is said to be the best in the
Eastern bloc, with a high degree of mechanisation and
the use of fertiliser. Cereals lead in production, although
potatoes and sugar beet are also important crops. Since
the war Czechoslovakia has concentrated on developing
heavy industry, including chemical plant and iron and
steel works, but industries like textiles, clothing, leather,
footwear, glass, ceramics and timber have expanded.
The manufacture of vehicles and building materials is
developing in importance.

Trade
Gross National Product: Kcs384,900 million.
Exports: Kcs46,651 million, chiefly machinery,
transport equipment, iron and steel, chemicals, footwear,
textile yarn, coal, ores, clothing.
Imports: Kcs50,716 million, chiefly machinery, foodstuffs,
manufactures, chemicals, transport equipment,
petroleum. *Chief trading partners:* USSR,
E. and W. Germany, Poland, Hungary, Yugoslavia,
Austria, Romania, UK, Bulgaria.
Inflation rate: Not available.

Prospects
The present five-year plan aims to increase productivity,
particularly in chemicals, engineering, power, textiles and
paper.

Currency
Crown (Kcs) = 100 halers. £ = Kcs17.59; $ = Kcs9.35.
(Tourist rates.)

Travel
Visas required.

Vaccinations
Not required.

Airlines
CSA, British Airways, Pan Am, Air France, JAT, Malev,
Air Canada, Air Algérie, Balkan, Interflug, LOT, Swissair,
Aeroflot, KLM, SAS.
Flying times: Copenhagen 1¼ hrs; London 2 hrs;
New York 9 hrs; Sydney 27 hrs.
Fares: Copenhagen F Dkr1,445 Y Dkr950;
London F £132 Y £88; New York F $756 Y $367;
Sydney F A$1,466 Y A$937.
Airport to city: 17 kms (11 mls). *Taxi fare:* Kcs70–80.

Duty-free allowances
250 cigarettes *or* 20 cigars *or* 50 grammes tobacco;
1 litre of spirits, 2 litres of wine.

Local time
GMT+1 hr.

Embassy phone numbers
Prague:

Denmark 254715	W. Germany 265541
Japan 530713	UK 533347
Switzerland 536772	USA 536641

Czechoslovakia

Hotels

Prague: Interhotel Alcron, Inter-Continental, International, Jalta, Interhotel Parkhotel. Prices up to Kcs540 per night.

International banks

None.

Credit cards

All major credit cards.

Office hours

08.00–16.00 Mon–Fri, although some offices work 06.00–14.00 or 07.00–15.00.

National holidays

1 Jan, Easter Monday, 1, 9 May, 25, 26 Dec.

Voltage

220 volts 50 cycles AC.

Communications

Tel: Kcs51 per 3 mins. *Telex:* Kcs21.60 per 3 mins. *Airmail:* 2–3 days. *Cables:* Kcs3.60 per word (7-word minimum).

Social customs

A relaxed atmosphere for Western visitors, but punctuality is important. Prior appointments are necessary. Czechoslovakians have a good sense of humour and Western visitors are most welcome. *Best buys:* Crystal, porcelain, costume jewellery, antiques and old books.

Denmark

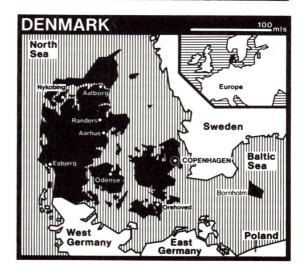

Area and population

43,022 sq kms (16,111 sq mls). Pop. 5 million. *Capital:* Copenhagen (Kobenhavn) (1.2 million). *Chief cities:* Aarhus (245,000), Odense (167,000), Aalborg (154,000), Esbjerg (79,000), Randers (63,000). *Ports:* Aalborg, Aarhus, Copenhagen, Esbjerg, Nykobing, Odense, Orehoved. *Airport:* Kastrup (Copenhagen).

Climate

Relatively mild winters and hot summers. Temperatures in Copenhagen range from −2° to 2.1°C (28.3° to 35.8°F) in Jan and 12° to 20.7°C (53.6° to 69.2°F) in July. *Clothing:* Lightweight in summer, but take a woollen suit or dress and a warm overcoat for winter.

People

Scandinavian. *Religion:* 95% Lutheran. *Distribution:* 45.6% urban.

Language

Danish. *English rating:* Excellent.

Economic background

In spite of limited natural resources, Denmark has built a prosperous economy, with a very large volume of foreign trade. About 70% of its land is given over to agriculture, more than half of it growing cereals. Dairy farming accounts for 8% of gross national product. So well developed is agriculture that Denmark produces enough food to feed not only its own people but 10 million others as well. Mechanisation has been extensive. Danish industry is based on light rather than heavy industries, chiefly metal and engineering, although electronics, chemicals, paper and printing, ship-building, textiles, furniture and cement are also important.

Trade

Gross National Product: US$40,000 million.
Exports: Dkr55,022 million, chiefly machinery and equipment, textiles, agricultural products.
Imports: Dkr74,962 million, chiefly machinery, fuels, chemicals, iron and steel, clothing, vehicles, paper.
Chief trading partners: W. Germany, Sweden, UK, Netherlands, USA, Norway, Belgium/Luxembourg, France, Japan, Italy, Finland, Iran, Switzerland.
Inflation rate: 12.2%.

Prospects

A very high rate of inflation has hurt the economy in recent years, but nevertheless Denmark remains fundamentally sound and Danish prosperity continues.

Currency

Kroner (Dkr) = 100 ore. £ = Dkr10.59; $ = Dkr5.63.

Travel

Visas not required.

Vaccinations

Not required unless coming from an infected area.

Airlines

All major airlines fly to Copenhagen.
Flying times: London $1\frac{3}{4}$ hrs; New York $7\frac{1}{2}$ hrs; Sydney 24 hrs. *Fares:* London F £154.50 Y £103; New York F $717 Y $347; Sydney F A$1,473 Y A$940. *Airport to city:* 10 kms (6 mls).
Taxi fare: Dkr38. *Bus fare:* Dkr8.

Duty-free allowances

Visitors from Europe: 200 cigarettes *or* 50 cigars *or* 250 grammes of tobacco; $\frac{3}{4}$ litre of spirits, 3 litres of wine. *Visitors from countries outside EEC:* 200 cigarettes *or* 50 cigars *or* 250 grammes of tobacco; $\frac{3}{4}$ litre of spirits, 2 litres of wine.

Local time

GMT+1 hr.

Embassy phone numbers

Copenhagen:
Australia 26.22.44
Canada 31.33.06
Sweden 14.22.42
Switzerland 14.17.96

Japan 15.38.35
Netherlands 15.62.93
Norway TR.19.85
W. Germany 26.16.22
UK 14.46.00
USA 12.31.44

Hotels

Copenhagen: Alexandra, Astoria, Bel Air, Botanique, Codan, Airport Hotel, Penta, d'Angleterre, 3 Falke, Grand, Imperial, Kong Frederik, Mercur, Nordland, Palace, Plaza, Richmond, Globetrotter, Royal Scandinavia, Scandis, Sheraton, Osterport. Prices range from US$35–40 in first class to US$45–52 in de luxe class.

International banks

Kjobenhavns Handelsbank, Den Danske Bank, Privatbanken i Kjobenhavn, Faellesbanken for Danmarks Sparekasser, Barclays International, Standard and Chartered.

Credit cards

All major credit cards.

Office hours

08.00 or 08.30–16.00 or 16.30 Mon–Fri.

National holidays

1 Jan, Maundy Thursday, Good Friday, Easter Monday, Store Bededag (fourth Friday after Easter), 16 Apr, 1 May, Ascension Day (May), Whit Monday (May *or* June), 5 June, 24, 25, 26 Dec.

Voltage

220 volts AC.

Communications

Tel: Dkr13 per 3 mins. *Telex:* Dkr1.60 per min, plus basic charge of Dkr14 and Dkr7 service charge.
Airmail: 2–3 days. *Cable:* Dkr1 per word (Dkr16 minimum charge).

Social customs

A traditional and sometimes formal business atmosphere is now giving way to less formality. Entertaining is frequent, both in homes and restaurants, and it is the custom to send flowers or chocolates to the hostess. Danish food is excellent, particularly smorrebrod (open sandwich) or kolde bord, a table full of Danish specialities, hot and cold. Beer is superb; types marked 'Export' are specially strong.
Best buys: Silverware, porcelain, glassware, home furnishings, furs and knitwear.

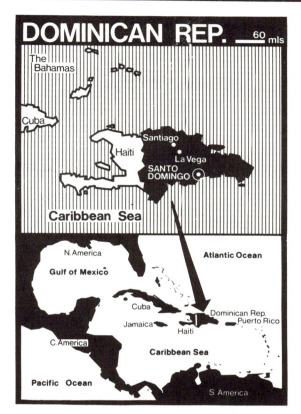

Area and population

48,430 sq kms (18,699 sq mls). Pop. 5 million.
Capital: Santo Domingo (817,000).
Chief cities: Santiago de los Caballeros (245,000),
La Vega (156,000), San Cristobal (106,000),
Puerto Plata (74,000). *Port:* Santo Domingo.
Airport: Las Americas (Santo Domingo).

Climate

Tropical. Santo Domingo temperatures rise to
37°C (98°F) in June–Oct, coming down to about
30°C (85°F) Nov–Apr. Dry season lasts Apr–Nov and
slight danger of hurricanes June–Nov.
Clothing: More formality than in most tropical countries,
but tropical-weight suits needed Mar–Nov.

People

Majority mixed blood; 15% European, 10% Negro.
Religion: Predominantly Roman Catholic.
Distribution: 60% rural.

Language

Spanish. *English rating:* Good.

Economic background

Traditionally dependent upon sugar, coffee, tobacco and
cocoa, which account for 80% of exports, the
Dominican Republic has been diversifying in recent
years. Even tourism, for which there are a number of
coastal developments, is beginning to forge ahead.
Efforts are being made, too, to encourage mining, notably
ferro-nickel, and light industry to try to break reliance on
agriculture. Some growth is foreseen in food processing
and packaging and import substitution industries.

Trade

Gross National Product: RD$2,342 million.
Exports: RD$650.8 million, chiefly sugar, coffee, cocoa,
tobacco, bauxite, molasses. *Imports:* RD$309.7 million,
chiefly wheat, vegetable oils, cars, tractors,
pharmaceutical products. *Chief trading partners:* USA,
Japan, Netherlands Antilles, W. Germany, Canada, Italy,
Puerto Rico, UK, Netherlands, Morocco.
Inflation rate: 8.5%.

Prospects

With the government committed to a firmly capitalist
policy, the Dominican Republic is experiencing better
economic times than under the Trujillo dictatorship.
Unemployment is still high, though, and industrial
progress will be only moderate.

Currency

Peso Oro (RD$) = 100 centavos. £ = RD$1.88;
$ = RD$1.00.

Travel

Visitor's card required. It can be purchased for $2
(payable in US dollars) from airlines or upon arrival in
the Dominican Republic.

Vaccinations

Smallpox.

Airlines

Iberia, Viasa, ALM, Pan Am.
Flying times: Copenhagen $19\frac{1}{4}$ hrs; London about
12 hrs (no direct flights; connections in Madrid,
New York or Miami); New York 4 hrs; Sydney 24 hrs.
Fares: Copenhagen F Dkr5,650 Y Dkr3,770; London
F £395.50 Y £253; New York F $226 Y $151;
Sydney F A$1,461 Y A$939.
Airport to city: 30 kms (18.5 mls). *Taxi fare:* RD$1.00.

Dominican Republic

Ecuador

Duty-free allowances

US$5.00 worth of cigarettes, cigars *or* tobacco; 1 bottle of spirits (opened); reasonable amount of perfume (opened).

Local time

GMT−5 hrs (−4 hrs in summer).

Embassy phone numbers

Santo Domingo: UK 682.3128.

Hotels

Santo Domingo: Embajador, Holiday Inn, Comercial, Hispaniola. Count on US$15 per day.

International banks

Royal Bank of Canada, Chase Manhattan Bank, First National City Bank, Bank of America, Banco de Boston Dominicano.

Credit cards

American Express, Diners Club.

Office hours

08.00–12.00 and 14.00–18.00 Mon–Fri. A few offices are open Sat mornings.

National holidays

1, 21, 26 Jan, 27 Feb, Good Friday, 1 May, Corpus Christi (May *or* June), 16 Aug, 24 Sept, 25 Dec.

Voltage

115 volts AC (220 volts for power appliances).

Communications

Tel: RD$5 per min (RD$15 minimum charge). *Telex:* RD$4 per min. *Airmail:* 2–3 days. *Cable:* 20.5 centavos per word.

Social customs

The Dominican Republic presents the visitor with a mixture of Spanish courtliness and American informality. Formal courtesy is given and is expected in return. Imported spirits are very expensive.

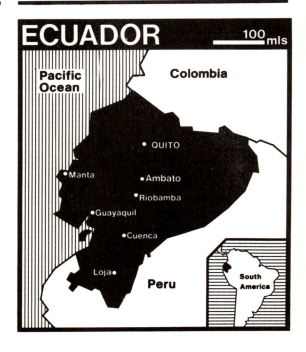

Area and population

270,670 sq kms (104,510 sq mls). Pop. 7 million. *Capital:* Quito (800,000). *Chief cities:* Guayaquil (1 million), Cuenca (100,000), Ambato (70,000), Manta (40,000). *Port:* Guayaquil. *Airports:* Mariscal Sucre (Quito), Simon Bolivar (Guayaquil).

Climate

While only 25 kms (18 mls) from the Equator, Quito is saved from excessive heat by its altitude (285 m, 9,202 ft). Average air temperature is 13°C (55.4°F). Much rain (147 cms, 58 ins) falls Feb–May and Oct–Nov, sometimes for days on end. The best time to visit is June–Oct. *Clothing:* European-weight for Quito, but something lighter is needed if visiting Guayaquil, the chief business city.

People

40% Amerindians, 40% mestizos, 10% Europeans, 10% Negroes. *Religion:* Roman Catholic. *Distribution:* 46% urban.

Language

Spanish. *English rating:* Fair.

Economic background

Primarily an agricultural country, Ecuador is the world's largest exporter of bananas. Although it has been limited in its economic progress by radically different climates, resources and population, as well as poor communications, newly-found oil and unexploited fish reserves could bring swift changes. A growing population (increasing yearly by 3–4%) plus membership of the Andean Group has encouraged industrial growth.

Trade

Gross National Product: $2,500 million (estimate).
Exports: $600 million, chiefly bananas, coffee, cocoa, fishery products, sugar.
Imports: $500 million (estimate), chiefly industrial plant and equipment, transport equipment, minerals, chemical products, paper, cereals and foodstuffs, pharmaceuticals, consumer durables.
Chief trading partners: W. Germany, Trinidad and Tobago, Chile, Panama, Canada, Colombia, Japan, Belgium/Netherlands/Luxembourg, Italy, UK, Sweden, Spain. *Inflation rate:* 12.7%.

Prospects

Oil and fish could lead to economic improvement, but the huge gap between rich and poor remains.

Currency

Sucre = 100 centavos. £ = 49.45 sucres; $ = 26.30 sucres.

Travel

No visas required, but a 90-day tourist card must be obtained either before or on arrival.

Vaccinations

Smallpox.

Airlines

Air France, Avianca, Iberia, KLM, Lufthansa, Braniff (from Miami).
Flying times: Copenhagen (no direct flights) $25\frac{1}{4}$ hrs; London 16 hrs; New York 5 hrs; Sydney 24 hrs.
Fares: Copenhagen F Dkr7,450 Y Dkr4,825; London F £512 Y £330; New York F $499 Y $322; Sydney F A$1,607 Y A$1,036.
Airport to city: 8 kms (5 mls). *Taxi:* 50 sucres.

Duty-free allowances

300 cigarettes *or* 50 cigars; 1 litre of spirits.

Local time

GMT−5 hrs.

Embassy phone numbers

Quito:

Denmark 54.21.16	UK 23.00.70
Switzerland 23.16.61	USA 3.00.20
W. Germany 23.26.60	

Hotels

Quito: Capitol Humboldt, Inter-Continental, Internacional Colon. *Guayaquil:* Humboldt Internacional, Internacional Atahualpa. Prices about $20.00 per night.

International banks

Bank of London and Montreal, First National City, Bank of America.

Credit cards

Barclaycard (Bank Americard), American Express, Diners Club.

Office hours

Vary slightly between Quito and Guayaquil. Offices and shops in Quito: 08.00–12.30 and 14.30–18.30 Mon–Fri, 08.30–12.30 Sat. In Guayaquil, hours are generally 08.00–12.00 and 15.30–18.30 Dec–Apr; many offices and shops close all day Sat.

National holidays

1 Jan, Carnival (3 days before Ash Wednesday), Maundy Thursday, Good Friday, 1, 24 May, 24 July, 10 Aug, 9, 12 Oct, 1, 2, 3 Nov, 6, 25, 26 Dec.

Voltage

110 volts AC.

Communications

Tel: 330 sucres per 3 mins. *Telex:* 295 sucres per 3 mins.
Airmail: 4–5 days. *Phone rating:* Poor.

Social customs:

Warning! Thieves and pickpockets are notorious. There are few places of entertainment. Wine (except local, which is not very good) is expensive, but the beer is excellent. Amoebic dysentery is prevalent. Drink only bottled water and do not eat salads or uncooked vegetables.

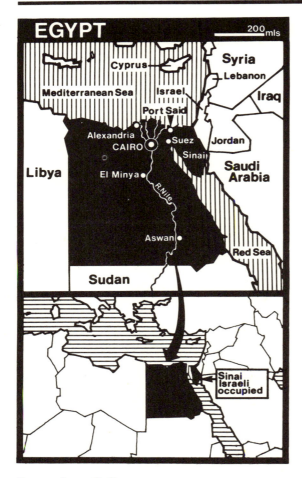

EGYPT
200 mls

Cyprus
Syria
Lebanon
Mediterranean Sea
Israel
Iraq
Port Said
Alexandria
CAIRO
Suez
Jordan
Sinai
Libya
El Minya
Saudi Arabia
R. Nile
Aswan
Red Sea
Sudan

Sinai Israeli occupied

Area and population
1,002,000 sq kms (386,900 sq mls).
Pop. 40 million.
Capital: Cairo (8.5 million).
Chief cities: Alexandria (3.2 m), Ismailia, Port Said,
Suez (populations unknown since the evacuation that
followed the June 1967 war). *Port:* Alexandria.
Airport: Cairo.

Climate
Sometimes intensely hot, with temperatures of up to
38°C (100°F) Apr–Oct, Nov–Mar is much cooler—about
18°C (65°F)—and nights can be cold.
Clothing: Lightweight, but medium-weight clothes and
overcoat are needed in winter.

People
Chiefly Hamitic stock. *Religion:* 90% Moslem,
7% Coptic Christian. *Distribution:* 42% urban.

Language
Arabic. English and French are commercial
languages. *English rating:* Good.

Economic background
With 96% of its land desert, Egypt's limited arable
land is fertile and crops can be grown more than once a
year. Agriculture employs more than half the population,
and provides 30% of Egypt's gross national product
and much of its foreign exchange earnings: chief crops
are cotton, rice, sugar cane, onions, potatoes and citrus
fruits. Industry has grown substantially since the war,
particularly in the production of cotton yarn and
textiles, edible oils, refined sugar, cigarettes, tyres,
paper, fertiliser and glass. There is some heavy industry.

Trade
Gross National Product: £E5,800 million.
Exports: £E668 million, chiefly cotton, rice, onions,
garlic, crude petroleum, footwear.
Imports: £E1,900 million, chiefly chemicals, wheat,
boilers, machinery, vehicles, textiles, iron and steel,
animal and vegetable oils.
Chief trading partners: USA, France, Australia, USSR,
W. Germany, Romania, Italy, Lebanon, UK, E. Germany,
Japan, Czechoslovakia, Poland. *Inflation rate:* 25.8%.

Prospects
Egypt is undertaking more industrialisation, including
plans for projects in engineering, electronics, chemicals,
textiles, food, mining, building and iron and steel.

Currency
£E = 100 piastres = 1,000 milliemes. £ = £E1.27;
$ = £E0.692. (Tourist rates.)

Travel
Visas required.

Vaccinations
Smallpox. Inoculations against other diseases
sometimes demanded. Inoculations against typhoid and
paratyphoid recommended.

Airlines
Egyptair, British Airways, TWA, KLM, SAS, Swissair,
Alitalia, Air France, Austrian, Gulf Air, Olympic, Tarom,
Balkan, JAL, JAT, LOT, Royal Air Maroc, Sabena,
Interflug.
Flying times: Copenhagen 6 hrs; London 4½ hrs;
New York 11½ hrs; Sydney 24 hrs.

Egypt

Fares: Copenhagen F Dkr3,560 Y Dkr2,420;
London F £283.50 Y £192.50; New York F $987
Y $597; Sydney F A$1,162 Y A$768.
Airport to city: 22.5 kms (14 mls). *Taxi fare:* £E1.

Duty-free allowances
400 cigarettes *or* 50 cigars *or* 250 grammes tobacco;
a reasonable quantity of spirits.

Local time
GMT+2 hrs.

Embassy phone numbers
Cairo:

Australia 28190	Switzerland 78171
Denmark 802001	W. Germany 806015
Japan 33963	UK 20850
Netherlands 802024	USA 28219
Sweden 913133	

Hotels
Cairo: Meridien, Mena House, Nile Hilton,
Sheraton, Shepheard's. Prices are about £E20 per night.

International banks
All nationalised.

Credit cards
All major credit cards.

Office hours
08.30–13.30 and 16.30–19.00 Sat–Thurs.

National holidays
All Moslem holidays plus 22 Feb, 8 Mar, 18 June,
23 July, 1 Sept, 6, 24 Oct, 23 Dec.

Voltage
220–440 volts 50 cycles AC.

Communications
Tel: £E3.69 per 3 mins. *Telex:* available at hotels.
Airmail: 5 days. *Cable:* 137 milliemes per word.
Phone rating: Poor.

Social customs
Be prepared to work in the mornings and evenings,
since afternoons are devoted to siesta. Cairo restaurants
can be excellent, but imported spirits are expensive.
Egyptian wines and beers are both good and inexpensive.
Best buys: Leatherware, carpets, antiques, ivory, copper,
brass, silk brocades.

El Salvador

Area and population
21,331 sq kms (8,236 sq mls). Pop. 4 million.
Capital: San Salvador (400,000).
Chief cities: Santa Ana (197,000), San Miguel (125,000),
Santa Tecla (59,000), Zacatecoluca (65,000).
Ports: Acajutla, La Union.
Airport: Ilopango (San Salvador).

Climate
Varies with altitude. Average rainfall in San Salvador
is 182 cm (72in). Average shade temperature is
23°C (73°F). Best time to visit is Nov–Jan.
Clothing: Tropical lightweight. Locals favour dark colours
and collar and tie.

People
92% mestizo, rest European and Indian stock.
Religion: 95% Roman Catholic. *Distribution:* 40% urban.

Language
Spanish. *English rating:* Fair.

Economic background
Small, densely populated, industrialised, El Salvador lives
chiefly on its coffee exports. Important, too, are
manufactured cotton goods, sugar, meat and shrimps.
A sound economy is being helped by industrialisation
and the manufacture of textiles, shoes, furniture,
chemicals, pharmaceuticals, building materials, cement
and food processing.

Trade
Gross National Product: 3,939 million colons.
Exports: 1,156 million colons, chiefly coffee, cotton,
shrimps, sugar. *Imports:* 1,409 million colons, chiefly
transport equipment, chemicals, fuels, lubricants,

industrial machinery. *Chief trading partners:* USA, Guatemala, Venezuela, Japan, W. Germany, Netherlands, Costa Rica, Nicaragua, Belgium/Luxembourg, Mexico, UK. *Inflation rate:* 14.5%.

Prospects
With world demand for coffee rising, and El Salvador meeting demand for its manufactured goods from the Central American Common Market, prospects are good.

Currency
Colon = 100 centavos. £ = 4.72 colons; $ = 2.51 colons.

Travel
While most businessmen do not require visas, a non-immigrant visa is required if goods are to be sold.

Vaccinations
Smallpox.

Airlines
Pan Am, Iberia, TACA.
Flying times: Copenhagen (no direct flight) $25\frac{1}{2}$ hrs; London (no direct flight) about 16 hrs; New York 6 hrs; Sydney 24 hrs. *Fares:* Copenhagen F Dkr6,520 Y Dkr4,175; London F £465.50 Y £302; New York F $386 Y $267; Sydney F A$2,063 Y A$1,344. *Airport to city:* 13 kms (8 mls). *Taxi fare:* US$1.60.

Duty-free allowances
400 cigarettes; 2 bottles of spirits.

Local time
GMT−6 hrs.

Embassy phone numbers
San Salvador: UK 21.9106.

Hotels
San Salvador: San Salvador, Grand, Ritz Continental, Camino Real, prices from 50 to 55 colons per night.

International banks
Bank of London and Montreal, First National City Bank.

Credit cards
American Express, Diners Club.

Office hours
08.00–12.00 and 14.00–18.00 Mon–Fri, 08.00–12.00 Sat.

National holidays
1 Jan, Holy Week, 14, 27 Apr, 1 May, Corpus Christi (May *or* June), 22, 29 June, First Week of Aug, 15 Sept, 12 Oct, 2, 5 Nov, 24, 25, 31 Dec.

Voltage
110 volts for lighting, 220 volts for power.

Communications
Tel: 37.50 colons per 3 mins. *Telex:* 36 colons per 3 mins. *Airmail:* 3–5 days. *Cable:* 1.20 colons per word.

Social customs
You will need a wallet full of visiting cards—and spares in your briefcase. There is much social and business handshaking. El Salvador is generally a healthy country, but drink only bottled water.

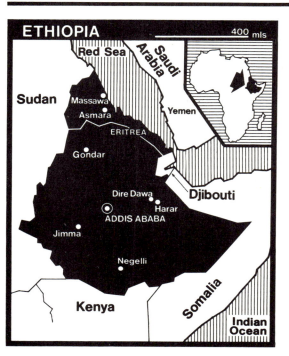

ETHIOPIA 400 mls
Red Sea
Saudi Arabia
Sudan
Massawa
Asmara
Yemen
ERITREA
Gondar
Dire Dawa
Harar
ADDIS ABABA
Djibouti
Jimma
Negelli
Kenya
Somalia
Indian Ocean

Haile Selassie and the institution of a military government, have not helped Ethiopia's economy, which is almost totally agricultural. The country was badly affected by the drought of 1972–5 and the situation remains critical. International aid has helped but Ethiopia's war in Eritrea depletes reserves. Industry is growing but slowly, dominated chiefly by textiles, food, beer, mineral waters, tobacco, sugar and shoes. The government has nationalised many foreign-owned manual enterprises.

Trade

Gross National Product: E$4,716 million.
Exports: US$267 million, chiefly coffee, hides and skins, vegetables, oil seeds, nuts, fruit, animal feeding stuffs.
Imports: US$273 million, chiefly machine and transport equipment, manufactures, chemicals, mineral fuel lubricants, food and live animals.
Chief trading partners: Italy, Japan, W. Germany, UK, USA, Iran, France, Czechoslovakia, Netherlands, Saudi Arabia, China. *Inflation rate:* 14.5%.

Prospects

Very poor indeed until Ethiopia settles its international and internal political problems. Ethiopia's mineral wealth is, however, being explored.

Currency

Ethiopian birr = 100 cents. £ = E$3.89; $ = E$2.06.

Travel

Visas required. At a cost of E$10, they are obtainable from Ethiopian embassies and consulates.

Vaccinations

Cholera, smallpox and yellow fever. Vaccination against typhus, typhoid and tetanus advisable but not essential.

Airlines

British Airways, Ethiopian Airlines, Alitalia, Air France, KLM, SAS, Swissair, TWA.
Flying times: Copenhagen $16\frac{1}{4}$ hrs; London 9 hrs; New York 18 hrs; Sydney 24 hrs. *Fares:* Copenhagen F Dkr5,510 Y Dkr4,100; London F £414.50 Y £292.50; New York F $1,082 Y $742; Sydney F A$1,128 Y A$746.
Airport to city: 8 kms (5 mls). *Bus fare:* E$2.

Duty-free allowances

100 cigarettes *or* 50 cigars *or* 250 grammes of tobacco; 1 litre of spirits *or* wine.

Area and population

1,221,900 sq kms (471,777 sq mls). Pop. 27.8 million.
Capital: Addis Ababa (900,000).
Chief cities: Asmara (250,000), Dire Dawa (67,000), Harar (48,000), Massawa (21,000). *Port:* Massawa.
Airports: Bole (Addis Ababa), Yohannes (Asmara).

Climate

Altitude saves Addis Ababa from the rigours of closeness to the equator. Temperatures range from 6°C (48°F) in Dec to 26°C (79°F) in Mar. Average humidity 68%.
Clothing: European summer clothes are usually worn, although raincoat and umbrella are needed during the rain from mid-June to Sept.

People

Hamitic and mixed Hamitic and Semitic origin, with expatriate communities. *Religion:* 50% Ethiopian Christian, 33% Moslem. *Distribution:* 6% urban.

Language

Amharic, but 30 other languages spoken.
English rating: Excellent.

Economic background

Problems of government, which followed the fall of

Local time
GMT+3 hrs.

Embassy phone numbers
Addis Ababa:

Canada 48335	Switzerland 447848
Denmark 447787	W. Germany 110433
Japan 448215	UK 151666
Netherlands 445597	USA 100666
Sweden 448110	

Hotels
Addis Ababa: Hilton, Ghion, Wabe Shebelle, Ethiopia, Ras. Prices about E$18 per night.

International banks
Commercial Bank of Ethiopia, Addis Ababa Bank.

Credit cards
American Express, Diners Club.

Office hours
09.00–13.00 and 15.00–18.00 Mon–Fri, 09.00–13.00 Sat. Varies slightly in Asmara.

National holidays
Religious holidays alter each year, so check before arrival. Fixed holidays: 2 Mar, 6 Apr, 1 May, 11, 12 Sept.

Voltage
220 volts.

Communications
Tel: E$23.55 per 3 mins. *Telex:* E$22.50 per 3 mins. *Airmail:* 3–4 days. *Cable:* E$1 per word.

Social customs
Most businessmen speak English or French. Much informal entertaining goes on in Addis Ababa.

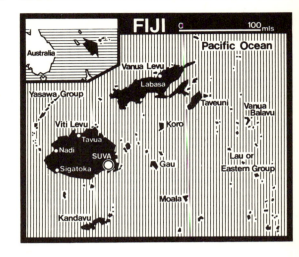

Area and population
18,272 sq kms (7,095 sq mls). Pop. 551,000.
Capital: Suva (66,000).
Chief cities: None but principal towns include Lautoka (13,000), Nadi (3,000), Ba (4,000).
Port: Suva. *Airport:* International (Nadi).

Climate
Tropical and sometimes steamy. Temperatures range from 18° to 32°C (65° to 90°F), and humidity is high. Heavy rain Dec–Apr. *Clothing:* Tropical clothing. Umbrella essential in rainy season.

People
Chiefly Fijians, Indians, with European and Chinese communities. *Religion:* Christian and Hindu. *Distribution:* 20% urban.

Languages
English, Fijian, Hindi and Cantonese.

Economic background
Tourism is now beginning to make a valuable contribution to the economy, which is still largely based on agriculture, chiefly sugar, copra, rice, bananas and other tropical fruits. Fiji's development programmes have been helped by UN and British aid. As well as the processing of the two main export crops, copra and sugar, other industries now include hotel development, cement, paint, cigarettes, confectionery, biscuits, beer, and mineral waters.

Trade
Gross National Product: F$302.4 million.
Exports: F$51.7 million, chiefly sugar, coconut oil, gold, fish, oil seed cake, bananas, timber.
Imports: F$131.5 million, chiefly mineral fuels. machinery, chemicals, wheat flour, metal products, photographic and optical goods.
Chief trading partners: Australia, UK, Japan, New Zealand, Singapore, USA, Canada.
Inflation rate: Not available.

Prospects
Development plans are continuing in the main islands of the 300-island group. Best prospects lie in tourism and light industry.

Currency
Fiji dollar = 100 cents. £ = F$1.59; $ = F$0.84.

Travel
Visas not required.

Vaccinations
Smallpox, unless visitor has resided in Australia, New Zealand and neighbouring Pacific territories for 14 days prior to departure for Fiji.

Airlines
British Airways, Air New Zealand, Qantas, Pan Am, CP Air, Air Pacific.
Flying times: Copenhagen 30 hrs; London 31 hrs; New York 18 hrs; Sydney 6 hrs.
Fares: Copenhagen F Dkr11,500 Y Dkr7,420; London F £886.50 Y £571.50; New York F $2,652 Y $1,640; Sydney F A$351 Y A$239.
Airport to Nadi: 5 kms (3 mls). *Taxi fare:* F$3.
Businessmen travelling on to Suva can fly from Nadi by Air Pacific, a 112.5 km (70 ml) journey.

Duty-free allowances
200 cigarettes *or* ½ lb tobacco; 1 quart of spirits *or* 2 quarts of wine.

Local time
GMT + 12 hrs.

Embassy phone numbers
Suva: UK 311033.

Hotels
Suva: Beachcomber, Southern Cross, Suva Travelodge. Prices from F$15 to 26 per night. *Nadi:* Travelodge, Hibiscus, Melanesian, Tanoa. Similarly priced.

International banks
Australia and New Zealand Bank, Bank of Baroda, Bank of New South Wales, Bank of New Zealand, First National City Bank, Barclays Bank.

Credit cards
American Express, Diners Club.

Office hours
08.00–13.00 and 14.00–16.00 Mon–Fri, 08.00–12.00 or 13.00 Sat.

National holidays
In addition to Moslem and Hindu holidays, 1 Jan, Good Friday, Easter Monday, Queen's Birthday (June), August Bank Holiday, Fiji Day (usually early Oct), Prince of Wales's Birthday (decided each year), 25, 26 Dec.

Voltage
240–415 volts AC.

Communications
Tel: $7.92 per 3 mins. *Telex:* $7.92 per 3 mins.
Airmail: 5 days. *Cable:* 18 cents per word (7-word minimum).

Social customs
It is cheaper to buy tropical clothing in Suva, where oppressive humidity makes for much discomfort. Islands are free from tropical diseases.

FINLAND 0 — 250 mls
Norway
Sweden
Tornio
USSR
Vaasa
Tampere
Baltic Sea
HELSINKI
Porkkala
Leningrad

price of wood. Half of Finland's revenue comes from the products of its vast forests. Finland was particularly hard hit by the world trade recession, which produced record trade deficits in successive years. The greatest part of its industry is based on wood processing, followed by metal and metal-working industries, textiles, glass, ceramics, and furniture. Much of Finland's heavy plant is imported.

Trade
Gross National Product: 82,800 million markka.
Exports: 20,248 million markka, chiefly paper, pulp, wood products, glass, manufactured goods, machinery, transport equipment, engineering products.
Imports: 27,974 million markka, chiefly vehicles, foodstuffs, fuel, petroleum, minerals, consumer goods.
Chief trading partners: USSR, Sweden, W. Germany, UK, USA, France, Denmark, Netherlands, Norway.
Inflation rate: 10.4%.

Prospects
There are signs that the economy is recovering. Further industrialisation is expected.

Currency
Markka or Finnmark = 100 pennis. £ = 7.93 markka; $ = 4.21 markka.

Travel
Visas not required.

Vaccinations
Not required.

Airlines
Aeroflot, British Airways, Finnair, Lufthansa, Swissair, SAS, Austrian, LOT, Interflug.
Flying times: Copenhagen 1¾ hrs; London 3 hrs; New York 10 hrs; Sydney 36 hrs.
Fares: Copenhagen F Dkr1,300 Y Dkr1,085; London F £215 Y £143; New York F $797 Y $390; Sydney F A$1,560 Y A$1,012.
Airport to city: 19 kms (12 mls). *Taxi fare:* 35 markka.

Area and population
305,475 sq kms (130,091 sq mls). Pop. 4.6 million.
Capital: Helsinki (504,000).
Chief cities: Tampere (165,000), Turku (163,000), Lahti (93,000), Oulu (89,000). *Ports:* Helsinki, Kemi, Kotka, Turku. *Airport:* Vantaa (Helsinki).

Climate
Winter is long and cold, with temperatures falling to −30°C (−22°F). Average summer temperature is 16°C (61°F). *Clothing:* Medium-weight clothing, even in winter, since homes and offices are well heated, but heavy outer clothes essential for cold months.

People
Finns. *Religion:* 90% Evangelical Lutherans.
Distribution: 50.5% urban.

Languages
Finnish and Swedish. *English rating:* Excellent.

Economic background
Even though Finland is a very industrialised country, producing all kinds of industrial and consumer goods, the economy is still greatly influenced by the world

Duty-free allowances
Visitors entering from EEC: 200 cigarettes *or* 250 grammes of cigars *or* tobacco; 0.75 litre of spirits *or* 1 litre of wine.
Visitors entering from outside Europe: 400 cigarettes *or* 500 grammes of cigars *or* tobacco; 2 litres of spirits *or* wine.

Finland

France

Local time
GMT+2 hrs.

Embassy phone numbers
Helsinki:

Canada 11141	Sweden 12151
Denmark 641948	W. Germany 602355
Japan 175445	UK 12574
Netherlands 661737	USA 11931
Norway 11234	

Hotels
Helsinki: Inter-Continental, Academica, Hesperia, Klaus Kurki, Marski, Seurahuone, Vaakuna. Prices up to 175 markka per night.

International banks
None.

Credit cards
All major credit cards.

Office hours
Winter: 08.00–16.15 Mon–Fri. *Summer:* 08.00–15.15.

National holidays
1, 7 Jan, Good Friday, Easter Monday, 1 May, Ascension Day (May), Whit Monday (May *or* June), 24 June, 4 Nov, 6, 24, 26 Dec.

Voltage
220 volts AC.

Communications
Tel: 3 markka per min. *Telex:* 9.50 markka per 3 mins. *Airmail:* 2–3 days. *Cable:* 9 markka plus 30 pennis per word.

Social customs
No.1 rule for all visitors: Do not drink and drive, for the penalty, even for visitors, is to be sent to the North to help build roads or landing strips. In business circles, the handshake is the formal introduction, even for children. Punctuality is expected. The sauna is the national pastime, but choose the temperature carefully. Finns like it hot. *Best buys:* Hats and shoes made from reindeer skins, linens, pottery, carved wood, unusual toys.

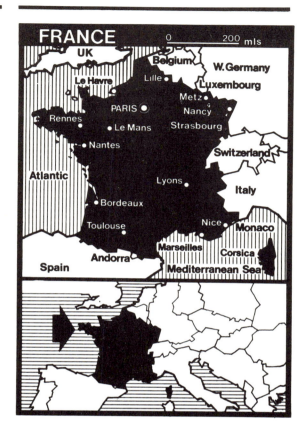

Area and population
550,787 sq kms (212,659 sq mls). Pop. 51.9 million (estimate).
Capital: Paris (9.2 million).
Chief cities: Lille (1.3 m), Lyons (Lyon) (1.1 m), Marseilles (Marseille) (1 m), Bordeaux (612,000), Toulouse (509,000), Nice (445,000), Grenoble (390,000). *Ports:* Le Havre, Cherbourg, Marseilles, Calais, Dieppe, Dunkirk, Rouen, St Malo, St Nazaire. *Airports:* Charles de Gaulle, Orly, Le Bourget (Paris).

Climate
Temperate, but varies considerably in different areas. Paris average temperatures range from 3°C (37°F) in winter to 19°C (66°F) in summer. *Clothing:* European clothing in Paris, but lightweight for Mediterranean and Basque coasts in summer.

People
Nordic, Alpine and Mediterranean.
Religion: Predominantly Roman Catholic.
Distribution: 63% urban.

Language
French. *English rating:* Good.

Economic background
Now one of the most industrialised nations in the world, France has produced a dynamic economy, which increased by 6% a year between 1963 and 1973. Some studies indicate that France will become the leading industrial power in Europe before the end of the century. The momentum of France's development halted briefly in 1975 because of the worldwide economic recession but, like the rest of the industrialised world, it is beginning to pick up again. While agriculture remains important, occupying about 12% of the labour force and providing 20% of France's export earnings, it is industry that is expanding rapidly, particularly in Paris, the North and the East.

Trade
Gross National Product: 1,442,000 million francs.
Exports: 273,000 million francs, chiefly machinery, chemicals, textiles, cars, steel, grain, aircraft, wines and spirits, perfume and fashion clothes.
Imports: 308,000 million francs, chiefly machinery, food, petroleum, chemicals, steel, non-ferrous metals, transport equipment, minerals, communications and electronic equipment, paper and woodpulp.
Chief trading partners: EEC nations, USA, Switzerland, Algeria, Saudi Arabia, Iraq, Spain, USSR.
Inflation rate: 9.2%.

Prospects
Economically, some of the best in the western world. Government and industry are working together to ensure constant development of trade, both at home and abroad.

Currency
Franc = 100 centimes. £ = Fr8.42; $ = Fr4.47.

Travel
Visas not required.

Vaccinations
Not required unless coming from an infected area.

Airlines
Air France, British Airways, British Caledonian, TWA, Air Canada, Swissair, KLM, SAS, JAL, and all major international airlines.
Flying times (to Paris): Copenhagen 2¾ hrs; London 1 hr; New York 7¾ hrs; Sydney 24 hrs.
Fares: Copenhagen F Dkr1,770 Y Dkr1,330; London F £58.50 Y £39; New York F $684 Y $325; Sydney F A$1,466 Y A$937.
Airport to city: Charles de Gaulle 23 kms (14.5 mls); Orly 14 kms (9 mls); Le Bourget 13 kms (8 mls).
Taxi fares: Approx Fr35–50.

Duty-free allowances
Visitors entering from EEC: 300 cigarettes *or* 75 cigars; 1.5 litres of spirits, 3 litres of wine.
Visitors entering from non-EEC European countries: 200 cigarettes *or* 50 cigars; 1 litre of spirits, 2 litres of wine.
Visitors entering from countries outside Europe: 400 cigarettes *or* 50 cigars; 1 litre of spirits, 2 litres of wine.

Local time
GMT+1 hr (+2 hrs Apr–Sept).

Embassy phone numbers
Paris:

Australia 720.33.04	Sweden 553.11.89
Canada 225.99.55	Switzerland 551.62.92
Denmark 723.54.20	W. Germany 359.33.51
Japan 924.83.59	UK 266.91.42
Netherlands 578.61.88	USA 265.74.60
Norway 359.68.65	

Hotels
Paris: Numerous, but the best include Bristol, Claridge, George V, Inter-Continental, Lancaster, Hilton, Penta, Plaza Athénée, Ritz. Prices vary but a good class 4-star hotel will cost about Fr300 per night.

International banks
Lloyds Bank International, International Westminster Bank, Barclays International, Crédit Lyonnais, Chase Manhattan, and other major banks.

Credit cards
All major credit cards.

Office hours
09.00–12.00 and 14.00–18.00 Mon–Fri.

France

National holidays
1 Jan, Easter Monday, 1 May, Ascension Day (May), Whit Monday (May or June), 14 July, 15 Aug, 1, 11 Nov, 25 Dec.

Voltage
220 volts AC 50 cycles in most areas.

Communications
Tel: Fr6.15 per 3 mins. *Telex:* 12.1 centimes per 6-second unit. *Airmail:* 1–2 days.
Cable: Fr1.08 per word.

Social customs
Handshaking is still the formal introduction and departure. Take special care if planning a visit in July or Aug, when Parisians take their holidays. Dinner parties are generally extremely formal and, if you are arranging one, take extra care in the placing of guests so as to denote their importance. Many French businessmen and government officials prefer to speak French even though their English may be excellent, and some insist on it. *Shopping:* Many shops give a 12–20% discount if you pay for your purchases for export in travellers cheques or dollars. *Best buys:* High fashion, handbags, leathergoods, cosmetics, cognac, champagne and local wines. Prices are among the highest in the world.

Gabon

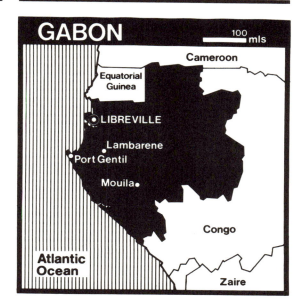

Area and population
267,000 sq kms (103,000 sq mls). Pop. 950,000.
Capital: Libreville (112,000).
Chief city: Port Gentil (45,000). *Ports:* Libreville, Port Gentil. *Airport:* Libreville.

Climate
Tropical and little variation. Temperatures range from 20° to 31.6°C (70° to 93°F). Very high humidity.
Clothing: Tropical all the year round.

People
Bantu origin. *Religion:* 50% Christians, remainder animist, with a small Moslem minority.
Distribution: 21% urban.

Language
French. *English rating:* Poor.

Economic background
Gabon's revenue comes from timber, minerals and oil, although the majority of the people depend on growing their own cassava and bananas. Much of the country is rain forest, which provides best quality plywood. It is floated down the Ogooué River to be processed at Port Gentil. Mining and oil have boomed and, together with minerals, account for more than 60% of total exports.

Trade

Gross National Product: 108,500 million CFAfrancs.
Exports: 1,174.4 million French francs, chiefly wood,
petroleum and manganese. *Imports:* 682.1 million
French francs, chiefly machinery, transport equipment,
metal products, tobacco, industrial chemicals.
Chief trading partners: France, USA, W. Germany, Italy,
UK, Netherlands, Antilles, Senegal. *Inflation rate:* 61.8%.

Prospects

Gabon's oil, minerals and wood have produced the
highest *per capita* income in Africa outside South Africa.
The government is working towards further development.

Currency

CFAfranc. £ = CFAfrs421; $ = CFAfrs223.

Travel

Visas required.

Vaccinations

Smallpox, yellow fever, cholera.

Airlines

Air Gabon, UTA, Air Afrique, Pan Am, Swissair, Sabena.
Flying times: Copenhagen 10¼ hrs; London (no direct
flights) 13 hrs; New York 14 hrs; Sydney 36 hrs.
Fares: Copenhagen F Dkr6,635 Y Dkr4,920;
London F £494 Y £355; New York F $1,045
Y $653; Sydney F A$1,368 Y A$886.
Airport to city: 12 kms (7.5 mls).
Taxi fare: Approx. CFAfrs500.

Duty-free allowances

200 cigarettes *or* 50 cigars; 1 litre of spirits; presents up
to US$1,800 in value.

Local time

GMT+1 hr.

Embassy phone numbers

Libreville: UK (honorary consul) 223.30.

Hotels

Libreville: Gambia, Inter-Continental. Prices up to
CFAfrs7,000 per night.

International banks

Banque de Paris et des Pays-Bas.

Credit cards

American Express, Barclaycard, Diners Club.

Office hours

07.30–16.30 Mon–Fri.

National holidays

1 Jan, 5, 12 Mar, Easter Monday, 1 May,
Ascension Day (May), Whit Monday (May *or* June),
15, 17 Aug, 1 Nov, 4, 25 Dec.

Voltage

220–380 volts 50 cycles.

Communications

Tel: CFAfrs2625 per 3 mins.
Telex: CFAfrs405 per min. *Airmail:* 3–7 days.
Cable: CFAfrs160 per word.

Social customs

Apart from much hand-shaking, there are no special
overall customs in Gabon, where the business
community is European-orientated. It is essential to
speak French, for little English is spoken outside of
hotels and travel agencies. *Best buys:* Wood carvings.

The Gambia

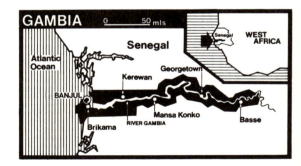

Area and population

10,381 sq kms (4008 sq mls). Pop. 494,000.
Capital: Banjul (formerly Bathurst) (40,000).
Chief cities: None, but towns smaller than Banjul
are Mansa Konko, Basse. *Port:* Banjul.
Airport: Yundum (Banjul).

Climate

One of the best in West Africa. During Dec–Apr the

average temperature is 24°C (75°F), with plenty of sunshine and no rain. During Mar–Oct the average temperature is 29°C (84°F). The rainy season is July–Oct. *Clothing:* Tropical suits or shorts, and shirt with or without tie. Lightweight suit for evening wear.

People
Various tribes, chiefly Mandingo, Wolof, Peul, Sarakole, Dialas—plus 500 Europeans. *Religion:* 90% Moslem. *Distribution:* 10% urban.

Language
English.

Economic background
The economy of The Gambia is based on one crop, groundnuts, produced by peasant farmers. The entire production is bought by the Gambia Produce Marketing Board. There is little industry other than factories involved in the production of lime juice, oil and kaolin.

Trade
Gross National Product: Not available.
Exports: 70 million dalasi (approx), almost entirely groundnuts. *Imports:* 67 million dalasi (approx.), chiefly food, textiles, clothing, machinery, transport equipment. *Chief trading partners:* UK, France, W. Germany, Switzerland, Italy, China, Japan, Senegal, Burma, Netherlands, USA. *Inflation rate:* Not available.

Prospects
Little prospect of further development, although tourism is growing, particularly from Scandinavia.

Currency
Dalasi = 100 bututs. £ = D3.99; $ = D2.12.

Travel
Commonwealth citizens need only a valid passport, but other visitors must possess a visa. A visitor's pass is issued on entry, valid for one month.

Vaccinations
Smallpox. Inoculation against the enteric group of fevers is recommended.

Airlines
British Caledonian, Sierra Leone Airways, Ghana Airways, Nigeria Airways.
Flying times: Copenhagen 11¼ hrs; London 10 hrs; New York 10 hrs; Sydney 24 hrs.

Fares: Copenhagen F Dkr5,510 Y Dkr3,905; London F £380.50 Y £264; New York F $861 Y $534; Sydney F A$1,612 Y A$1,079.
Airport to city: 29 kms (18 mls). *Taxi fare:* D5.

Duty-free allowances
½ lb of tobacco; 1 quart of spirits, 2 quarts of wine *or* beer.

Local time
GMT.

Embassy phone numbers
Banjul: UK 244.6.

Hotels
Banjul: Atlantic, Banjul, Carlton, Sunwing. Prices range from D20 to 25 per night.

International banks
Standard Bank of West Africa.

Credit cards
None.

Office hours
08.00–12.00 and 14.00–1700 Mon–Thurs, 08.00–12.00 and 13.00 Fri. 08.00–12.00 Sat.

National holidays
In addition to Moslem holidays, 1 Jan, 18 Feb, Good Friday, Easter Monday, 1 May, 15 Aug, 25, 26 Dec.

Voltage
230–240 volts AC.

Communications
Tel: D5 per 3 mins. *Telex:* Limited availability.
Airmail: 2–3 days. *Cable:* 45 bututs per word.

Social customs
Other than some Moslem customs, none of significance.

EAST GERMANY 0 ——— 100 mls

Denmark

Kiel

Rostock

Hamburg

West
Berlin

Magdeburg

East
Berlin

Poland

Halle

Leipzig

Dresden

West
Germany

Czechoslovakia

Area and population
108,178 sq kms (41,768 sq mls). Pop. 17 million.
Capital: Berlin (1.1 million).
Chief cities: Leipzig (571,000), Dresden (508,000),
Karl-Marx-Stadt (304,000), Magdeburg (276,000),
Rostock (210,000). *Ports:* Rostock, Stralsund, Wismar.
Airport: Schönefeld (Berlin).

Climate
Temperate. May–Sept temperatures rise to 33°C (91°F),
but fall to 16°C (3°F) in winter. *Clothing:* Lightweight
for summer but warm suits, dresses and overcoats for
winter.

People
Germanic. *Religion:* 82% Protestant, 12% Roman
Catholic. *Distribution:* 74% urban.

Language
German. *English rating:* Poor.

Economic background
A planned economy has stressed heavy industry for
many years. All imports are strictly controlled by state

buying organisations, much of it financed through barter,
counter-purchase and compensation trading. All foreign
trading is the responsibility of Foreign Trade Enterprises,
which act on the authority of the Ministry of Foreign
Trade. One of the best ways of learning about the market
is by visiting the twice-yearly Leipzig Fair, held each
March and September. The March fair concentrates on
heavy industry, and the one in September on
petrochemicals and light industry.

Trade
Gross National Product: 187,200 million marks.
Exports: 30,443.2 million marks, chiefly
machinery, railway rolling stock, chemicals, fertilisers,
pesticides, fuel oil, building materials, ships, vehicles,
clothing, textiles. *Imports:* 33,569.5 million marks,
chiefly mineral ores, coal, rolled steel, tyres, crude oil,
wood, cotton, wool, paper, pulp, foodstuffs, raw skins.
Chief trading partners: USSR, W. Germany,
Czechoslovakia, Poland, Hungary, Netherlands,
Romania, Switzerland, Bulgaria, UK.
Inflation rate: Not available.

Prospects
Little is officially revealed, but East Germany's standard
of living is regarded as the highest in the Eastern Bloc.
The country's annual growth rate is estimated at 4%.

Currency
Mark = 100 pfennigs. £ = M3.89; $ = M2.06. Rate of
exchange is strictly controlled and no East German
currency, known as Ostmarks, may be taken out of the
country.

Travel
Visas required.

Vaccinations
Not required.

Airlines
Interflug, Aeroflot, LOT and other Eastern Bloc airlines,
SAS. Western passengers may fly direct to East Berlin
from Copenhagen, from London by LOT, or travel to
West Berlin by British Airways, Air France or Pan Am
and cross into East Berlin by road.
Flying times: Copenhagen 1 hr; London 1¾ hrs;
New York 9 hrs; Sydney 24 hrs.
Fares (to West Berlin): Copenhagen F Dkr950
Y Dkr635; London F £114.50 Y £76; New York F $721
Y $353; Sydney F A$1,466 Y A$937.
Airport to city: 19 kms (12 mls).

East Germany

Duty-free allowances
200 cigarettes *or* 250 grammes of cigars *or* tobacco; coffee up to 500 grammes; 1 litre of spirits *or* wine.

Local time
GMT+1 hr.

Embassy phone numbers
Berlin:
Denmark 229.1202   UK 220.2431
Japan 220.2481

Hotels
Berlin: Berolina, Stadt Berlin, Unter den Linden.
Leipzig: Astoria, International, Am Ring, Stadt Leipzig, Zum Löwen. Prices vary but up to M70 per night.

International banks
None.

Credit cards
Diners Club.

Office hours
08.00–16.00 Mon–Fri.

National holidays
1 Jan, Good Friday, 1 May, Whit Monday (May *or* June), 7 Oct, 25–26 Dec.

Voltage
220 volts AC 50 cycles.

Communications
Telex: M3.60 per 3 mins. *Airmail:* 3–4 days.
Cable: 15 pfennigs per word.

Social customs
Traditionally, no-one ever concludes a deal on a first visit to East Germany. Numerous visits and much patience are required. All entertaining is done in hotels and restaurants.

West Germany

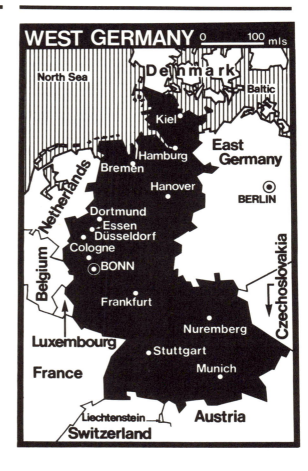

Area and population
248,882 sq kms (96,094 sq mls). Pop. 61.5 million, including West Berliners.
Capital: Bonn (278,800).
Chief cities: West Berlin (2.2 million), Hamburg (1.8 m), Munich (München) (1.3 m), Cologne (Köln) (1 m), Dortmund (700,000), Düsseldorf (700,000), Essen (700,000), Frankfurt (700,000), Bremen (600,000), Stuttgart (600,000), Hanover (Hannover) (600,000), Duisburg (600,000) Nuremberg (Nürnberg) (500,000).
Ports: Bremen, Hamburg. *Airports:* Frankfurt/Main, Fuhlsbüttel (Hamburg), Munich Riem, Lohausen (Düsseldorf), Tegel (West Berlin).

Climate
Temperate. Cold winters with temperatures ranging from −10° to 0°C (15° to 32°F) and with hot summers up to about 20°C (68°F). *Clothing:* Lightweight for

summer but warm clothing for winter, including heavy shoes and heavy top-coat.

People
Germanic. *Religion:* 51% Protestant, 46% Roman Catholic. *Distribution:* 79% urban.

Language
German. *English rating:* Excellent.

Economic background
The greatest economic power in Europe, West Germany achieved its prominence in the so-called Economic Miracle that followed the end of the war in 1945. So strong has its industry and exporting achievement become that its currency is among the hardest in the world and subject to revaluations. Based on huge mineral resources of coal, petroleum, natural gas and iron ore, manufacturing is the most important sector of the economy, accounting for 43% of domestic product. Every conceivable kind of product is made. While mining is declining in importance, contributing less than 4% of the domestic product, agriculture is still a vital part of the economy, even though, as in much of Europe, farmers are continuing a drift into industry. Increasing mechanisation and the improvement of farm structures have provided a firm agricultural base.

Trade
Gross National Product: DM1,123,200 million.
Exports: DM256,172 million, chiefly non-electrical machinery, chemicals, vehicles, electrical machinery, iron and steel, textile and yarn fabrics, precision instruments.
Imports: DM221,637 million, chiefly non-electrical machinery, petroleum, non-ferrous metals, chemicals, iron and steel, fruit and vegetables, textile yarns and fabrics. *Chief trading partners:* France, Netherlands, Belgium/Luxembourg, Italy, USA, Austria, UK, Switzerland, Sweden, USSR, Iran, Japan, Saudi Arabia. *Inflation rate:* 2.9%.

Prospects
Badly hit by the world recession, West Germany is recovering and the current upturn is expected to continue. The economy continues to depend on exports.

Currency
Deutschmark (DM) = 100 pfennigs. £ = DM3.89; $ = DM2.06.

Travel
Visas not required.

Vaccinations
Not required unless travelling from an infected area.

Airlines
All major international airlines.
Flying times (to Frankfurt): Copenhagen 1¼ hrs; London 1 hr; New York 7¼ hrs; Sydney 28 hrs.
Fares (to Frankfurt): Copenhagen F Dkr1,405 Y Dkr935; London F £82 Y £54.50; New York F $717 Y $343; Sydney F A$1,466 Y A$937.
Airport to city: Frankfurt 10 kms (6 mls); Hamburg 12 kms (7.5 mls); Munich 10 kms (6 mls); Düsseldorf 8 kms (5 mls); West Berlin 8 kms (5 mls).
Taxi fares: Frankfurt DM20–25; Hamburg DM15; Munich DM15; Düsseldorf DM12; West Berlin DM12.

Duty-free allowances
Visitors living outside Europe: 400 cigarettes *or* 100 cigars *or* 500 grammes of tobacco; 1 litre of spirits *or* 2 litres of wine.
Residents or visitors living inside Europe: 200 cigarettes *or* 50 cigars *or* 250 grammes of tobacco; 1 litre of spirits *or* 2 litres of wine.

Local time
GMT+1 hr.

Embassy phone numbers
Frankfurt:

Denmark 724861	Switzerland 725941
Netherlands 752021	UK 720406
Norway 7991	USA 740071
Sweden 722607	

Berlin:

Australia 883.5095	Sweden 885.70.91
Denmark 261.24.95	Switzerland 394.40.21
Japan 832.70.26	UK 309.52.95
Netherlands 883.51.73	USA 832.40.87
Norway 261.15.71	

Munich:

Denmark 22.04.41	Sweden 22.64.00
Japan 89.57.06	Switzerland 34.70.63
Netherlands 59.41.03	UK 39.40.15
Norway 22.41.70	USA 2.30.11

Hotels
Frankfurt: Frankfurter Hof, Inter-Continental, Sheraton, Airport, Parkhotel, Frankfurt, Plaza.
Hamburg: Vier Jahreszeiten, Atlantic, Hamburg Plaza,

Inter-Continental, Reichshof, Europäischer Hof.
Munich: Grand Hotel Continental, Bayerischer, Hilton,
Sheraton, Vier Jahreszeiten.
Düsseldorf: Eden, Esplanade, Grafadolf, Hilton,
Inter-Continental, Savoy, Steingenberger Parkhotel.
West Berlin: Am Zoo, Ambassador, Hilton, Kempinsky,
Palace, Parkhotel Zellermayer, Savoy.
Prices up to DM170 per night.

International banks

All international banks are represented.

Credit cards

All major credit cards

Office hours

Slight variations in different parts of Germany, but
generally 08.00–17.30 Mon–Fri.

National holidays

Regional holidays plus 1 Jan, Good Friday, Easter
Monday, 1 May, Ascension Day (May), Whit Monday
(May *or* June), Corpus Christi (May *or* June)
(except Berlin, Hamburg, Hanover), 17 Jun, 15 Aug
(except Berlin, Hamburg, Hanover), 1 Nov
(except Berlin, Hamburg, Hanover, Hesse), 22 Nov,
25, 26 Dec.

Voltage

220 volts AC.

Communications

Tel: DM5.40 per 3 mins. *Telex:* DM2.40 per 3 mins.
Airmail: 1–2 days. *Cable:* 60 pfennigs per word
(7–word minimum).

Social customs

Formality and politeness in business circles, as well as
promptness in keeping appointments. Entertainment is
plentiful and varied, and Germans are generous hosts.
In general, Germans like to be addressed by their
title. *Best buys:* Leather goods of all kinds, cameras,
binoculars, porcelain, cutlery, chocolates.

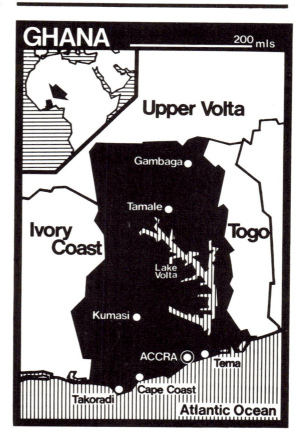

Area and population

238,530 sq kms (92,000 sq mls). Pop. 9 million.
Capital: Accra (900,000).
Chief cities: Takoradi (58,000), Tema (74,000),
Kumasi (260,000), Tamale (84,000),
Cape Coast (52,000). *Ports:* Takoradi, Tema.
Airport: Kotoka (Accra).

Climate

Tropical. Average temperature is 30°C (73°F),
Humidity 80%. Temperature never falls below
23°C (73°F) in Accra. Coolest time is June–Sept, but
this is also the rainy season. *Clothing:* This is a
trousers-and-shirt society, with safari suits becoming
popular. A lightweight suit is needed for business
appointments.

People

Chiefly Sudanic stock. Main peoples Akan, Daganbi,
Ga, Ewe. *Religion:* 42% Christian, 12% Moslem, rest
animist. *Distribution:* 66% rural.

Language
English.

Economic background
With the aim of achieving economic self-reliance, the government has pursued a policy aimed at overcoming such basic problems as high unemployment, low productivity, low savings and investment, and high private and government consumption. Cocoa is still the most important export commodity and fluctuations in world prices can hit balance of payments. Strict import controls conserve foreign exchange and, with few exceptions, imports are subject to specific licences.

Trade
Gross National Product: 2,820,000 million cedis.
Exports: 840 million cedis, chiefly cocoa, logs, gold, timber, diamonds, manganese ore, bauxite.
Imports: 943 million cedis, chiefly food, machinery, transport equipment, chemicals, mineral fuels, crude materials, manufactures, oils and fats.
Chief trading partners: UK, W. Germany, USA, Japan, France, China, Switzerland, Netherlands, USSR.
Inflation rate: 51.1%.

Prospects
The government intends to maintain a mixed economy and to encourage foreign investment. Chances of more trade are still dependent upon availability of foreign currency and the world price of cocoa.

Currency
Cedi = 100 pesawas. £ = 2.60 cedis; $ = 1.38 cedis.

Travel
Visas required by all non-Commonwealth visitors except W. Germans. However, Commonwealth visitors must have entry permits issued by Ghanaian High Commissions.

Vaccinations
Smallpox, yellow fever, cholera.

Airlines
Air Afrique, Air Mali, Alitalia, British Caledonian, Ethiopian, KLM, Lufthansa, Nigeria, Pan Am, Swissair, UTA.
Flying times: Copenhagen 10 hrs; London 7½ hrs; New York 11 hrs; Sydney 24 hrs.
Fares: Copenhagen F Dkr6,595 Y Dkr4,315; London F £463 Y £297; New York F $976 Y $604; Sydney F A$1,433 Y A$915.

Airport to city: 10 kms (6 mls). *Taxi fare:* 3 cedis.
Airport tax: 3 cedis payable on departure.

Duty-free allowances
400 cigarettes *or* tobacco equivalent; 1 quart spirits.

Local time
GMT.

Embassy phone numbers
Accra:

Australia 77972	Switzerland 28125
Canada 28555	W. Germany 21311
Denmark 21369	UK 64651
Japan 75616	USA 66811

Hotels
Accra: Ambassador, Continental, Meridian, Washington. Prices about 10–20 cedis per night.

International banks
Standard Bank of Ghana (Standard and Chartered), Barclays Bank of Ghana, Ghana Commercial Bank.

Credit cards
American Express, Diners Club.

Office hours
08.00–12.00 and 14.00–17.00 Mon–Fri. Some firms open 08.00–12.00 Sat.

National holidays
1, 13 Jan, 6 Mar, Good Friday–Easter Monday, 1 July, 25–26 Dec.

Voltage
230–250 volts.

Communications
Tel: 12 cedis per 3 mins. *Telex:* 12.54 cedis per 3 mins.
Airmail: 3 days. *Cable:* 36 pesawas per word.

Social customs
There are many private cocktail and dinner parties. Ghanaians are an exuberant people, given to noise and bright colours. Visitors may take unused foreign currency out of Ghana only if its importation has been declared on Form T5 upon entry. Unused local currency must be reconverted to foreign currency on departure.

Ratings
Safety excellent, food poor.

GREECE

0   200 mls

Bulgaria
Yugoslavia
Albania
Kavalla
Thessaloniki
Yannina
Corfu
Volos
Aegean Sea
Turkey
ATHENS
Patras
Ionian Sea
Kalamai
Rhodes
Crete   Iraklion
Mediterranean Sea

Area and population
130,883 sq kms (50,534 sq mls). Pop. 8 million.
Capital: Athens (2.5 million).
Chief cities: Thessaloniki (Salonica) (703,000),
Patras (110,000), Iraklion (79,000), Volos (51,000).
Ports: Piraeus (Athens), Patras.
Airports: Ellinikon (Athens), Micra (Thessaloniki).

Climate
Mediterranean. Athens temperatures rarely fall below
freezing and in summer temperatures of 38°C (100°F)
and slightly over are common. 50%–70% humidity.
Clothing: Normal European clothing plus overcoat for
winter, lightweight for summer.

People
94% Greek, 4% Turkish. *Religion:* Greek Orthodox.
Distribution: 54% urban.

Language
Greek. *English rating:* Good.

Economic background
Like its neighbour Turkey, Greece has an
agricultural-based economy with a developing industrial
base. The main industries at present are manufactured

goods, textiles and cement. In order to encourage
industrial expansion the government is working on a
five-year development plan. Other important revenue
earners are Greek shipping, with a gross tonnage of
about 30 million, and tourism.

Trade
Gross National Product: 575,000 million drachma.
Exports: 74,174 million drachma, chiefly tobacco,
currants, cotton, unprocessed aluminium, iron, nickel,
citrus fruits. *Imports:* 172,041 million drachma,
chiefly machinery, iron and steel, crude oil, meat,
vehicles. *Chief trading partners:* W. Germany,
Saudi Arabia, Japan, Italy, USA, France, UK,
Netherlands, Syria, Libya, USSR, Yugoslavia.
Inflation rate: 13.4%.

Prospects
Greece's future development will come with fuller
membership of the EEC, now under discussion. Further
industrialisation is anticipated.

Currency
Drachma = 100 lepta. £ = Dr68.99; $ = Dr36.69.

Travel
No visas required.

Vaccinations
Not required unless coming from an infected area.

Airlines
British Airways, Tarom, Olympic, Alitalia, Austrian,
LOT, Qantas, Sabena, Air France, Lufthansa, UTA,
El Al, KLM, Gulf Air, MEA, Kuwait, Swissair,
Pakistan International, TWA, Cyprus.
Flying times: Copenhagen $4\frac{1}{4}$ hrs; London $3\frac{1}{2}$ hrs;
New York 11 hrs; Sydney 36 hrs.
Fares: Copenhagen F Dkr3,085 Y Dkr 2,210;
London F £201 Y £158; New York F $846 Y $489;
Sydney F A$1,317 Y A$895.
Airport to city (Athens): 10 kms (6 mls).
Taxi fare: 100 drachma. *Bus fare:* 26 drachma.

Duty-free allowances
200 cigarettes *or* $\frac{1}{2}$ lb cigars *or* tobacco; 1 bottle of
spirits, 1 bottle of wine.

Local time
GMT+2 hrs (+3 hrs Apr–Sept).

Greece

Embassy phone numbers
Athens:

Australia 604611	Sweden 724504
Canada 739511	Switzerland 730365
Denmark 713012	W. Germany 742801
Japan 715343	UK 736211
Netherlands 711361	USA 712951
Norway 746173	

Hotels
Athens: Hilton, Acropole Palace, Amalia, Athenee Palace, Caravel, Grand Bretagne, King George V, Kings Palace, Mont Parnes, Royal Olympic, St George Lycabettus. Prices for good-class hotels are about Dr1,300 per night.

International banks
Grindlays, National Westminster, Barclays Bank International, First National City, Chase Manhattan, Bank of America, Bank of Nova Scotia.

Credit cards
All major credit cards.

Office hours
08.00–12.00 and 14.00–18.00 Mon–Fri, 08.00–12.00 Sat.

National holidays
Greek Orthodox holidays (movable, so check before departure), plus 1, 6 Jan, 25 Mar, 15 Aug, 28 Oct, 25, 26 Dec.

Voltage
220 volts AC.

Communications
Tel: Dr36.70 per min. *Telex:* Dr14+50% per min. *Airmail:* 2–3 days. *Cable:* Dr7 per word+7 drachma fee+8% surcharge (7-word minimum).

Social customs
It is best, if possible, to avoid visiting Athens during the tourist season because hotels and restaurants are packed. Be prepared to drink endless cups of strong Greek coffee during business talks. There is much entertaining at hotels and restaurants.

Grenada: see West Indies

Guatemala

Area and population
108,889 sq kms (42,042 sq mls). Pop. 5.7 million.
Capital: Guatemala City (720,000).
Chief cities: Quezaltenango (46,000), Escuintla (38,000), Puerto Barrios (20,000), Mazatenango (24,000).
Ports: Santo Tomas de Castilla (chief Caribbean port), San Jose (Pacific coast).
Aitport: La Aurora (Guatemala City).

Climate
Varies with altitude and season. In Guatemala City the Nov–Jan temperature ranges from 28° to 30°C (82° to 86°F), coming down to 4° to 7°C (39° to 45°F) at night. Daytime temperatures range up to 34°C (93°F) in Mar–May.
Clothing: Tropical-weight suits necessary for the humid coastal regions, but medium-weight for Guatemala City and other highland towns.

People
45% Amerindian, remainder of mixed blood, with small numbers of Europeans and Negroes.
Religion: Predominantly Roman Catholic.
Distribution: 34% urban.

Language
Spanish. *English rating:* Fair.

Economic background

The most populous of the Central American republics, Guatemala has a steadily growing economy based on coffee, cotton, bananas and sugar. Industry is expanding, too. Protective tariffs are helping rubber, paper, textiles and pharmaceuticals to replace imports. Oil has been discovered, further exploration is still going on, and nickel mining is expected to become important.

Trade

Gross National Product: 3,097,000 million quetzales.
Exports: 623.6 million quetzales, chiefly coffee, bananas, cotton, sugar. *Imports:* 732.6 million quetzales, chiefly industrial machinery, chemicals, pharmaceuticals, building materials.
Chief trading partners: USA, Venezuela, Japan, El Salvador, W. Germany, Mexico, UK, Netherlands, Costa Rica, Australia. *Inflation rate:* 8%.

Prospects

Growing at a steady rate of between 5% and 7%, the economy of Guatemala is now leaning more towards industry, even though agriculture is still the mainstay.

Currency

Quetzal = 100 centavos (at par with US dollar).
£ = 1.88 quetzales.

Travel

Visas are required, and are obtainable from Guatemalan consulates. Since there is no consulate in the UK, applications should be made to consulates either in Paris (73 Rue de Courcelles, Paris 8. Tel: 2277863) or Brussels (Boulevard Saint Michel 3, 1040 Brussels. Tel: 736.03.40). Thirty-day visas can also be obtained at New York or Miami consulates.

Vaccination

Smallpox.

Airlines

Pan Am, Sabena, KLM, Iberia, Aviateca (Guatemala's national airline which connects with major international airlines in Miami), TACA, SAHSA, Mexicana.
Flying times: Copenhagen (no direct flights) 30 hrs; London (no direct flights) 13 hrs; New York $4\frac{1}{2}$ hrs; Sydney 24 hrs. *Fares:* Copenhagen F Dkr6,520 Y Dkr4,175; London F £465.50 Y £302; New York F $386 Y $267; Sydney F A$2,063 Y A$1,344. *Airport to city:* 6.4 kms (4 mls). *Taxi fare:* 3 quetzales.

Duty-free allowances

80 cigarettes *or* tobacco equivalent;
2 bottles of spirits.

Local time

GMT−6 hrs.

Embassy phone numbers

Guatemala City: UK 61329 and 64375.

Hotels

Guatemala City: Camino Real, Conquistador Sheraton, Ritz Continental. Prices about US$25 per night.

International banks

Bank of London and Montreal, Bank of America.

Credit cards

American Express, Diners Club.

Office hours

08.00–12.00 and 14.00–18.00 Mon–Fri,
08.00–12.00 Sat.

National holidays

1 Jan, Holy Week (starting Wednesday before Good Friday), 1 May, 30 June, 1 July, 15 Aug, 15 Sept, 13, 20 Oct, 1 Nov, 24, 25, 31 Dec.

Voltage

110 volts AC.

Communications

Tel: 18 quetzales per 3 mins. *Telex:* 12 quetzales per 3 mins. *Airmail:* 4–6 days. *Cables:* 60 cents per word.

Social customs

Guatemala is a very conservative country, particularly where dress and manners are concerned. Take dark but lightweight clothes for evening wear. The best guide to South America, *The South American Handbook*, advises visitors to Guatemala City not to park on the street at night or the car will be broken into, and 'in the town of Pancajche the police are biased against long-haired men'.

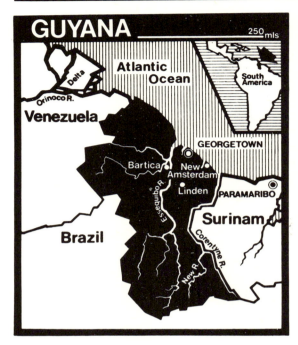

GUYANA 250 mls

Atlantic Ocean

South America

Orinoco R.

Venezuela

Delta

GEORGETOWN

Bartica
New Amsterdam
Linden
PARAMARIBO

Essequibo R.

Surinam

Brazil

Corentyne R.

New R.

and little industry. The government's Industrial Development Corporation is trying to encourage new industries, and boost current facilities for shipbuilding, engineering, fruit, tinned foods, brewing, rum-distilling, and building materials. In the meantime, the economy relies heavily on the world price for sugar, rice, bauxite and alumina.

Trade
Gross National Product: $400 million (estimate)
Exports: $140 million, chiefly unrefined sugar, bauxite, alumina, rice, timber. *Imports:* $170 million, chiefly manufactured goods, machinery and transport equipment, food, chemicals, fuels and lubricants.
Chief trading partners: Caribbean Community, Japan, UK, USSR, USA, Canada, Netherlands, W. Germany.
Inflation rate: Not available.

Prospects
Much will depend on the government's success in attracting new industries.

Currency
Guyana dollar = 100 cents. £ = GU$4.79; $ = GU$2.54.

Travel
Visas not required.

Vaccination
Smallpox.

Airlines
Air France, Pan Am, British Airways, BWIA, KLM.
Flying times: Copenhagen 18 hrs; London 13 hrs; New York $5\frac{1}{2}$ hrs; Sydney 24 hrs.
Fares: Copenhagen F Dkr6,565 Y Dkr4,300; London F £450.50 Y £300.50; New York F $413 Y $276; Sydney F A$2,011 Y A$1,344.
Airport to city: 40 kms (25 mls). *Taxi fare:* GU$25.

Duty-free allowances
200 cigarettes *or* tobacco equivalent; $\frac{1}{8}$ gallon of spirits.

Local time
GMT −3 hrs.

Embassy phone numbers
Georgetown: UK 65881.

Area and population
215,000 sq kms (82,990 sq mls). Pop. 800,000.
Capital: Georgetown (195,000).
Chief cities: New Amsterdam (25,000),
Linden (35,000). *Port:* Georgetown.
Airport: Timehri (Georgetown).

Climate
Shade temperatures of 27°C (80°F) throughout the year, rising to about 31°C (87°F). Two wet seasons are mid-Apr to mid-Aug and mid-Nov to Jan.
Average rainfall is 228 cms (90 ins) per year.
Clothing: Tropical-weight throughout the year.

People
50% East Indians, 35% African, 1% Europeans, the remainder Chinese and Amerindians.
Religion: 57% Christian, 34% Hindu, 9% Moslem.
Distribution: Mainly urban.

Language
English.

Economic background
The economy is based on sugar and rice, helped by minerals, timber and cattle. Consequently, Guyana is faced with the problem of a rapidly growing population

Guyana

Haiti

Hotels
Georgetown: Guyana Pegasus, Park, Tower.
Prices all about GU$20–25 per night.

International banks
Royal Bank of Canada, Barclays Bank International,
Chase Manhattan, Bank of Baroda, Bank of Nova Scotia.

Credit cards
Barclaycard, American Express, Diners Club.

Office hours
Government offices: 08.00–11.30 and
13.00–16.00 Mon–Fri, 08.00–12.00 Sat.
Banks: 08.00–12.00 Mon–Fri, 08.00–11.00 Sat.
Department stores and offices: 08.00–11.30 and
13.00–16.00 Mon–Fri, 08.00–11.30 Sat.

National holidays
Moslem and Hindu holidays plus 1 Jan, 23 Feb,
Good Friday–Easter Monday, 1 May, 3 July, 7 Aug,
25, 26 Dec.

Voltage
110 volts.

Communications
Rates not available but international telephone, telex
and cable facilities are available. Cables can be sent
from Cable & Wireless situated in the Bank of Guyana
Building in Georgetown.

Social customs
European business customs prevail in the business
community, which is boosted by the presence of up to a
dozen international companies. Unfortunately,
Georgetown has acquired a reputation for violence,
particularly after dark, and care should be taken not to
walk alone. Take one of the plentiful taxis that ply the
city streets at reasonable prices.
Best buys: Beaten brasswork and Amerindian curios,
such as bows and arrows, and blowpipes.

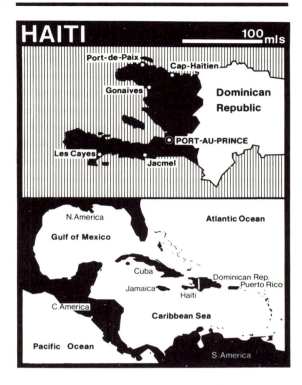

Area and population
27,750 sq kms (10,700 sq mls). Pop. 4.7 million.
Capital: Port-au-Prince (500,000).
Chief cities: Cap-Haïtien (50,000), Gonaïves (14,000),
Les Cayes (14,000), Port-de-Paix (6,500).
Port: Port-au-Prince. *Airport:* François Duvalier
International (Port-au-Prince).

Climate
Tropical. Temperatures range from
24° to 35°C (75° to 95°F). High humidity.
Worst time to visit is May–Sept. *Clothing:* Tropical suits
or cotton dresses throughout the year.

People
95% African origin. *Religion:* Predominantly Roman
Catholic, but voodoo practised. *Distribution:* 12% urban.

Language
French, but most people speak only Creole.
English rating: Poor.

Economic background
One of the poorest countries in the world, Haiti has only
begun to develop slowly in recent years. Its economy is

almost entirely agricultural, based on coffee and sisal, but since 1970 there has been a noticeable improvement. A hydro-electric scheme has brought energy, and development aid is now coming in from the United Nations, USA, France, Canada and W. Germany. Tourism is developing quickly, bringing in much needed foreign exchange.

Trade

Gross National Product: 2,241 million gourdes.
Exports: US$50 million, chiefly coffee, sisal, bauxite, sugar, shellfish, fruit. *Imports:* US$70 million, chiefly wheat, fish, fats and oils, paper, cotton, fabrics, vehicles, petroleum, machinery, electrical equipment, raw materials. *Chief trading partners:* Japan, Canada, France, W. Germany, UK, Curacao, Belgium, Netherlands, Italy, Switzerland.
Inflation rate: Not available.

Prospects

New roads, development aid and increased tourism offer prospects of greater prosperity than Haiti has ever known.

Currency

Gourde = 100 centimes. £ = 9.40 gourdes;
$ = 5.00 gourdes.

Travel

Visas not required but visitors must buy a US$2 tourist card on arrival.

Vaccinations

Smallpox (except travellers coming from USA and Canada).

Airlines

Pan Am, American, Eastern, Air France, ALM.
Flying times: Copenhagen (no direct flights) 16½ hrs; London (no direct flights) 12 hrs (approx); New York 4½ hrs; Sydney 24 hrs.
Fares: Copenhagen F Dkr5,650 Y Dkr3,810; London F £393.50 Y £256.50; New York F $240 Y $160; Sydney F A$1,451 Y A$933.
Airport to city: 12.8 km (8 mls). *Taxi fare:* US$3.50.

Duty-free allowances

200 cigarettes *or* 50 cigars *or* 250 grammes of tobacco; 1 litre of spirits.

Local time

GMT−5 hrs.

Embassy phone numbers

Port-au-Prince: UK 21227 and 23921.

Hotels

Port-au-Prince: Castel D'Haiti, Beau Rivage, Sans Souci, Oloffson, Splendid, Plaza, Park. Prices up to US$30 per night. For businessmen, Sans Souci is most conveniently located.

International banks

Royal Bank of Canada, First National City Bank of New York, Bank of Nova Scotia, Bank of Boston, Banque Nationale de Paris, First National Bank of Chicago.

Credit cards

American Express, Diners Club.

Office hours

07.00–16.00 in summer, 08.00–17.00 in winter, Mon–Fri.

National holidays

1, 2 Jan, Carnival (Feb), Good Friday, 14 Apr, 1, 18, 22 May, Ascension (May), 22 June, 15 Aug, 17 Oct, 1, 2, 18 Nov, 5, 25 Dec.

Voltage

110–220 volts.

Communications

Tel: US$15.00 per 3 mins.
Telex: US$12.00 per 3 mins. *Airmail:* 4–5 days.
Cable: US$0.44 per word (7-word minimum).

Social customs

Most business entertaining goes on in hotels and restaurants. US currency circulates freely in Haiti. If the humidity of Port-au-Prince becomes too tiring, the hill resort of Kenscoff, 25 kms (17 mls) away, where the air is cool, is a pleasant relief.

HONDURAS 250 mls

Mexico
Belize
Caribbean Sea
Guatemala
Porto Cortes
San Pedro Sula
TEGUCIGALPA
El Salvador
Nicaragua
Pacific Ocean

Area and population
108,067 sq kms (43,227 sq mls). Pop. 3 million.
Capital: Tegucigalpa (400,000).
Chief cities: San Pedro Sula (175,000),
Puerto Cortes (27,000). *Ports:* Amapala, Puerto Cortes.
Airport: Toncontin (Tegucigalpa).

Climate
Very hot and humid in other regions, but
Tegucigalpa is pleasant, with an average mean
temperature of 23°C (74°F). The dry season is Dec–May.
Clothing: Lightweight for most of the year, but
something warmer for Nov–Feb.

People
90% mestizo, with European, Negro and Indian
minorities. *Religion:* Roman Catholic.
Distribution: 28% urban.

Language
Spanish. *English rating:* Good.

Economic background
One of the poorest of Central American countries,
Honduras's economy was further hit by the 1974
hurricane which caused extensive damage to its banana
and coffee crops. About 75% of Hondurans live off the
land and industry has made little progress. The
government is working on development plans,
proceeding with offshore oil exploration and some
mining projects. It hoped for much improvement by
joining the Central American Common Market but left
when it found there were no advantages for Honduras.

Trade
Gross National Product: 1,937 million lempiras.

Exports: 339.4 million lempiras, chiefly foodstuffs, crude
materials, manufactured articles, beverages, tobacco,
combustible lubricants.
Imports: 441.3 million lempiras, chiefly manufactured
goods, machinery and transport equipment, chemicals,
food, mineral fuels. *Chief trading partners:* USA,
Guatemala, Japan, Nicaragua, Costa Rica, W. Germany,
Venezuela, UK, Belgium, Dominican Republic.
Inflation rate: Not available.

Prospects
With most of its people living at bare subsistence level
and only a small minority at West European standards,
there is little immediate prospect of industrial progress.
Some development plans are under way.

Currency
Lempira (Lps) = 100 centavos. £ = Lps3.79.
By law the value of the lempira is fixed at one-half of
the US dollar.

Travel
Visas not required.

Vaccinations
Smallpox. Tetanus and typhoid inoculations
recommended.

Airlines
SAHSA, TAN, which connect at Belize, Guatemala City,
Mexico City, Miami, New Orleans, Panama City and
San Jose (Costa Rica).
Flying times: Copenhagen 28 hrs; London 15 hrs;
New York 6 hrs; Sydney 36 hrs. *Fares:* Copenhagen
F Dkr6,520 Y Dkr4,175; London F £465.50 Y £302;
New York F $386 Y$267;
Sydney F A$2,063 Y A$1,344.
Airport to city: 4.8 kms (3 mls). *Taxi fare:* Lps4.

Duty-free allowances
200 cigarettes; 2 bottles of spirits.

Local time
GMT–6 hrs.

Embassy phone numbers
Tegucigalpa: UK 2.0479.

Hotels
Tegucigalpa: Honduras Maya, Lincoln, Prado,
Boston, Savoy. Prices up to US$20 per night.

Honduras

International banks
None.

Credit cards
American Express, Barclaycard, Diners Club.

Office hours
08.00–12.00 and 13.30–17.00 Mon–Fri,
08.00–11.00 Sat.

National holidays
1 Jan, 3 Feb, Maundy Thursday to Easter Monday,
14 Apr, 1 May, 15 Sept, 3, 12, 21 Oct, 25 Dec.

Voltage
110 volts or 220 volts AC.

Communications
Tel: Lps18 per min. *Telex:* Lps28.50 per 3 mins.
Airmail: 4–7 days. *Cable:* Lps1.30 per word.

Social customs
Nothing significant in the way of business manners.
Care should be taken with food and water because
dysentery is prevalent. Drink only boiled water.

Hong Kong

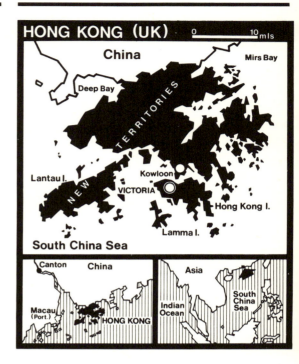

Area and population
1,030 sq kms (398 sq mls). Pop. 4.4 million.
Capital: Victoria.
Chief cities: None. *Port:* Hong Kong.
Airport: Kai Tak.

Climate
Tropical but variable. Temperatures range from
15°C (60°F) in Feb to 28°C (82°F) in July. Expect gales
with heavy rain May–Nov.
Clothing: European-weight clothing for winter,
light- or tropical-weight in summer.

People
98% Chinese. *Religion:* Confucianism, Buddhism,
Taoism.

Languages
English and Cantonese.

Economic background
Hong Kong has a flourishing economy, depending on
its exports and trading with almost every country in the
world. Even the 1975 recession did not affect it as badly
as other parts of South East Asia. The economy is based
mainly on textiles and clothing, and electronics have

played an increasingly important part in recent years. Almost 90% of all goods produced in Hong Kong are exported.

Trade
Gross National Product: £1,000 million (estimated).
Exports: HK$30,000 million (not including re-exports) chiefly clothing, textiles, fabrics, electronic equipment, footwear, scientific instruments, travel goods.
Imports: HK$34,000 million, chiefly textile yarns, fabrics, electrical machinery, pearls and precious stones, non-electrical machinery. *Chief trading partners:* Japan, China, USA, Taiwan, UK, W. Germany, Singapore, Indonesia. *Inflation rate:* Not available.

Prospects
Hong Kong is expected to remain one of South East Asia's leading trading and financial centres in the foreseeable future.

Currency
Dollar = 100 cents. £ = HK$8.77; $ = HK$4.66.

Travel
Visas not required for visits of up to 3 months.

Vaccinations
Smallpox; cholera vaccination recommended. If travelling from an infected area, an international certificate of vaccination against yellow fever is required.

Airlines
Air France, Air India, Alitalia, British Airways, Cathay Pacific, Garuda, JAL, KLM, Lufthansa, Korean, Pan Am, Qantas, Swissair, Thai, TWA.
Flying times: Copenhagen $17\frac{1}{4}$ hrs; London 18 hrs; New York 24 hrs; Sydney 6 hrs.
Fares: Copenhagen F Dkr9,645 Y Dkr5,645; London F £743.50 Y £435; New York F $1,799 Y $1,131; Sydney F A$830 Y A$593.
Airport to city: 7.5 km (4.5 mls). *Taxi fare:* HK$3.55.

Duty-free allowances
200 cigarettes *or* 50 cigars; 1 quart of spirits *or* 1 quart of wine.

Local time
GMT+8 hrs.

Embassy phone numbers
Australia 5.227171	Sweden 5.227125
Canada 5.451041	W. Germany 5.221031
Japan 5.450153	UK 5.229541
Netherlands 5.227710	USA 5.239011
Norway 5.226381	

Hotels
Mandarin, Hong Kong, Hilton, Caravelle, Furama, Hyatt Regency, Peninsula, Sheraton, Excelsior.
Good class hotels charge HK$175–300 per night.

International banks
Chartered Bank, Barclays Bank International, Hong Kong and Shanghai Banking Corporation.

Credit cards
American Express, Bank Americard, Diners Club.

Office hours
09.00–17.00 Mon–Fri, 09.00–12.30 Sat.

National holidays
Chinese festivals are variable, but fixed holidays include 1 Jan, 5 Apr, Good Friday, Easter Monday, 1 July, First Monday in Aug, 25, 26 Dec.

Voltage
200 volts 50 cycles AC.

Communications
Tel: HK$43.80 per 3 mins. *Telex:* HK$18.20 per min.
Airmail: 3–4 days. *Cable:* HK$1.45 per word.

Social customs
A very hospitable environment with many cocktail parties and much entertaining in private houses.
Best buys: Cameras, hi-fi, suits and shirts. Beware of unlicensed taxis (no meters).

HUNGARY

Czechoslovakia, Austria, Poland, Italy, Switzerland, Brazil, Romania, France, UK, Yugoslavia, Iraq.
Inflation rate: Not available.

Prospects
While the development of agriculture remains an important aim, modernization of industry continues, particularly chemicals and petrochemicals.

Currency
Forint (Fts) = 100 fillers.   £ = Fts36.33; $ = Fts19.32. (Tourist rates.)

Area and population
93,030 sq kms (35,919 sq mls). Pop. 10.5 million.
Capital: Budapest (2 million).
Chief cities: Miskolc (191,000), Debrecen (173,000), Pecs (158,000), Gyor (111,000), Szeged (133,000).
Airport: Ferihegy (Budapest).

Travel
Visas required.

Vaccinations
Smallpox.

Climate
Moderately continental. Winter temperatures range from 0°C (32°F), summer temperatures up to 23°C (73°F) in July. *Clothing:* Lightweight in summer, but a warm overcoat is needed in winter.

Airlines
British Airways, Malev, Pan Am, SAS, KLM, Lufthansa, Swissair, Air France, Balkan, CSA, Finnair, Interflug, JAT, LOT, Tarom, Aeroflot.
Flying times: Copenhagen 3 hrs; London 2½ hrs; New York 10 hrs; Sydney 24 hrs. *Fares:* Copenhagen F Dkr2,155 Y Dkr1,370; London F £162 Y £108; New York F $828 Y $429; Sydney F A$1,435 Y A$922.
Airport to city: 16 kms (10 mls). *Taxi fare:* Fts 60–80.

People
96% Hungarian, with German, Slovak, Gypsy, Serbian and Croatian minorities. *Religion:* 65% Roman Catholic, 25% Protestant, 3% Eastern Orthodox.
Distribution: 45% urban.

Duty-free allowances
250 cigarettes *or* 50 cigars *or* 250 grammes of tobacco; 1 litre of spirits, 2 litres of wine.

Language
Hungarian. *English rating:* Fair.

Local time
GMT+1 hr.

Economic background
An industrial and agricultural country, Hungary is poor in raw materials and to counter this it has mechanised farming and developed industry to the point at which manufacturing accounts for about a half of the national income. Hungary must export in order to pay for its raw materials. Hungary produces machinery (almost half of the industrial output) as well as textiles, clothing, paper, pharmaceuticals and food.

Embassy phone numbers
Budapest:
Japan 150.043	UK 182.888
Switzerland 229.491	USA 329.375
	W. Germany 224.204

Hotels
Budapest: Hilton, Duna Inter-Continental, Grand Hotel, Margitsziget, Grand Hotel Gellert, Grand Hotel Royal. Prices up to Fts840 per night.

Trade
Gross National Product: Fts369.900 million.
Exports: Fts204,839 million, chiefly machinery, vehicles, tractors, food, textiles. *Imports:* Fts230,056 million, chiefly raw materials, machinery, semi-finished products.
Chief trading partners: USSR, E. and W. Germany,

International banks
Hungarian International Bank.

Credit cards
All major credit cards.

Office hours

08.00–16.00 Mon–Fri, 08.00–12.00 Sat.

National holidays

1 Jan, Easter Monday, 4 Apr, 1 May, 20 Aug, 7 Nov, 25, 26 Dec.

Voltage

220–380 volts AC/single and 3 phase 50 cycles.

Communications

Tel: Fts63.50 per 3 mins. *Telex:* Fts11 per min (3 mins minimum). *Airmail:* 7–10 days.
Cable: Fts37.10 for 7 words.

Social customs

Generous hospitality greets the Western visitor, Hungarians are friendly and possess a sense of humour. There is much handshaking. Budapest restaurants serve excellent food and wine—the white is particularly good, especially Tokaj. *Best buys:* Embroidery, lace, dolls in national costume, wooden articles, and long-playing records.

Iceland

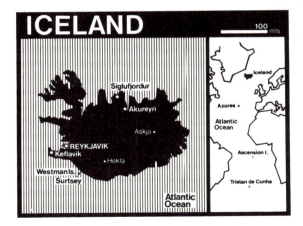

Area and population

103,000 sq kms (39,758 sq mls). Pop. 220,000.
Capital: Reykjavik (84,300).
Chief cities: Kopavogur (13,000), Akureyri (12,000), Hafnarfjördhur (12,000). *Port:* Reykjavik.
Airport: Keflavik (Reykjavik).

Climate

Comparatively mild climate for a country so far north. January temperature is about −0.6°C (31°F) and in July 11°C (52°F). *Clothing:* Warmer clothing is needed than elsewhere in Europe. Take a raincoat.

People

Northern European. *Religion:* 97% Evangelical Lutheran. *Distribution:* 70% urban.

Language

Icelandic. *English rating:* Excellent.

Economic background

Based heavily on fishing. Iceland's modern industry has developed since the country began to diversify. Cement, nitrate fertiliser and diatomite is produced, as well as knitwear, blankets, furs, skins, paint and clothing. Tourism is particularly important as a source of foreign exchange and Icelandic Airlines (Loftleidir) has become a major international carrier.

Trade

Gross National Product: Kr93,600 million.
Exports: Kr73,500 million, chiefly fish and fish products, shrimps, lobsters, fish meal, aluminium.
Imports: Kr85,660 million, chiefly transport equipment, petroleum, machinery, textile yarns, iron and steel.
Chief trading partners: USSR, W. Germany, USA, UK, Denmark, Norway, Sweden, Netherlands, Australia, Japan, Portugal, Italy, Poland.
Inflation rate: Not available.

Prospects

New industrial projects are under way.

Currency

Krona = 100 aura. £ = Kr491.85; $ = Kr261.62.

Travel

Visas not required.

Vaccinations

Not required.

Airlines

British Airways, Loftleidir, SAS.
Flying times: Copenhagen 3 hrs; London 2½ hrs; New York 6 hrs; Sydney 24 hrs. *Fares:* Copenhagen F Dkr2,075 Y Dkr1,600; London F £154 Y £102.50; New York F $560 Y $232; Sydney F A$1,654 Y A$1,067.
Airport to city: 51 mls (32 mls). *Taxi fare:* Kr4,300.

Iceland

Duty-free allowances
200 cigarettes *or* their weight equivalent in cigars *or* tobacco; 1 litre of spirits *or* 2 litres of wine.

Local time
GMT.

Embassy phone numbers
Reykjavik: UK 15883.

Hotels
Reykjavik: Borg, City, Esja, Gardur, Holt, Loftleidir, Saga. Prices about US$30 per night.

International banks
None.

Credit cards
All major credit cards.

Office hours
09.00–12.00 and 13.00–17.00 Mon–Fri.

National holidays
1 Jan, Maundy Thursday, Good Friday, Easter Monday, First Day of Summer (Apr), 1 May, Ascension Day (May), Whit Monday (May *or* June), 17 June, First Monday in Aug, 24, 25, 26, 31 Dec.

Voltage
220–380 volts AC.

Communications
Tel: Kr990 per min. *Telex:* Kr450 per 3 mins.
Airmail: 2–3 days. *Cable:* Kr39 per word.
(Kr675 minimum plus 4% tax).

Social customs
Formal customs in business circles. Names in the telephone directory are listed alphabetically by Christian name because sons and daughters take their father's Christian name plus '-son' or '-dottir' as surnames.
Best buys: Hand-made wood or whalebone carvings, sweaters, sheepskins.

India

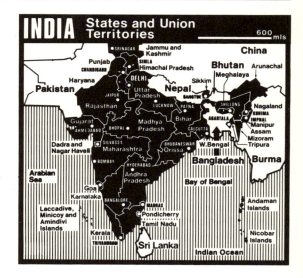

Area and population
3,053,597 sq kms (1,178,995 sq mls). Pop. 600 million.
Capital: New Delhi (4 million).
Chief cities: Calcutta (11 million), Bombay (6m), Madras (3.1m), Bangalore (1.6 m), Ahmedabad (1.7m), Kanpur (1.3m), Poona (1.1m). *Ports:* Bombay, Calcutta, Madras. *Airports:* Palam (New Delhi), Dum Dum (Calcutta), Santa Cruz (Bombay), Meenambakkan (Madras).

Climate
Extremes—from humid tropical to even dry Arctic.
Delhi: Temperatures are moderate, but in Nov–Feb can drop to 5°C (41°F). From May onwards temperatures rise to 45°C (113°F). Monsoon: June–Sept.
Calcutta: Apr–June very hot—up to 45°C (113°F). Monsoon: June–Sept. Best time to visit is Nov–Mar, when temperatures range up to 24°C (75.2°F).
Bombay: No extremes but humidity worst Apr–June. Temperatures rarely exceed 33°C (91.4°F). Monsoon: June–Sept.
Madras: Temperatures up to 40°C (104°F). Best time to visit: Nov–Mar. Worst time: Sept–Nov.

People
Aryan and Dravidian stock. *Religion:* 83% Hindu, 10% Moslem, 2% Christian. *Distribution:* 18% urban.

Languages
Hindi plus 16 official languages according to state.
English rating: Excellent.

Economic background

India has made considerable industrial progress in recent years. The best of its industry is very good and India has gone a considerable way towards self-sufficiency in basic engineering products. Few people who have not visited India realise its industrial achievement or that in the years ahead it is likely to become an important competitor in world markets. The Indian economy is now healthier than it has been for many years and business confidence is buoyant. Half the national income is derived from agriculture, the remainder being generated by mining and manufacturing. India is particularly strong in steel production.

Trade

Gross National Product: 633,750 million rupees.
Exports: 32,986 million rupees, chiefly jute, tea, ores, cotton manufactures, iron and steel, leather, fruit, animal feedstuffs, pearls and precious stones, machinery and transport equipment. *Imports:* 44,681 million rupees, chiefly machinery, cereals, fertilisers, textile fibres, iron and steel manufactures, petroleum, organic chemicals.
Chief trading partners: USA, Iran, Japan, USSR, W. Germany, Saudi Arabia, UK, Poland, Iraq, Netherlands. *Inflation rate:* 3.4%.

Prospects

With the economy closely related to the vagaries of the weather and the availability of foreign exchange, the improved economic situation is a fragile development that could suffer reverses.

Currency

Rupee = 100 paisa. £ = R15.28; $ = 8.12.

Travel

Visas not generally required.

Vaccinations

While vaccinations against smallpox and cholera are not required, they are strongly recommended. Visitors arriving from yellow fever areas must possess a valid international certificate of vaccination.

Airlines

Aeroflot, Air France, Air India, Alitalia, British Airways, JAL, KLM, Kuwait, Lufthansa, PIA, Pan Am, Qantas, SAS, Thai.
Flying times (to Delhi): Copenhagen 7¾ hrs; London 10 hrs; New York 19 hrs; Sydney 8 hrs.
Fares (to Delhi): Copenhagen F Dkr6,205 Y Dkr3,975;
London F £478 Y £306.50; New York F $1,451 Y $900; Sydney F A$943 Y A$673.
Airport to city: Delhi 14.5 kms (9 mls). *Taxi fare:* R25. Bombay 29 kms (18 mls). *Taxi fare:* R30. Calcutta 13 kms (8 mls). *Taxi fare:* R25.

Duty-free allowance

200 cigarettes *or* 50 cigars *or* 250 grammes of tobacco; 1 bottle of spirits.

Local time

GMT+5½hrs.

Embassy phone numbers

Bombay:

Australia 294741	Sweden 262583
Japan 363853	Switzerland 293550
Denmark 268181	W. Germany 296023
Netherlands 296840	UK 274874
Norway 214254	USA 363611

Hotels

Bangalore: Ashoka, Bangalore. *Bombay:* Ambassador, Oberoi-Sheraton, Taj Mahal Inter-Continental.
Calcutta: Oberoi Grand, Park, Ritz Inter-Continental.
Madras: Connemara, Savera. *New Delhi:* Claridges, Imperial, Janpath, Ashoka, Oberoi Inter-Continental, Quitab, Rajdoot. Prices up to R300 per night.

International banks

Bank of Baroda, Bank of India, British Bank of the Middle East, Central Bank of India, Chartered Bank, Citibank, Hong Kong and Shanghai Banking Corporation.

Credit cards

All major credit cards.

Office hours

Variable from city to city but generally 09.30–17.00 Mon–Sat.

National holidays

Many and varied according to city and should always be checked before arrival. Fixed holidays include 26 Jan, 15 Aug.

Voltage

220 volts AC.

Communications
Tel: R84 per 3 mins. *Telex:* R72 per 3 mins.
Airmail: 6–7 days. *Cable:* R2 per word
(7-word minimum).

Social customs
An intensely religious country, India's social customs
apply on that basis. Simple rules to remember are: the
cow is sacred to Hindus, who are also vegetarian and
may be teetotal. Moslems do not eat pig flesh, or drink
spirits. Sikhs and Parsees do not smoke.

Indonesia

Area and population
1.9 million sq kms (575,000 sq mls). Pop. 130 million.
Capital: Jakarta (5.8 million).
Chief cities: Surabaya (1.2 m), Bandung (1.1 m),
Denpasar, Medan (620,000), Ujung Pandang
(formerly Makassar). *Ports:* Jakarta, Surabaya.
Airport: Halim International (Jakarta).

Climate
Tropical. Temperatures range from 24° to 32°C
(75°–90°F). High humidity. Dry season lasts May–Sept,
wet season Oct–Apr. *Clothing:* Tropical. Jackets not
normally worn during the day, but businessmen may
prefer to do so as an act of courtesy.

People
Predominantly Malays; Papuans in West Irian.
Religion: 80% Moslem, remainder Hindu, Christian,
Buddhist. *Distribution:* 15% urban.

Language
Bahasa Indonesia. *English rating:* Good.

Economic background
Potentially a wealthy country, Indonesia suffered serious
economic setbacks until a military government took
power in 1966 and introduced reforms. The country is
now completing its second five-year plan, which
includes priority development targets such as agriculture,
education, infrastructure and health services. Indonesia is
one of the world's top producers of tin and rubber and
the leading oil producer in the Far East.

Trade
Gross National Product: US$22,480 million.
Exports: US$7,102.5 million, chiefly petroleum,
petroleum products, tin ore, copra, coffee, tobacco.
Imports: US$4,769.8 million, chiefly textiles, machinery,
transport equipment, rice, fertilisers, chemicals.
Chief trading partners: Japan, USA, W. Germany,
Singapore, UK, Netherlands. *Inflation rate:* 10.9%.

Prospects
Indonesia is still the recipient of large amounts of US and
international aid. Public investment has been cut and
Indonesia is passing through a period of consolidation.

Currency
Rupiah = 100 sen. £ = 780.2 rupiahs; $ = 415 rupiahs.

Travel
Visas required.

Vaccination
Smallpox, cholera.

Airlines
Garuda, Cathay Pacific, Lufthansa, JAL, KLM, MAS,
Qantas, SAS, SIA, Thai.
Flying times: Copenhagen $16\frac{1}{4}$ hrs; London 17 hrs;
New York 27 hrs; Sydney $7\frac{1}{2}$ hrs. *Fares:* Copenhagen
F Dkr8,920 Y Dkr5,500; London F £693.50 Y £428;
New York F $1,703 Y $1,902; Sydney F A$555 Y A$395.
Airport to city: 13 kms (8 mls). *Taxi fare:* 1500 rupiahs.

Duty-free allowances
200 cigarettes *or* 50 cigars, 1 bottle of spirits.

Local time
West Zone (incl. Jakarta): GMT+7 hrs.
Central Zone: GMT+8 hrs. *East Zone:* GMT+9 hrs.

Indonesia

Embassy phone numbers
Jakarta:

Australia 50511	Sweden 46953
Canada 47841	Switzerland 47921
Denmark 46406	W. Germany 48074
Japan 50061	UK 41091
Netherlands 54831	USA 40001
Norway 54556	

Hotels
Jakarta: Asoka, Hilton, Inter-Continental, Indonesia, Kartika Plaza, President, Ramayana City, Sabang Metropolitan. *Denpasar:* Bali. *Surabaya:* Mirama. Prices vary, but a good-class hotel is about US$30 per night.

International banks
Chartered, Hong Kong and Shanghai, European Asian Bank.

Credit cards
American Express, Diners Club.

Office hours
08.30–16.00 Mon–Sat, but most offices close 12.00 on Fri. Some firms also close 12.30 Sat.

National holidays
All Moslem holidays, plus 1 Jan, Good Friday, Ascension Day (May), 17 Aug, 25 Dec.

Voltage
110 volts.

Communications
Tel: 5,940 rupiahs per 3 min. *Telex:* Available. *Airmail:* 4–7 days.

Social customs
Patience is more than a virtue in Indonesia—it is a necessity. Business decisions take time. Businessmen, even in the state trading organisations, are very hospitable, so anticipate an exchange of small gifts. Use only the right hand for giving and receiving.

Iran

Area and population
1,648,000 sq km (630,000 sq mls). Pop. 30 million. *Capital:* Tehran (4 million). *Chief cities:* Esfahan (600,000), Tabriz (510,000), Mashad (580,000), Abadan (320,000), Shiraz (370,000), Ahvaz (300,000), Kerman (90,000), Arak (80,000). *Ports:* Khorramshahr, Abadan, Bandar-e-Abbas. *Airport:* Mehrabad (Tehran).

Climate
Tehran temperatures range from 3°C (34°F) in Jan to more than 38°C (100°F) in summer. Average humidity 59%. With the exception of the Gulf and Caspian areas, which are extremely hot and humid, the climate is the same throughout the country. Normally a short rainy season occurs in spring and in early winter.
Clothing: Light tropical suits are needed in summer but ordinary European clothing is suitable for the winter. Women need light cotton or silk dresses in summer and clothing as worn in Europe during winter. For visits Mar–May and Sept–Oct, take an overcoat for evening wear.

People
50% Iranian; 35% Turkic origin. *Religion:* 98% Moslem. *Distribution:* 31% urban.

Language
Farsi (Persian). *English rating:* Good.

Economic background
A series of radical land and social reforms, introduced by the Shah in the early 1960s, cleared the way for Iran's economy to undergo a period of rapid transformation and sustained growth. In the past ten years Iran's GNP has grown at an annual rate of 11.2%. Iran plans to triple *per capita* income to US$1500 by the end of 1979, creating two million new jobs. The pattern of trade between Iran and the rest of the world is likely to be affected by the large number of bilateral trade agreements that have been concluded in the past three years. The biggest of these, with the United States, provides for US exports to Iran of US15,000 million over the next five years.

Trade
Gross National Product: 3,085,000 million rials.
Exports: 1,213,027 million rials, chiefly crude petroleum, carpets, cotton, fruit, hides and skins, metallic ores.
Imports: 448,075 million rials, chiefly machinery, iron and steel, textile fibres, chemicals, pharmaceuticals, vehicles, paper, rubber. *Chief trading partners:* USA, W. Germany, Japan, UK, France, Italy, USSR, Belgium, Netherlands, Iraq. *Inflation rate:* 17.6%.

Prospects
In order to expand Iran still needs to buy goods from abroad. Iran is keen to attract foreign investment in sectors of manufacturing industry where local expertise is lacking.

Currency
Rial = 100 dinars. £ = 132 rials; $ = 70.21 rials.

Travel
Visas not required by UK citizens.

Vaccinations
Smallpox. Inoculation against typhoid and paratyphoid strongly recommended.

Airlines
Air France, Alitalia, British Airways, El Al, Gulf Air, Iran Air, KLM, Kuwait, Lufthansa, MEA, Pan Am, Qantas, Sabena, SAS, Swissair, Syrian, UTA.
Flying times: Copenhagen $6\frac{1}{4}$ hrs; London 6 hrs; New York $13\frac{1}{4}$ hrs; Sydney 24 hrs. *Fares:* Copenhagen F Dkr4,720 Y Dkr3,270; London F £376 Y £260; New York F $1,126 Y $700; Sydney F A$1,029 Y A$678. *Airport to city:* 11 kms (7 mls). *Taxi fare:* 400 rials.

Duty-free allowances
200 cigarettes *or* 50 cigars *or* 250 grammes of tobacco; 1 litre of spirits *or* 1 litre of wine.

Local time
GMT+4 hrs (+5 hrs in summer).

Embassy phone numbers
Tehran:

Australia 824554	Sweden 828305
Canada 648306	Switzerland 47319
Denmark 315832	W. Germany 314111
Japan 42848	UK 645011
Netherlands 626206	USA 60511
Norway 828819	

Hotels
Tehran: Arya-Sheraton, Commodore, Evin, Inter-Continental, Park, Royal Tehran Hilton, Semiramis, Tehran International, Tehran Kings, Tehran Palma, Versailles. Prices range from 2,000 to 3,000 rials per night.

International banks
Irano–British Bank, Bank of Iran and the Middle East, International Bank of Iran and Japan, Iranians Bank, International Bank of Iran, Bank Melli Iran.

Credit cards
American Express, Diners Club.

Office hours
Variable but chiefly 08.00–17.00. Some firms close Thurs afternoon and all day Fri.

National holidays
All Moslem, plus other movable holidays. Fixed holidays include 1 Jan, 21–25 Mar, 2 Apr, 5 Aug, 26 Oct.

Voltage
220 volts AC.

Communications
Tel: 900 rials per 3 mins. *Telex:* 1,000 rials per 3 mins.
Airmail: 4–5 days. *Cable:* 27 rials per word (7-word minimum).

Social customs
Iranians are noted for their hospitality and tolerance. Wealthy and senior businessmen live a European social way of life. Punctuality for social engagements is not strictly observed.

Iraq

Area and population
438,446 sq kms (168,040 sq mls). Pop. 11 million.
Capital: Baghdad (3 million).
Chief cities: Basra (1 million), Mosul (892,000), Kirkuk (586,000), Sulaimaniya (538,000), Kut (381,000). *Port:* Basra.
Airport: International (Baghdad).

Climate
Two contrasting seasons—dry, hot summer May–Oct, when temperatures range from 35°C (95°F) to 49°C (120°F), and cool winter Dec–Mar, with temperatures down to 10°C (49°F). *Clothing:* Light tropical clothing although woollens and raincoat needed Dec–Mar.

People
Arabs, with minorities of Kurds, Persians, Turkomans, Assyrians, Armenians and Jars. *Religion:* 90% Moslem; 3% Christian. *Distribution:* 58% urban.

Languages
Arabic and Kurdish.

Economic background
With an agricultural economy until industrial expansionist policies began in the 1950s, Iraq has used its oil revenue to develop both industry and agriculture. The chief crop is the date (Iraq is one of the world's largest producers) but there are other important crops, such as barley, wheat and beans, and there are good-sized herds of sheep, goats and cattle. The oil industry is nationalised. In industry, textiles are increasing but Iraq produces many other products, including farm implements, sheet-metal work, batteries, electric plugs and transformers, and there are assembly lines for tractors and trucks.

Trade
Gross National Product: ID1,484 million (1971).
Exports: US$8,000 million, chiefly oil, farm products, livestock, cement. *Imports:* US$2,000 million, chiefly machinery, iron and steel, vehicles, foodstuffs, clothing, pharmaceuticals. *Chief trading partners:* W. Germany, Japan, France, UK, USA, Italy, Australia, Denmark, USSR, Canada, Sweden, Belgium/Luxembourg, Brazil, China, India. *Inflation rate:* 20.1%.

Prospects
Oil income is enabling Iraq to continue its policy of increased industralisation and improvement of agriculture. In the five years to 1980 Iraq plans to invest about US$60,000 million in development plans.

Currency
Dinar (ID) = 20 dirhams = 1,000 fils. £ = ID0.557; $ = ID0.296.

Travel required.
Visas required.

Vaccinations
Smallpox and cholera.

Airlines
British Airways, Iraqi, CSA, Lufthansa, Alitalia, Gulf, KLM, Swissair, SAS, Balkan, Sabena, Air India, Thai, MEA, Air France, PIA.
Flying times: Copenhagen 8 hrs; London $5\frac{1}{4}$ hrs; New York 19 hrs; Sydney 24 hrs. *Fares:* Copenhagen F Dkr4,285 Y Dkr2,995; London F £341.50 Y £235.50; New York F $1,076 Y $648; Sydney F A$1,061 Y A$703. *Airport to city:* 17 kms (11 mls). *Taxi fare:* ID1.5.

Irish Republic

Duty-free allowances
200 cigarettes *or* 50 cigars *or* 250 grammes of tobacco;
1 litre of spirits *or* 1 litre of wine.

Local time
GMT+3 hrs.

Embassy phone numbers
Baghdad:
Japan 95156   UK 32121

Hotels
Baghdad: Ali Babi, Andalus Palace, Baghdad,
Ali-Abbasi, Ambassador, Khayam, Carlton, Dar Al Salam,
Sahorah, Orient Palace, Ramses, Diwan.
Hotel accommodation is difficult to obtain. Prices about
ID8 per night.

International banks
None.

Credit cards
All major credit cards.

Office hours
Summer: 08.00–14.00 Sat–Wed, 08.00–13.00 Thurs.
Winter: 08.30–14.30 Sat–Wed, 08.00–13.30 Thurs.

National holidays
All Moslem holidays plus 1, 6 Jan, 8 Feb, 21 Mar, 1 May,
14, 17 July.

Voltage
220 volts 50 cycles AC.

Communications:
Tel: ID3 per 3 mins. *Telex:* 120 fils per word.
Airmail: 5–10 days. *Cable:* 160 fils per word.

Social customs
Most Iraqi businessmen speak English and French.
Patience is required in obtaining an interview. There is
frequent hand-shaking. *Best buys:* Copperware, silks,
bracelets.

Area and population
68,893 sq kms (26,599 sq mls). Pop. 3 million.
Capital: Dublin (778,000).
Chief cities: Cork (134,000), Limerick (63,000),
Waterford (33,000), Galway (29,000),
Dundalk (23,000), Drogheda (20,000), Sligo (14,000),
Wexford (13,000). *Ports:* Cork, Drogheda, Dublin,
Galway, Greenore, Limerick, New Ross, Rosslare,
Waterford. *Airports:* Dublin, Shannon.

Climate
Temperate, with temperatures ranging from 4°C (39°F)
in winter to 26°C (78.8°F) in summer. *Clothing:* As
elsewhere in Europe, but take an umbrella.

People
Irish, with Anglo-Irish minority. *Religion:* 95% Roman
Catholic. *Distribution:* 50% urban.

Languages
Gaelic (Irish) and English.

Economic background

A mixed economy, with agriculture as its mainstay. In recent years, largely through government incentive schemes, industry has been developing as Dutch, Japanese and German firms took advantage of Ireland's membership of the European Economic Community to set up subsidiary manufacturing units. Ireland has become a major producer of pharmaceuticals. Nevertheless, unemployment remains a major factor.

Trade

Gross National Product: £2,878 million.
Exports: £1,441 million, chiefly meat, livestock, textiles, machinery, transport equipment, dairy products, ores, pharmaceuticals. *Imports:* £1,699 million, chiefly machinery and transport, chemicals, grains, food, textiles, metal and metal products. *Chief trading partners:* UK, USA, W. Germany, France, N. Ireland, Netherlands, Italy, Sweden, Kuwait, Belgium/Luxembourg, Japan, Finland, Canada, Spain. *Inflation rate:* 8.3%.

Prospects

The government is trying to cut the rate of unemployment and of inflation. It has called, too, for a reduction in the trade deficit.

Currency

£ = 100 pence. £ = £1; $ = £0.53.

Travel

Visas not required.

Vaccinations

Not required.

Airlines

All major international airlines.
Flying times: Copenhagen 2 hrs; London 1 hr; New York 7 hrs; Sydney 24 hrs. *Fares:* Copenhagen F Dkr2,190 Y Dkr1,560; London F £51 Y £34; New York F $630 Y $284; Sydney F A$1,509 Y A$965.
Airport to city: Dublin 8.8 kms (5.5 mls).
Taxi fare: £1.50.

Duty-free allowances

Residents of other EEC countries: 300 cigarettes *or* 75 cigars *or* 400 grammes tobacco; 1.5 litres of alcoholic beverages *or* 3 litres of wine.
Residents of European countries outside the EEC: 200 cigarettes *or* 50 cigars *or* 250 grammes tobacco; 1 litre of alcoholic beverages *or* 2 litres of wine.

Residents of countries outside Europe: 1,000 cigarettes *or* 200 cigars *or* 2.5 lbs tobacco; $\frac{1}{3}$ gallon of alcoholic beverages *or* $\frac{1}{3}$ gallon of wine.

Local time

GMT (+1 hr Mar–Oct).

Embassy phone numbers

Dublin:

Australia 761517	Sweden 694544
Canada 781988	Switzerland 692515
Denmark 760122	W. Germany 693011
Japan 694244	UK 695211
Netherlands 693444	USA 764061
Norway 782444	

Hotels

Dublin: Burlington, Gresham, New Jury's, Royal Hibernian, Shelbourne. Prices up to £16 per night.

International banks

None.

Credit cards

All major credit cards.

Office hours

09.30–17.30 Mon–Fri.

National holidays

1 Jan, 17 Mar, Good Friday, Easter Monday, First Monday in Aug, Last Monday in Oct, 25, 26 Dec.

Voltage

220 volts AC, but 380–220 volts AC in industry.

Communications

Tel: 57.6p per 3 mins. *Telex:* 8p per min.
Airmail: 1–2 days. *Cable:* 75p for 12 words.

Social customs

While business customs will strike the visitor as being more casual than in Britain, Irish businessmen are shrewd by nature. *Best buys:* Waterford crystal, Donegal tweed, linens, Arklow pottery, Beleek china, knitwear.

Economic background

Agriculture, mining and quarrying, industry and, increasingly, tourism are the main components of Israel's economy. The largest source of foreign currency is diamond-cutting and polishing, followed by tourism. In recent years, there has been a great expansion in the cultivation of citrus, and industry has grown rapidly.

Trade:

Gross National Product: US$11,716 million.
Exports: US$2,000 million, chiefly polished diamonds, fruit, textiles, vegetables, fertilisers, rubber, plastics, chemicals, electronic equipment. *Imports:* US$6,000 million, chiefly rough diamonds, transport equipment, machinery and electrical equipment, iron and steel, foodstuffs, chemicals, petroleum, grain.
Chief trading partners: USA, UK, W. Germany, Netherlands, Belgium, France, Switzerland.
Inflation rate: 34.2%.

Prospects

Rising inflation has affected Israel's ability to expand. Industrialisation is expected to continue with the help of overseas investments but this has been limited by the threat of the Arab trade boycott, which works against Western concerns investing in Israel.

Currency

Israeli pound (£I) = 100 agoroth.
£ = £I33.83; $ = £I17.99.

Travel

Visas not normally required.

Vaccinations

Not normally required.

Airlines

Air France, Alitalia, Austrian, British Airways, El Al, Lufthansa, Turkish, TWA, KLM, Olympic, SAS, Swissair, Tarom, Sabena.
Flying times: Copenhagen $4\frac{1}{2}$ hrs; London $4\frac{1}{4}$ hrs; New York $13\frac{1}{4}$ hrs; Sydney 26 hrs. *Fares:* Copenhagen F Dkr3,625 Y Dkr2,580; London F £286 Y £194; New York F $1,015 Y $597; Sydney F A$1,133 Y A$750.
Airport to city: 19 kms (12 mls). *Taxi fare:* £I30.

Duty-free allowances

250 cigarettes *or* 250 grammes of tobacco products; 2 litres of wine and 1 litre of other alcoholic beverages.

Area and population

20,700 sq kms (7,992 sq mls), not including occupied Arab lands. Pop. 3.2 million.
Capital: Jerusalem (300,000).
Chief cities: Tel Aviv (450,000), Haifa (250,000).
Ports: Ashdod, Haifa. *Airport:* Lod-Ben Gurion International (Tel Aviv).

Climate

Sub-tropical, with hot, dry summers. Mean annual temperatures range from 20° to 21°C (68° to 70°F) but may rise to 49°C (120°F) in the south.
Clothing: Lightweight the year round. Sunglasses recommended.

People

90% Jews, 10% Arabs. *Religion:* Judaism, with Christian and Moslem minorities. *Distribution:* 82% urban.

Languages

Hebrew and Arabic. *English rating:* Excellent.

Israel

Local time
GMT+2 hrs.

Embassy phone numbers
Tel Aviv:

Australia 231263	Sweden 242105
Canada 28721	Switzerland 244121
Denmark 440405	W. Germany 243111
Japan 24926	UK 249171
Netherlands 51177	USA 56171
Norway 55208	

Hotels
Jerusalem: American Colony, King David, Moriah, National Palace, St George International, Diplomat, Jerusalem Hilton, Inter-Continental, Mount Scopus, Shalom. *Tel Aviv:* Dan, Grand Beach, Hilton Tel Aviv, Plaza Tel Aviv, Ramada-Continental, Avia. Prices up to US$28–32, depending on season.

International banks
Barclays.

Credit cards
All major credit cards.

Office hours
June-Oct: 07.30–14.30 Sun–Thurs.
Nov–May: 08.00–13.00 and 15.00–18.00 Sun–Thurs. Some offices open on Friday morning.

National holidays
Dates vary but generally 1 Jan, Purim (2 days in Mar), Passover (8 days in Apr), Independence Day (Apr *or* May), Shavuot (May *or* June), New Year (2 days in Sept *or* Oct), Yom Kippur (Sept *or* Oct), 2 more days in Oct. Christian and Moslem holidays are observed by those minorities.

Voltage
220 volts AC.

Communications
Tel: £l30 per 3 mins. *Telex:* £l30 per 3 mins. *Airmail:* 2–3 days. *Cable;* 85 agoroth per word.

Social customs
Varied, but in general Jewish customs regarding the Sabbath (Saturday) and Kosher eating are followed. *Best buys:* Cloth, pottery, jewellery, precious stones and beaten brassware.

Italy

Area and population
301,253 sq kms (116,314 sq mls). Pop. 56 million.
Capital: Rome (Roma) (3 million).
Chief cities: Milan (Milano) (4 million), Naples (Napoli) (1.5 m), Turin (Torino) (1.2 m), Genoa (Genova) (850,000), Bari (400,000), Palermo (388,000), Venice (Venezia) (363,000), Trieste (272,000). *Ports:* Genoa, Leghorn (Livorno), Naples, Trieste, Venice.
Airports: Leonardo da Vinci (Rome), Malpensa (Milan).

Climate
Rome climate is pleasant throughout the year. Average temperatures in spring and summer range from 18° to 30°C (62° to 85°F) and in autumn and winter from 5° to 18°C (40° to 62°F). *Clothing:* Lightweight from May to Sept, warmer clothes in autumn and winter.

People
Southern European. *Religion:* Roman Catholic.
Distribution: 48% urban.

Language
Italian. *English rating:* Good.

Economic background
From almost total disruption caused by the war, Italy's economy has been growing uninterruptedly for 30 years, and Italy is now regarded as one of the world's top ten industrial nations. With success based firmly on trade, Italy has produced one of the best modern manufacturing industries in Europe, particularly in steel, vehicles and electrical appliances. Agriculture has remained important especially in the South. While wages are lower than in other parts of Europe, there are wide divergences in rates paid in the industrial North and the agricultural South. In recent years Italy has suffered from excessive inflation and unfavourable trade balances.

Trade
Gross National Product: 97,427,000 million lire.
Exports: 30,904,000 million, chiefly industrial machinery, office machines, vehicles, footwear, textiles, foodstuffs, fruits, knitwear, iron and steel, spirits.
Imports: 36,305,000 million, chiefly crude oil, minerals, machinery, chemicals, meat, feed grains.
Chief trading partners: W. Germany, France, USA, Saudi Arabia, Netherlands, Libya, Belgium/Luxembourg, UK, USSR, Iraq, Iran, Switzerland. *Inflation rate:* 12.6%.

Prospects
Basically sound, but inflation remains a continuing problem.

Currency
Lira. £ = 1,597 lire; $ = 849 lire.

Travel
Visas not required.

Vaccinations
Not required.

Airlines
All major international airlines.
Flying times (to Rome): Copenhagen $2\frac{1}{4}$ hrs; London $2\frac{1}{4}$ hrs; New York 8 hrs; Sydney 22 hrs.
Fares: Copenhagen F Dkr2,610 Y Dkr1,820; London F £169.50 Y £117.50; New York F $797 Y $416; Sydney F A$1,397 Y A$894.
Airport to city: Rome (Leonardo da Vinci) 35.4 kms (22 mls); Milan (Malpensa) 46 kms (29 mls).
Taxi fare: Rome 7,000 lire; Milan 10,000 lire.

Duty-free allowances
Visitors living in Europe: 200 cigarettes *or* 250 grammes of cigars; $\frac{1}{2}$ litre of spirits *or* 1 bottle of wine.
Visitors living elsewhere: 400 cigarettes *or* 250 grammes of cigars; a bottle of spirits *or* 2 bottles of wine.

Local time
GMT+1 hr (+2 hrs late May–Sept).

Embassy phone numbers
Rome:

Australia 841241	Sweden 8441947
Canada 855341	Switzerland 803641
Denmark 856642	W. Germany 860341
Japan 317941	UK 4755551
Netherlands 873141	USA 4674
Norway 572537	

Hotels
Rome: Cavalieri Hilton, Eden, Excelsior, Flora, Grand, Hassler, Parco dei Principi. *Milan:* Carlton Senato, Cavour, Duomo, Excelsior-Gallia, Grand et de Milan, Grand Plaza, Hilton, Select. Good-class hotels in Rome and Milan now cost up to 70,000 lire per night.

International banks
Banca Commerciale Italiana, Credito Italiano, Banco di Roma, Banca Nazionale del Lavoro, Banco di Napoli, Banco di Sicilia.

Credit cards
All major credit cards.

Office hours
Northern Italy: 08.30–12.45 and 15.00–18.30 Mon–Fri.
Central and Southern Italy: 08.30–12.45 and 16.30 or 17.00–20.00 Mon–Fri.

National holidays
1 Jan, Easter Monday, 25 Apr, 1 May, 5 June, 15 Aug, 1, 6 Nov, 8, 25, 26 Dec.

Voltage
220 volts AC.

Communications
Tel: 600 lire per min plus VAT. *Telex:* 1,240 lire per min. *Airmail:* 7–10 days. *Cable:* 3,350 lire for minimum 3 words and 118.80 lire for each additional word.

Social customs
Hand-shaking is the custom, both on arrival and departure. In the North particularly, there is a growing respect for punctuality, and visiting cards have become obligatory. Business entertaining over lunch is now more common than before.

Ivory Coast

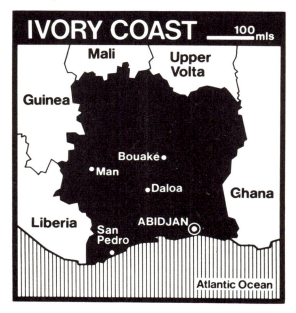

Area and population
322,463 sq kms (127,800 sq mls). Pop. 6.7 million.
Capital: Abidjan (950,000).
Chief cities: Bouaké (175,000), Korhogo (45,000), Daloa (60,000), Grand Bassam (26,000).
Ports: Abidjan, San Pedro. *Airport:* Port Bouet (Abidjan).

Climate
Tropical. Temperatures in Abidjan range from 23° to 30°C (73° to 86°F). Average humidity: 82%.
Clothing: Lightweight suits for business calls, otherwise trousers, shirt and tie. Women need cotton dresses.

People
60% African ethnic groups, plus minorities of French, Lebanese, Syrians and Italians. *Religion:* 60% animist, 22.8% Moslem, 13.5% Christian.
Distribution: 29% urban.

Language
French. *English rating:* Poor.

Economic background
One of the world's largest producers of coffee, Ivory Coast is primarily an agricultural country. Besides coffee, its chief crops are cocoa, timber and bananas. The production of palm oil and rubber is increasing. Industry, which began in French colonial times, is developing with the help of aid from France. Much of it is food processing, but there are textile and car-assembly plants.

Trade
Gross National Product: CFAfrs573,000 million.
Exports: CFAfrs392,501 million, chiefly coffee, wood, cocoa, bananas, pineapples.
Imports: CFAfrs311,607 million, chiefly machinery, transport, and electrical equipment, petroleum.
Chief trading partners: France, USA, Netherlands, W. Germany, Japan, Iran, Italy, UK, Spain, Mali.
Inflation rate: 17.9%.

Prospects
Further industrialisation is continuing.

Currency
CFAfranc. £ = CFAfrs421; $ = CFAfrs223.

Travel
Visas not required.

Vaccinations
Smallpox. Yellow fever and cholera inoculations recommended.

Airlines
Air Afrique, Alitalia, Air Zaire, British Caledonian, KLM, Pan Am, Sabena, Swissair.
Flying times: Copenhagen $9\frac{1}{2}$ hrs; London 11 hrs; New York 12 hrs; Sydney 30 hrs. *Fares:* Copenhagen F Dkr6,595 Y Dkr4,315; London F £463 Y £297; New York F $966 Y $596; Sydney F A$1,484 Y A$952.
Airport to city: 16 kms (10 mls). *Taxi fare:* CFAfrs1,000.

Duty-free allowances
200 cigarettes *or* 400 grammes of tobacco; 1 bottle of spirits.

Local time
GMT.

Ivory Coast

Embassy phone numbers
Abidjan: UK 22.66.15.

Hotels
Abidjan: Ivoire, du Parc, Tiama, Akwaba, Palm Beach.
Prices up to CFAfrs8,000 per night.

International banks
All the main French banks.

Credit cards
American Express, Diners Club.

Office hours
08.00–12.00 and 14.30–17.30 Mon–Fri.
08.00–12.00 Sat.

National holidays
Moslem holidays plus 1 Jan, Easter Monday,
1 May, Ascension Day (May), Whit Monday (May *or*
June), 15 Aug, 1 Nov, 7, 25 Dec.

Voltage
230 volts AC.

Communications
Tel: CFAfrs2,613 per 3 mins. *Telex:* Available at hotels.
Airmail: 4–7 days. *Cable:* CFAfrs129.31 per word.

Social customs
French manners, both business and social, prevail
in Abidjan.

Jamaica

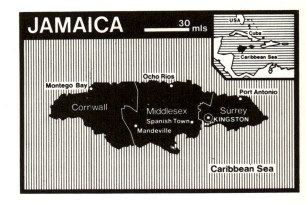

Area and population
11,525 sq kms (4,411 sq mls). Pop. 2 million.
Capital: Kingston (113,700).
Chief cities: None, but towns include Port Royal,
Port Antonio, Ocho Rios, Spanish Town, Mandeville.
Port: Kingston. *Airports:* Norman Manley International
(Kingston), Donald Sangster International
(Montego Bay).

Climate
Tropical. Kingston temperatures are about 27°C (80°F)
and rarely vary. *Clothing:* Lightweight clothing the year
round. Jackets need only be worn for formal
appointments.

People
90% African and mixed stock.
Religion: 75% Protestant, 5% Roman Catholic.
Distribution: 36% urban.

Language
English.

Economic background
One of the world's largest producers of bauxite and
alumina, Jamaica depends also on sugar, bananas and
citrus for its export earnings. Tourism is steadily
contributing to revenue.

Trade
Gross National Product: J$2,119 million.
Exports: J$664 million, chiefly alumina, bauxite, sugar,
fruit, clothing, coffee, pimento.
Imports: J$850 million, chiefly machinery, oil, transport
equipment, chemicals, mineral fuels, textile yarns, fabrics,
base metals. *Chief trading partners:* USA, Venezuela, UK,

Canada, Trinidad and Tobago, Japan, Norway, USSR.
Inflation rate: 16.9%.

Prospects
Jamaica's development will depend largely on agriculture and industry. Strict import restrictions have been imposed in order to save foreign exchange.

Currency
Jamaican dollar (J$) = 100 cents. £ = J$2.91. J$ is linked to the US$.

Travel
Visas not required.

Vaccinations
Smallpox.

Airlines
British Airways, Air Jamaica, Air Canada, Lufthansa, BWIA, American.
Flying times: Copenhagen 15½ hrs; London 10 hrs; New York 3¾ hrs; Sydney 24 hrs. *Fares:* Copenhagen F Dkr5,650 Y Dkr3,810; London F £399.50 Y £259; New York F $250 Y $167; Sydney F A$1,960 Y A$1,267. *Airport to city:* 17.5 kms (11 mls). *Taxi fare:* J$12.

Duty-free allowances
200 cigarettes *or* 50 cigars *or* ½ lb of tobacco; 1 quart of spirits and 1 quart of wine.

Local time
GMT−5 hrs (−4 hrs end Apr–end Oct).

Embassy phone numbers
Kingston: UK 926.9050.

Hotels
Kingston: Jamaica Pegasus, Sheraton-Kingston, Skyline. Prices vary according to season.

International banks
Barclays Bank Jamaica, Bank of Montreal Jamaica, Bank of Nova Scotia Jamaica, First National City Bank, Royal Bank of Jamaica, First National City Bank of Chicago, Scotia Bank of Jamaica.

Credit cards
All major credit cards.

Office hours
08.30–16.00 Mon–Fri.

National holidays
1 Jan, Ash Wednesday, Good Friday, Easter Monday, 23 May, 7 Aug, Third Monday in Aug, 16 Oct, 25, 26 Dec.

Voltage
110–220 volts AC.

Communications
Tel: J$6 per 3 mins. *Airmail:* 3–5 days.
Telex: J$6 per 3 mins. *Cable:* 14 cents per word.

Social customs
Easy-going business atmosphere and no special customs of any note. If you are carrying samples, remember that they need an import licence. Kingston has acquired a bad reputation for violence, particularly after dark.

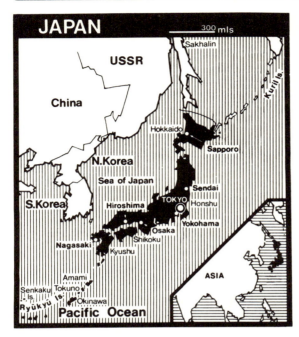

Area and population

372,488 sq kms (143,818 sq mls). Pop. 112 million.
Capital: Tokyo (8.6 million).
Chief cities: Yokohama (2.6 m), Osaka (2.7 m),
Kobe (1.3 m), Nagoya (2.1 m), Kyoto (1.4 m),
Kita-Kyushu (1.1 m), Fukuoka (1 m), Sapporo (1.2 m).
Ports: Kobe, Moji, Naha, Nagoya, Osaka, Otaru, Shinizu,
Yokohama. *Airports:* Narita and Haneda (Tokyo), Osaka.

Climate

Varied. Tokyo temperatures range from −1°C (30°F) in
winter to 35°C (95°F) in summer.
Clothing: European-weight clothing from mid-Oct to
Apr, but lightweight for summer.

People

Mongoloid. *Religion:* Buddhism and Shintoism.
Distribution: 72.2% urban.

Language

Japanese. *English rating:* Good.

Economic background

Now the world's third largest economic power, after the
United States and the USSR, Japan's growth expanded
at the rate of 12% a year in the 1960s. Its exports of
manufactured goods now account for 7% of the world's
total exports. It is the leading shipbuilder, and its
important industries include crude steel, synthetic rubber,
aluminium, plastics, cement, cars, refined copper and
cotton yarn. It has some of the world's biggest and most
advanced industrial plants. It must, however, import most
of its raw materials and about half its food.

Trade

Gross National Product: 132,725,000 million yen.
Exports: 19,934,618 million yen, chiefly ships, cars, iron
and steel, textiles, electronic equipment.
Imports: 19,229,169 million yen, chiefly oil, minerals,
metal ores and scrap, food.
Chief trading partners: USA, Saudi Arabia, Australia, Iran,
Indonesia, Canada, United Arab Emirates, Kuwait,
S. Korea, China, Liberia, Australia, Taiwan, USSR,
W. Germany, Hong Kong. *Inflation rate:* 4.5%.

Prospects

Japan's economy has faltered in recent years, largely
because of the oil price increases, Unemployment is still
relatively high.

Currency

Yen. £ = 383 yen; $ = 203 yen.

Travel

Visas not required.

Vaccinations

Smallpox. Typhoid and cholera certificates required if
entering through infected countries.

Airlines

All international airlines.
Flying times (to Tokyo): Copenhagen $12\frac{1}{4}$ hrs;
London $15\frac{1}{2}$ hrs; New York $13\frac{3}{4}$ hrs; Sydney 10 hrs.
Fares: Copenhagen F Dkr11,240 Y Dkr6,800;
London F £913.50 Y £552.50; New York F $2,087
Y $1,330; Sydney F A$993 Y A$700.
Airport to city: Tokyo: Narita 70 kms (43.4 mls),
Haneda 19 kms (12 mls); Osaka 16 kms (10 mls).
Taxi fare: Narita 11,200 yen, Haneda 3,000 yen;
Osaka 3,000 yen.

Duty-free allowances

400 cigarettes *or* 100 cigars *or* 500 grammes of tobacco;
3 bottles of spirits *or* 3 bottles of wine.

Local time

GMT+9 hrs.

Japan

Embassy phone numbers
Tokyo:

Australia 453.0251	Sweden 582.6891
Canada 408.2101	Switzerland 473.0121
Denmark 404.2331	W. Germany 473.0151
Netherlands 431.5126	UK 265.5511
Norway 446.5201	USA 583.7141

Hotels
Tokyo: Akasaka Tokyu, Grand Palace, Hilton, Imperial, Marunouchi, New Japan, New Otani, Palace, Takanawa Prince, Ginza Tokyu, Okura, Pacific, New Plaza.
Osaka: Hanshin, New Hankyu, Royal, International, Plaza. Prices 8,000–12,000 yen per night.

International banks
All international banks.

Credit cards
All major credit cards.

Office hours
09.00–17.00 Mon–Fri.

National holidays
1, 15 Jan, 11 Feb, 21 Mar, 29 Apr, 3, 5 May, 15, 23 Sept, 10 Oct, 3, 23 Nov.

Voltage
100 volts AC 50 cycles in Tokyo, 100 volts AC 60 cycles in Osaka.

Communications
Tel: 3,240 yen per 3 mins. *Telex:* 1,080 yen per min. *Airmail:* 4–6 days. *Cable:* 192 yen for 7 words.

Social customs
Visiting cards are essential for any business visit to Japan. Preferably they should be printed in Japanese, as well as the language of the visitor—a service that is offered by Japanese Airlines, British Airways and other international carriers. Expect lavish entertainment, and stay long enough in Japan to establish good personal relations. While visitors are not expected to understand all Japanese manners and customs, Japanese like to be addressed by the suffix San, which equates to Mr. Hence Mr Yomomoto becomes Yomomoto-san. Walking in your shoes on Japanese floors in restaurants and homes is considered bad manners. A simple rule of thumb to follow is: stone floors: shoes; wooden floors: slippers; matting: socks or stockings.

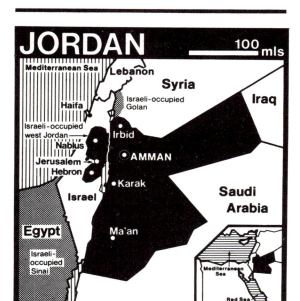

Area and population
95,000 sq kms (37,730 sq mls) pre-1947, but 5,607 sq kms (2,165 sq mls) lost in 1967 war with Israel. Pop. 2.5 million.
Capital: Amman (750,000).
Chief cities: Irbid (116,000), Zarqa (232,000). Jerusalem, Hebron and Nablus, all on the West Bank, are occupied by Israel. *Port:* Aqaba. *Airport:* Amman.

Climate
Mediterranean and desert. Amman temperatures range from 16°C (44°F) in winter (Nov–Mar) to 31°C (81°F) in summer (May–Sept). *Clothing:* European winter clothes Nov–Mar, lightweight suits May–Sept.

People
Arab. *Religion:* 90% Moslem, 10% Christian. *Distribution:* 51% urban.

Language
Arabic. *English rating:* Good.

Economic background
Dependent on foreign aid since its independence in 1946, Jordan was striving for self-sufficiency until the June 1967 war struck the economy. The war, and the fact that Jordan's population has been swollen by 500,000 refugees, has resulted in trade deficits, although the government is making progress in encouraging

tourism and export industries. Jordan is mostly dependent upon agricultural and phosphate exports, plus the products of light industries.

Trade
Gross National Product: JD352 million.
Exports: JD40.1 million, chiefly phosphates, fruit and vegetables, olive oil, cereals, cement, marble.
Imports: JD234 million, chiefly food, machinery, vehicles, crude petroleum, textiles.
Chief trading partners: W. Germany, USA, Saudi Arabia, UK, Japan, Italy, Lebanon, Romania, France, Syria, Egypt, Greece, Netherlands, Turkey, Iran.
Inflation rate: 26.2%.

Prospects
Even though Jordan's future rests mainly on a solution to the Middle East's political problems, the government is undertaking development plans which, considering the circumstances, have done well in recent years.

Currency
Dinar (JD) = 1,000 fils. £ = JD0.567; $ = JD0.301.

Travel
Visas required.

Vaccinations
Requirements vary but during the pilgrimage to Mecca all travellers must have smallpox and cholera certificates.

Airlines
British Airways, Royal Jordanian, Lufthansa, Gulf, MEA, KLM, Air France, Kuwait.
Flying times: Copenhagen 6¾ hrs; London 5 hrs; New York 15 hrs; Sydney 24 hrs. *Fares:* Copenhagen F Dkr3,560 Y Dkr2,420; London F £283.50 Y £192.50; New York F $987 Y $597; Sydney F A$1,133 Y A$750.
Airport to city: 5.5 kms (3.5 mls). *Taxi fare:* JD2.

Duty-free allowances
200 cigarettes *or* 50 cigars *or* 200 grammes of tobacco: 1 bottle of spirits *or* 2 bottles of wine.

Local time
GMT+2 hrs.

Embassy phone numbers
Amman: UK 37374.

Hotels:
Amman: Inter-Continental, Grand Palace, Philadelphia, Jordan Tower. Prices up to JD20.500 per night.

International banks
Arab Bank, British Bank of the Middle East, First National City Bank, Chase Manhattan.

Credit cards
All major credit cards.

Office hours
May–Oct: 08.00–13.00 and 15.30–19.30.
Nov–Apr: 08.30–13.30 and 15.00–18.30. Moslem firms close on Fridays, Christian firms on Sundays.
In Ramadan, Moslem firms open 09.00–16.00.

National holidays
All Moslem holidays plus 15 Jan, 22 Mar, 1, 25 May, 12 July, 11 Aug, 14 Nov.

Voltage
Domestic: 220 volts AC. Industrial: 220–380 volts AC.

Communications
Tel: JD3 per 3 mins. *Telex:* JD2.320 per 3 mins.
Airmail: 2–4 days.

Social customs
Most Jordanian businessmen observe Western customs, and are hospitable. Coffee and cold drinks are always offered and should not be refused. During Ramadan Western visitors should not drink or smoke during business sessions. *Best buys:* Silver, copper, leather, rugs, coral from the Red Sea, glassware.

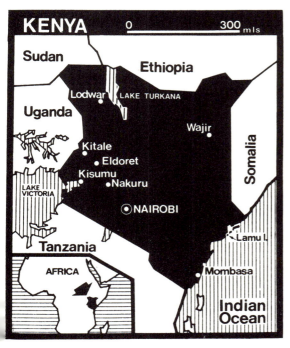

Area and population

582,646 sq kms (224,960 sq mls). Pop. 13.8 million.
Capital: Nairobi (736,000).
Chief city: Mombasa (246,000). *Port:* Mombasa.
Airport: Embakasi (Nairobi).

Climate

Tropical and humid on the coast, temperate on the plateau. Nairobi temperatures rarely rise above 27°C (80°F) and vary little. Rain falls Apr–June and Oct–Nov. *Clothing:* Summer-weight clothing plus light raincoat.

People

40 tribes, the largest being Kikuyu, plus 100,000 Asians, 28,000 Arabs and 40,000 Europeans. *Religion:* 50% animist, 30% Christian, rest Hindu and Moslem. *Distribution:* 92% rural.

Language

Swahili. *English rating:* Excellent.

Economic background

Badly hit by the steep increase in oil prices, Kenya has a growing economy, based largely on agriculture and, more recently, tourism. Kenya has few minerals, but industry is developing, chiefly in food processing, fruit canning, dairy products and brewing. Other sectors comprise paper, tobacco, rubber and textiles.

Trade

Gross National Product: US$2,600 million.
Exports: 3,376 million shillings, chiefly coffee, tea, pyrethrum, sisal, horticultural products, tea, meat and meat preparations. *Imports:* 6,748 million shillings, chiefly machinery, transport equipment, manufactured goods, lubricants, chemicals. *Chief trading partners:* UK, Iran, W. Germany, USA, Netherlands, Zambia, Italy, Canada, Japan. *Inflation rate:* 8.8%.

Prospects

Kenya's main development plan was drafted before the oil crisis. Since then its trade deficit has increased and Kenya has received international monetary aid. Kenya welcomes overseas investment.

Currency

Shilling (Shs) = 100 cents. £ = Shs14.58; $ = Shs7.75.

Travel

Visitor's pass, usually acquired on arrival.

Vaccinations

Smallpox and yellow fever.

Airlines

British Airways, Kenya Airways, Lufthansa, Swissair, Alitalia, KLM, El Al, SAS, Sabena, Olympic, Pan Am, Air France.
Flying times: Copenhagen 9¾ hrs; London 9 hrs; New York 20 hrs; Sydney 24 hrs. *Fares:* Copenhagen F Dkr7,205 Y Dkr4,635; London F £528.50 Y £333.50; New York F $1,213 Y $802; Sydney F A$1,128 Y A$746. *Airport to city:* 13.5 kms (8.5 mls). *Taxi fare:* 70 shillings.

Duty-free allowances

200 cigarettes *or* 50 cigars *or* ½ lb tobacco; 1 bottle of spirits *or* 1 bottle of wine.

Local time

GMT+3 hrs.

Embassy phone numbers

Nairobi:

Australia 34666	Sweden 29042
Canada 34033	Switzerland 28735
Denmark 31088	W. Germany 26661
Japan 32955	UK 335944
Netherlands 27111	USA 34141

Hotels
Nairobi: Ambassador, Hilton, Inter-Continental, Milimani, New Stanley, Norfolk, Panafric.
Mombasa: Bahari Beach, Coral Beach, Nyali Beach, Silver Beach. Prices up to about Shs400 per night.

International banks
Standard Bank, Barclays International, Grindlays, Kenya Commercial Bank, National Bank of Kenya, Commercial Bank of Africa.

Credit cards
All major credit cards.

Office hours
08.30–12.30 and 14.00–16.30 Mon–Fri,
08.30–12.00 Sat.

National holidays
1 Jan, Good Friday, Easter Monday, 1 May, 1 June, 20 Oct, 12, 25, 26 Dec.

Voltage
240 volts AC. Industrial: 415 volts.

Communications
Tel: Shs45 per 3 mins. *Telex:* Shs60 per 3 mins.
Airmail: 3–4 days. *Cable:* Shs2.60 per word
(7-word minimum).

Social customs
European customs prevail in business circles.
Best buys: Kamba woodcarvings and soapstone vases.

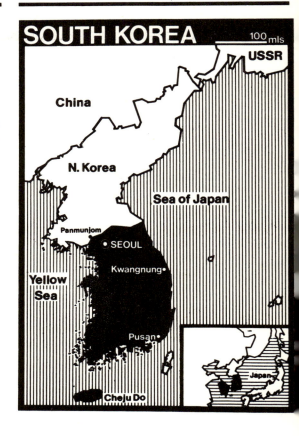

Area and population
98,477 sq kms (38,022 sq mls). Pop. 35 million.
Capital: Seoul (7 million).
Chief cities: Pusan (2.4 m), Taegu (1.3 m),
Inchon (797,000), Kwangju (606,000), Taejon (1.3 m).
Ports: Inchon, Pusan, Ulsan. *Airports:* Kimpo (Seoul).

Climate
Cold winters, hot summers. Temperatures in Seoul average −5°C (23°F) in Jan, and in Aug reach 25°C (78°F). *Clothing:* Lightweight May–Sept, but heavier clothes plus warm topcoat and fur hat with ear-flaps in winter.

People
Mongoloid. *Religion:* Christianity, Buddhism, Shamanism, Confucianism. *Distribution:* 32% urban.

Language
Korean. *English rating:* Good.

Economic background

South Korea's economy has progressed rapidly in manufacturing and mining, and under a number of five-year plans Korea hopes to achieve agricultural self-sufficiency. There has been much development in heavy industries, including shipbuilding and steel, and chemicals. Exports have climbed spectacularly, and South Korea recovered quickly from the 1973 oil crisis.

Trade

Gross National Product: US$18,702 million.
Exports: US$5,081 million, chiefly clothing, textiles, plywood, electrical machinery, iron and steel, footwear, raw silk, ships. *Imports:* US$7,274 million, chiefly petroleum, food, wood, wheat, rice, raw cotton, textile machinery, chemicals. *Chief trading partners:* Japan, USA, Saudi Arabia, Kuwait, Australia, W. Germany, UK, Canada, Hong Kong, Netherlands, Iran.
Inflation rate: 12.4%.

Prospects

South Korea is now in its fourth five-year plan, which is due to end in 1981, and there will be considerable investment in the chemical, iron and steel, machinery, electronics and shipbuilding industries.

Currency

Won. £ = 912 won; $ = 484 won.

Travel

Visas not required.

Vaccinations

Smallpox. Cholera recommended.

Airlines

Korean Air Lines, Air France, JAL, Northwest, Cathay Pacific, SIA.
Flying times: Copenhagen 16 hrs; London 24 hrs; New York 31 hrs; Sydney 14 hrs. *Fares:* Copenhagen F Dkr11,240 Y Dkr6,800; London F £913.50 Y £552.50; New York F $2,087 Y $1,330; Sydney F A$993 Y A$700.
Airport to city: 26 kms (16 mls). *Taxi fare:* 1,500 won.

Duty-free allowances

400 cigarettes *or* their cigar *or* tobacco equivalents; 2 bottles of spirits.

Local time

GMT+9 hrs.

Embassy phone numbers

Seoul:

Australia 73.4527	W. Germany 22.4037
Denmark 22.9648	UK 75.7341
Japan 73.5626	USA 72.2601
Switzerland 73.7876	

Hotels

Seoul: Ambassador, Chosun, King Sejong, New Korea, Seoul Plaza, Seoul Tokyu. Prices up to US$30 per night.

International banks

Chartered, Hong Kong and Shanghai.

Credit cards

All major credit cards.

Office hours

09.30–12.00 and 13.00–17.00 Mon–Fri, 09.30–13.00 Sat.

National holidays

1, 2, 3 Jan, 1 Mar, 5 Apr, 5 May, 6 June, 17 July, 15 Aug, 1, 3, 9 Oct, 25 Dec.

Voltage 100 and 220 volts AC.

Communications

Tel: 7,200 won per 3 mins. *Telex:* 4,320 won per 3 mins. *Airmail:* 3–9 days. *Cable:* 4,708 won for 22 words.

Social customs

Business entertainment is lavish and business depends upon good personal relationships. Most entertainment is offered in restaurants, only rarely in homes.
Dual-language business cards are essential and can be obtained within 2–3 days in Seoul. Use your right hand in giving and receiving.

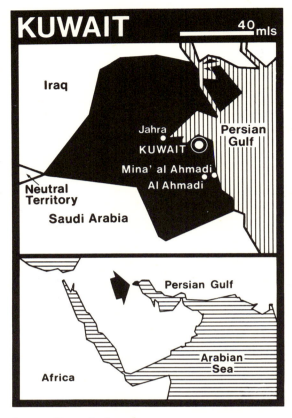

Area and population

24,281 sq kms (9,375 sq mls). Pop. 862,200.
Capital: Kuwait City (700,000).
Chief cities: None, but notable towns include Fahahil, Sulaibikhat, Jahra and Al Ahmadi. *Port:* Kuwait City.
Airport: Kuwait.

Climate

May–Oct average shade temperature is 38°C (100°F) and July–Aug can reach 50°C (122°F). In Jan temperatures fall to between 7° and 20°C (45° and 68°F), and nights can be cold. Humidity 60%–80%.
Clothing: Tropical-weight during summer months but European clothing from Nov to mid–Mar.

People

Arab origin but less than half born in Kuwait.
Religion: 95% Moslem, 4% Christian.
Distribution: 94% urban.

Language

Arabic. *English rating:* Good.

Economic background

A rich oil state, with oil reserves expected to last more than a hundred years, Kuwait is trying to diversify into industry, but is hampered by a lack of natural raw materials. Attempts are being made to build up Kuwait as a banking centre, but little can be done to promote agriculture because of the weather and the lack of water. Nevertheless, Kuwait, with its relatively small population, can live on its oil revenues for the foreseeable future.

Trade

Gross National Product: 3,229 million dinars.
Exports: 3,500 million dinars, chiefly crude oil, petroleum products. *Imports:* 700 million dinars, chiefly foodstuffs, building materials, vehicles, industrial equipment, electrical products. *Chief trading partners:* USA, Japan, W. Germany, UK, Italy, France, Spain, Australia, India, Lebanon, Singapore, Italy, Netherlands, Taiwan, South Korea. *Inflation rate:* 7.4%.

Prospects

Excellent. Kuwait has one of the biggest *per capita* incomes in the world.

Currency

Dinar = 1,000 fils. £ = KD0.515;
$ = KD0.273.

Travel

Visas or entry permits required.

Vaccinations

Smallpox. TAB inoculation recommended.

Airlines

British Airways, Kuwait, Iran Air, Gulf Air, Air France, Swissair, KLM, Olympic, CSA, SAS, Lufthansa, MEA, Tunis Air, JAT, Air India, Royal Air Maroc, Alitalia, Saudia.
Flying times: Copenhagen 7½ hrs; London 6 hrs; New York 13 hrs; Sydney 24 hrs. *Fares:* Copenhagen F Dkr4,720 Y Dkr3,270; London F £376 Y £260; New York F $1,137 Y $700; Sydney F A$1,032 Y A$681.
Airport to city: 16 kms (10 mls). *Taxi fare:* KD2.

Duty-free allowances

No limit on cigarettes, cigars or tobacco.
No alcohol permitted.

Local time

GMT+3 hrs.

Kuwait

Embassy phone numbers
Kuwait City:
Denmark 423376   UK 439220
Japan 424051   USA 424156
Sweden 44725

Hotels
Kuwait City: Bristol, Golden Beach, Hilton,
Messilah Beach, Sheraton, Universal. About KD12–15
per night.

International banks
British Bank of the Middle East.

Credit cards
American Express, Barclaycard, Diners Club.

Office hours
Winter: 07.00–12.00 and 14.00–17.00 Sat–Wed,
07.00–12.30 Thurs. *Summer:* 07.30–12.00 and
15.00–18.00 Sat–Wed, 07.30–12.30 Thurs.

National holidays
All Moslem holidays plus 1 Jan, 25 Feb.

Voltage
240 volts AC.

Communications
Tel: KD2.200 per 3 mins. *Telex:* KD3.222 per 3 mins.
Airmail: 5 days. *Cable:* 98 fils per word
(7-word minimum).

Social customs
Be prepared for much patience in waiting for business
appointments. Expect, too, to drink many cups of strong
Turkish coffee or soft drinks. As Kuwait boomed into an
oil capital, so more Western-style business customs
developed but in this strongly Moslem country always
give and accept with the right hand. Dinner is usually
served late and guests usually leave immediately after
dinner.

Lebanon

Area and population
10,230 sq kms (3,950 sq mls). Pop. 2.5 million
(plus about 400,000 Palestinian refugees).
Capital: Beirut (1 million).
Chief cities: Tripoli, Sidon, Tyre (no recent population
figures). *Ports:* Beirut, Tripoli.
Airport: International (Beirut).

Climate
Generally sub-tropical with hot, dry summers and mild
winters. Beirut temperatures range from 13°C (56°F) in
winter to 27°C (81°F) and higher in summer. Almost
all rain falls Nov–Apr. *Clothing:* Medium-weight in
winter and lightweight in summer. In spite of the
humidity, the business community favours jacket and tie.

People
No proper census since 1932, but ethnically indigenous
Lebanese contain Phoenician, Greek, Byzantine,
Crusader and Arab stock. Large immigrant communities
include Armenians, Palestinians, Syrians and Jordanians.
Religion: Moslem and Christian.
Distribution: Not available.

Languages
Arabic and French. *English rating:* Excellent.

Economic background

Now badly damaged by years of civil war and the Israeli invasion of its southern borders, Lebanon miraculously survives as an economic entity. During the internecine fighting, many factories and enterprises continue to operate. Agriculture employs half the work force, and industry, despite Lebanon's lack of mineral resources, continues to produce sufficient for its home market and some for export. Leading industries include furniture, chemicals, pharmaceuticals and plastics. Until the latest outbreak of civil war, Beirut was the Middle East's leading centre for banking and civil engineering.

Trade

Gross National Product: £L6,365 million (1972). *Exports:* No official figures available but products exported include fruit, vegetables, textiles, chemicals, pharmaceuticals, furniture. *Imports:* No figures available but products imported include vehicles and parts, machinery, oil, consumer goods, building materials. *Chief trading partners:* Saudi Arabia, Syria, UK, France, W. Germany, Kuwait, USA, Jordan. *Inflation rate:* 25% (est.).

Currency

Lebanese pound (£L) = 100 piastres. £ = £L5.49; $ = £L2.92.

Travel

Visas required.

Vaccinations

Smallpox.

Airlines

All major international carriers. *Flying times:* Copenhagen 6 hrs; London $4\frac{1}{4}$ hrs; New York 11 hrs; Sydney 21 hrs. *Fares:* Copenhagen F Dkr3,560 Y Dkr2,420; London F £283.50 Y £192.50; New York F $987 Y $597; Sydney A$1,133 Y A$750. *Airport to city:* 16 kms (10 mls). *Taxi fare:* £L25.

Duty-free allowances

500 cigarettes *or* 25 cigars *or* 200 grammes of tobacco; 1 litre of alcoholic beverages.

Local time

GMT+2 hrs.

Embassy phone numbers

Beirut: UK 221550.

Hotels

Beirut: Many hotels closed as a result of the civil war, but among those still open are Bristol, Carlton, Commodore, Mayflower. Prices up to US$40 per night.

International banks

British Bank of the Middle East.

Credit cards

Not being accepted at present.

Office hours

Summer: 08.00–13.00 Mon–Fri, 08.30–12.30 Sat. *Winter:* 08.30–13.00 and 15.00–18.00 Mon–Fri, 08.30–12.30 Sat.

Public holidays

Moslem holidays, plus 1 Jan, 9 Feb, 22 Mar, Good Friday (Western and Orthodox), Easter Monday, 1, 6 May, Ascension (May), 15 Aug, 1, 22 Nov, 25, 31 Dec.

Voltage

110 volts AC but some 220 volts AC.

Communications

Current rates are not available, but all communications are still working. Overseas telephone calls are difficult and it is best to rely on Telex, which is available in most hotels.

Social customs

Lebanon is the most westernised of Middle East nations. Despite the troubles, a fairly easy atmosphere prevails. Restaurants are gradually returning to normal, and they tend to be packed. Allow plenty of check-in time at Beirut Airport where strict security and customs procedures are in force.

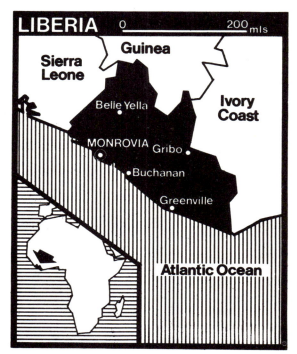

LIBERIA
0 — 200 mls

Sierra Leone
Guinea
Belle Yella
Ivory Coast
MONROVIA Gribo
Buchanan
Greenville
Atlantic Ocean

through the government's encouragement of overseas investment in manufacturing plants. Only light industry exists at present, and iron ore comprises 71% of exports.

Trade
Gross National Product: US$516 million.
Exports: US$400 million, chiefly iron ore, rubber, diamonds. *Imports:* US$288 million, chiefly manufactured goods, machinery, transport equipment, foodstuffs. *Chief trading partners:* USA, Saudi Arabia, UK, W. Germany, Japan, Netherlands, Italy, Belgium/Luxembourg, France.
Inflation rate: Not available.

Prospects
While attempts are being made to modernise agriculture, Liberia's best prospects appear to be through increasing industry and mining.

Currency
Dollar = 100 cents. £ = $1.88; $ = $1.00.

Travel
Visitor's visa required.

Vaccinations
Smallpox, yellow fever and cholera.

Airlines
British Caledonian, KLM, Swissair, Sabena, Pan Am, Iberia.
Flying times: Copenhagen 11¾ hrs; London 8 hrs; New York 9 hrs; Sydney 24 hrs. *Fares:* Copenhagen F Dkr6,315 Y Dkr4,210; London F £444.50 Y £288.50; New York F $932 Y $583; Sydney F A$1,546 Y A$1,003.
Airport to city: 60 kms (38 mls).
Taxi fare: $5 a seat or $15 for exclusive use.

Duty-free allowances
1 lb of tobacco products: 1 quart of spirits.

Local time
GMT.

Embassy phone numbers
Monrovia: UK 21055.

Hotels
Monrovia: Ducor Inter-Continental, Pan American, Carlton, Travellers Roost, Palm Hotel. Prices up to $30 per night.

Area and population
112,820 sq kms (43,700 sq mls). Pop. 1.65 million.
Capital: Monrovia (150,000).
Chief cities: None, but towns include Buchanan, Robertsport, Voinjama, Gbarnga, Sanniquellie, Tchien, Greenville and Harper. *Ports:* Buchanan, Monrovia.
Airport: Roberts International (Monrovia).

Climate
Warm and humid. Monrovia's temperatures range from 21° to 32°C (70° to 90°F), with humidity 85%–90%. Wet season: May–Oct. *Clothing:* Formal but tropical-weight. Liberians prefer dark business suits. Sunglasses needed.

People
90% indigenous African. *Religion:* 91% animist, 8% Christian, 1% Moslem. *Distribution:* 14% urban.

Language
English.

Economic background
Nearly three-quarters of Liberia's people live on subsistence agriculture, although industry is growing

Liberia

International banks
First National City Bank of New York, Bank of Liberia, Chase Manhattan.

Credit cards
All major credit cards.

Office hours
08.00–12.00 and 14.00–16.00 Mon–Fri.

National holidays
1, 7 Jan, 11 Feb, 9, 15 Mar, 14 Apr, Good Friday, Easter Monday, 14, 25 May, 26 July, 24 Aug, 2, 29 Nov, 1, 25 Dec.

Voltage
110–120 volts AC.

Communications
Tel: $9 per 3 mins. *Telex:* $9.32 per 3 mins.
Airmail: 4–6 days. *Cable:* 29 cents per word.

Social customs
European social customs prevail, and most entertaining is done in hotels. Note, however, that the cost of living is much higher in Liberia than elsewhere in West Africa.

Libya

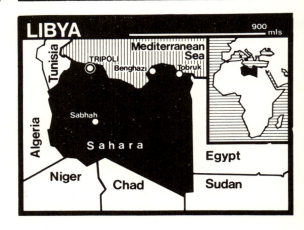

Area and population
1,748,700 sq kms (675,200 sq mls). Pop. 2.2 million.
Capital: Tripoli (709,000).
Chief cities: Benghazi (331,000), Zawia (244,000) Misurata (179,000), Homs-Kussebat (162,000), Gharian (155,000). *Ports:* Tripoli, Benghazi.
Airports: Tripoli International, Benina International (Benghazi).

Climate
Hot, arid desert climate. July and Aug temperatures reach 29°C (85°F) in Benghazi and 30°C (86°F) in Tripoli. In the coolest months, Jan and Feb, Benghazi temperatures rarely fall below 10°C (50°F) and Tripoli's below 8°C (47°F). *Clothing:* European-weight clothing is needed Nov–Mar, lightweight clothing for summer.

People
Racial mixtures of Arabs and Berbers.
Religion: 97% Moslem. *Distribution:* 25% urban.

Language
Arabic. *English rating:* Good.

Economic background
Oil has brought great wealth to Libya, with revenues of about 2,000 million Libyan dinars a year. The government is trying to modernise agriculture – the country's principal revenue-earner before the discovery of oil. New factories are being built as a result of the oil wealth, joining already established plants that produce cigarettes, paint, cement, olive oil, soft drinks and biscuits.

Trade

Gross National Product: 3,000 million Libyan dinars.
Exports: 2,445 million Libyan dinars, chiefly crude oil, barley, olives, citrus fruits, almonds, tomatoes, tobacco.
Imports: 817 million Libyan dinars, chiefly capital equipment, machinery, iron and steel pipes, tubes and fittings, manufactured goods, food.
Chief trading partners: Italy, W. Germany, France, Japan, UK, USA, Lebanon, Greece, Spain, Belgium, Romania, Netherlands, Brazil, Argentina, Bahamas, Switzerland.
Inflation rate: 7.9%.

Prospects

Libya is spending much of its oil wealth on developing the economy, and there are numerous projects under way.

Currency

Libyan dinar (LD) = 1,000 dirhams. £ = LD0.556; $ = LD0.295.

Travel

Visas required. All details must be written in Arabic.

Vaccination

Smallpox and cholera. Certificates should also be in Arabic.

Airlines

British Caledonian, Libyan Arab Airlines, Air Algérie, Alitalia, CSA, JAT, Lufthansa, Saudia, Royal Air Maroc, Tarom, UTA, Swissair.
Flying times (to Tripoli): Copenhagen $5\frac{1}{4}$ hrs; London 3 hrs; New York 15 hrs; Sydney 24 hrs.
Fares (to Tripoli): Copenhagen F Dkr3,325 Y Dkr2,525; London F £199 Y £132; New York F $822 Y $456; Sydney F A$1,323 Y A$843.
Airport to city: 35 kms (21 mls). *Taxi fare:* LD5.

Duty-free allowances

200 cigarettes *or* $\frac{1}{2}$ kilogramme of tobacco *or* cigars. Import of all spirits strictly prohibited.

Local time

GMT+2 hrs.

Embassy phone number

Tripoli: UK 31191.

Hotels

Tripoli: Libya Palace, Mediterranean, Beach, Grand, Marhaba. *Benghazi:* Omar Khayam, Gezira Palace.

Hotel accommodation is difficult to obtain. Prices up to LD10 per night.

International banks

None.

Credit cards

American Express, Diners Club.

Office hours

09.00–13.00 and 16.00–19.30 Sun–Thurs.

National holidays

All Moslem holidays plus 8, 28 Mar, 25 May, 11 June, 23 July, 1 Sept, 7 Oct.

Voltage

125 volts AC in Western Province, 200 volts AC in Eastern Province.

Communications

Tel: LD1.350 per 3 mins. *Telex:* Not generally available. *Airmail:* 3–5 days. *Cable:* 85 dirhams per word (7-word minimum).

Social customs

All Moslem customs prevail. Only soft drinks are on sale at all times, and the month of Ramadan is strictly observed, with no eating, drinking or smoking from dawn to dusk. In recent times the authorities have become more strict in observance of Moslem customs. Businessmen leaving Libya are sometimes charged income tax at the rate of LD1 per day based on the number of days spent in Libya.

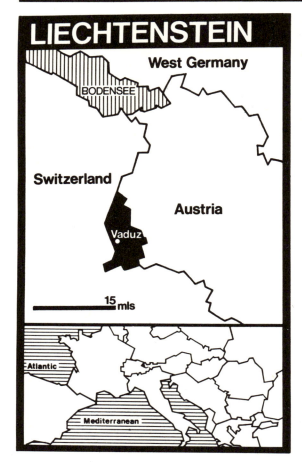

Area and population
160 sq kms (61.8 sq mls). Pop. 24,250.
Capital: Vaduz.
Airports: None. Vaduz is reached by bus from Buchs, Switzerland.

Climate
In winter the temperature rarely falls below −15°C (5°F) and in summer rises up to 28°C (82°F).
Clothing: Warm clothing for winter, lightweight for summer.

People
European stock. *Religion:* 90% Roman Catholic.

Language
German. *English rating:* Good.

Economic background
With no natural resources, almost all raw materials have to be imported. While there is no heavy industry, light industry has boomed in the tiny principality, and there are metal-working, pharmaceuticals, food-processing and consumer goods industries. Liechtenstein is joined to the Swiss customs union, through which much of its trade is conducted. Agriculture is important to much of the population.

Trade
Gross National Product: US$266,750,000. Liechtenstein's trade is not separated from that of Switzerland, to which to all intents and purposes it is linked.

Currency
Swiss franc (see Switzerland).

Travel
Visas not required.

Vaccinations
Not required.

Airlines
There is no air service. Visitors enter Liechtenstein by bus from the Swiss railway station of Buchs. Nearest international airport: Zurich.

Duty-free allowances
Same as Switzerland.

Local time
GMT+1 hr.

Hotels
Park Hotel Sonnenhof. Price is SFr85 per night.

International banks
None.

Credit cards
Same as Switzerland.

Office hours
Same as Switzerland.

National holidays
1, 6 Jan, 2 Feb, 19, 25 Mar, Easter Monday, 1 May, Ascension (May), Whit Monday (May *or* June), 15 Aug, 1 Nov, 25, 26 Dec.

Voltage
Same as Switzerland.

Communications
Same as Switzerland.

Social customs
Same as Switzerland.

Luxembourg

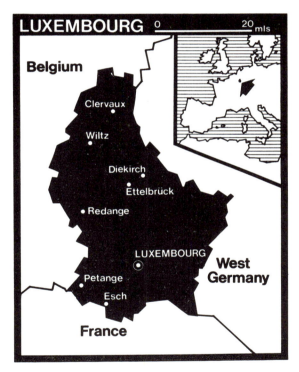

Area and population
2,578 sq kms (999 sq mls). Pop. 358,500.
Capital: Luxembourg City (78,500).
Chief cities: None, but towns include Esch-sur-Alzette
(29,000), Ettelbrück (6,000). *Airport:* Findel
(Luxembourg City).

Climate
Temperatures in Luxembourg City range from 3°C (37°F)
in Jan to 19°C (67°F) in July. *Clothing:* European.

People
French–German mixture. *Religion:* 97% Roman Catholic,
3% Jewish and Protestant. *Distribution:* 68% urban.

Languages
Luxemburgish (a German dialect) and French. German
is the commercial language. *English rating:* Good.

Economic background, Trade, Prospects
See Belgium.

Currency
Luxembourg franc = 100 centimes. At par with Belgian
franc. £ = 61.20 francs; $ = 32.55 francs.

Travel
Visas not required.

Vaccinations
None.

Airlines
British Airways, Luxair, Sabena, CSA, Loftleidir,
Finnair, Caribbean.
Flying times: Copenhagen $4\frac{1}{4}$ hrs; London 70 mins;
New York 12 hrs; Sydney 28 hrs. *Fares:* Copenhagen
F Dkr1,680 Y Dkr1,195; London F £67 Y £44.50;
New York F $700 Y $337; Sydney F A$1,466 Y A$937.
Airport to city: 6 kms (3 mls). *Taxi fare:* 80 francs.

Duty-free allowances
Visitors living in Europe: 300 cigarettes *or* 75 cigars *or*
400 grammes of tobacco; 1.5 litres of spirits and 3 litres
of wine. *Visitors living outside Europe:* 400 cigarettes *or*
100 cigars *or* 400 grammes of tobacco, 1 litre of spirits,
2 litres of wine.

Local time
GMT+1 hr (+2 hrs Apr–Sept).

Embassy phone numbers
Luxembourg City: UK 29864.

Hotels
Luxembourg City: Alfa, Kons, Cravat, Continental,
Molitor, Eldorado, Holiday Inn, Aerogolf. Prices about
800 francs per night.

International banks
Banque Internationale à Luxembourg, Kredietbank,
Caisse d'Épargne de l'État, Banque Lambert.

Madagascar

Credit cards
All major credit cards.

Office hours
08.00–12.00 and 14.00–18.00 Mon–Fri.

National holidays
1 Jan, Carnival Monday (Feb), Easter Monday,
1 May, Ascension Day (May), Whit Monday
(May or June), 23 June, 15 Aug, Luxembourg Fair
(end Aug or beginning Sept), 1, 2 Nov, 25, 26 Dec.

Voltage
220 volts AC.

Communications
See Belgium.

Social customs
See Belgium.

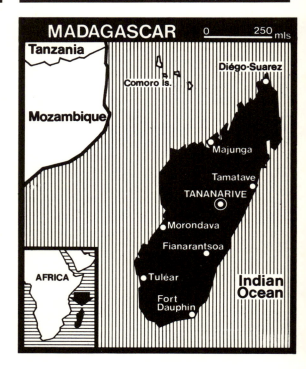

Area and population
592,183 sq kms (228,642 sq mls). Pop. 8 million.
Capital: Tananarive (400,000).
Chief cities: None, but towns include Tamatave (55,000),
Majunga (50,000), Diégo-Suarez (41,000).
Ports; Diégo-Suarez, Tamatave.
Airport: Ivato (Tananarive).

Climate
Hot, wet season Nov–Apr, cooler, drier season May–Oct,
hottest in Dec, 20° to 28°C (68° to 82°F). July is coolest
month, 12° to 25°C (54° to 77°F). Monsoons and
cyclones are prevalent. *Clothing:* Normal weight
May–Oct, tropical Nov–Mar. Sunglasses and raincoat are
needed.

People
Mainly Indonesian origin plus French, Indian and
Chinese minorities. *Religion:* 50% Christian, remainder
Moslem and animist. *Distribution:* 10% urban.

Languages
French and Malagasy. *English rating:* Poor.

Economic background
Predominantly agricultural, with rice as the main crop.

Madagascar

Madagascar still retains close connections with France, from which it gained independence in 1960. Apart from rice, main crops are coffee, vanilla, cloves, sugar cane, sisal and pepper. The government is trying to modernise cattle farming. Industry is still largely in its infancy, although it has grown since independence, and there are now an oil refinery, a paper mill, cotton mills, car-assembly plants, and a pharmaceutical factory.

Trade
Gross National Product: FMG273,100 million.
Exports: FMG41,864 million, chiefly coffee, vanilla, sugar, rice, raffia. *Imports:* FMG51,753 million, chiefly transport equipment, textiles, chemicals, pharmaceuticals, machinery and electrical apparatus. *Chief trading partners:* France, W. Germany, Japan, USA, Italy, UK, Malaysia. *Inflation rate:* 3.5%.

Prospects
Much investment is needed to expand industry, a requirement that is understood by the government.

Currency
Franc Malagasy (FMG). £ = FMG421; $ = FMG223.

Travel
Malagasy regulations require the automatic expulsion of visitors arriving without a visa. Early application for a visa is advised.

Vaccinations
Smallpox. Yellow fever and cholera certificates are required if arriving from an infected area.

Airlines
Air France, Air Madagascar, Alitalia.
Flying times: Copenhagen 18 hrs; London 9 hrs; New York 20 hrs; Sydney 24 hrs. *Fares:* Copenhagen F Dkr7,775 Y Dkr5,585; London F £573.50 Y £409; New York F $1,388 Y $930; Sydney F A$1,029 Y A$776. *Airport to city:* 17 kms (11 mls). *Taxi fare:* FMG300.

Duty-free allowances
Reasonable amounts of tobacco products and spirits.

Local time
GMT+3 hrs.

Embassy phone numbers
Tananarive: UK 25151.

Hotels
Tananarive: Colbert, Madagascar-Hilton, Select, Hotel de France. Prices up to FMG5,000 per night.

International banks
None.

Credit cards
All major credit cards.

Office hours
08.00–11.30 and 14.00–17.30 Mon–Fri, 08.00–11.30 Sat.

National holidays
1 Jan, 29 Mar, Good Friday, Easter Monday, 1 May, Ascension Day (May), Whit Monday (May or June), 26 June, 1 Nov, 25 Dec.

Voltage
110 or 220 volts AC.

Communications
Tel: FMG2,612 per 3 mins. *Telex:* FMG2,507 per 3 mins. *Airmail:* 4–6 days. *Cable:* FMG155.72 per word.

Social customs
French business customs prevail, but the atmosphere is easy and unhurried. *Best buys:* Turtle shells, coral objects.

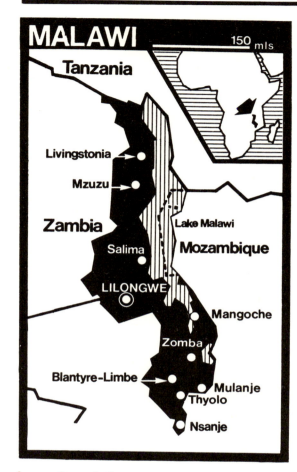

Area and population

118,485 sq kms (45,747 sq mls). Pop. 5 million.
Capital: Lilongwe (87,000).
Chief cities: Blantyre (180,000), Zomba (20,000),
Mzuzu (8,700). *Airport:* Chileka (Blantyre).

Climate

Entirely within the tropics, Malawi enjoys temperatures
of 24° to 33°C (75.2° to 91.4°F), with humidity up to
81%. Hottest months are Oct and Nov, immediately
before the start of the rains. There is little rain Apr–Aug.
Clothing: Summer-weight clothing is suitable for much
of the year but tropical-weight may be preferred during
the very hot period, Oct–Feb. See *Social customs.*

People

Bantu, with 7,000 Europeans and 12,000 Asians.
Religion: 50% Christian, 33% Moslem, rest animist.
Distribution: 5% urban.

Languages

English and Chichewa.

Economic background

Almost entirely an agricultural country, Malawi derives
its export revenue from maize, tobacco, tea, groundnuts,
cotton and sugar, and industry plays only a small part in
providing employment. Tea is a major export crop and
is grown chiefly on European estates. Malawi has few
mineral resources, although natural forests are extensive.

Trade

Gross National Product: 656 million kwacha.
Exports: 119.6 million kwacha, chiefly tobacco, tea,
groundnuts, maize, cassava, cotton fibre, beans, peas.
Imports: 218.3 million kwacha, chiefly cotton yarns and
fabrics, paper, man-made fibres, clothing, iron and steel,
boilers, machinery, vehicles.
Chief trading partners: UK, South Africa, Rhodesia,
Japan, USA, Netherlands. *Inflation rate:* Not available.

Prospects

The government has plans to expand manufacturing and
attract foreign investment.

Currency

Kwacha (K) = 100 tambala (t). £ = K1.57; $ = K0.83.

Travel

Visas not generally required. See *Social customs.*

Vaccinations

Not generally required.

Airlines

Air Malawi, British Caledonian, South African Airways.
Flying times: Copenhagen 16 hrs; London 13½ hrs;
New York 23 hrs; Sydney 30 hrs. *Fares:* Copenhagen
F Dkr7,720 Y Dkr4,940; London F £566.50 Y £359.50;
New York F $1,213 Y $802; Sydney F A$1,030 Y A$788.
Airport to city: 18 kms (11 mls). *Taxi fare:* K2.

Duty-free allowances

200 cigarettes *or* 225 grammes of cigars *or* tobacco;
1 bottle of spirits, 1 bottle of wine and 2 pints of beer.

Local time

GMT+2 hrs.

Malawi

Embassy phone numbers
Blantyre: UK 33022.

Hotels
Blantyre: Mount Soche, Ryall's.
Lilongwe: Lilongwe Hotel.
Zomba: Ku Chawe. Prices about K12 per night.

International banks
National Bank of Malawi (a merger of Standard Bank and Barclays in which the Malawi government holds a 49% share), Commercial Bank of Malawi (owned by the government of Malawi with a 30% holding by the Bank of America).

Credit cards
All major credit cards.

Office hours
Variable, but offices usually open 07.30–16.00 with 1½ hrs for lunch Mon–Fri, 07.30–12.00 Sat.

National holidays
1 Jan, 3 Mar, Good Friday, Easter Monday, 14 May, 6 July, First Monday in Aug, 17 Oct, 25, 26 Dec.

Voltage
230–240 volts AC.

Communications
Tel: K9 per 3 mins. *Telex:* Available.
Airmail: 3 days. *Cable:* 24t per word (7-word minimum).

Social customs
Rigorous clothing regulations are in force. Men are forbidden to have long hair or to wear bell bottom trousers. Hair must not trespass below an imaginary line drawn round the head at the level of the mouth. Under the Decency of Dress (Amendment) Act 1974, bell bottom trousers are defined as 'any flared trousers so made that the circumference of each leg thereof measured along the bottom edge is greater than six-fifths of the circumference of such leg measured at its narrowest point parallel to the aforesaid bottom edge'. Another act forbids women to wear clothing that exposes any part of the body between the lowest part of the kneecap and the waist. Women are not allowed to wear trousers or shorts. Visitors to Malawi who break the clothing and hair laws are likely to be forbidden entry.

Malaysia

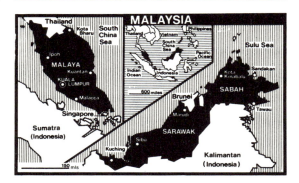

Area and population
329,736 sq kms (127,136 sq mls). Pop. 10 million.
Capital: Kuala Lumpur (707,000).
Chief cities: Georgetown (Penang) (332,000), Butterworth (61,000), Ipoh (248,000), Klang (113,000). Johore Bahru (136,000), Malacca (86,000).
Ports: Penang, Port Kelang, Pasir Gudang.
Airport: Subang (Kuala Lumpur).

Climate
Tropical, with high humidity, heavy rainfall and little variation in daytime temperatures. Temperature at night falls to 24°C (75°F) and rises in the day to 35°C (95°F).
Clothing: Lightweight. Jackets are needed only for formal occasions.

People
45% Malay, 36% Chinese, 9% Indian.
Religion: Principally Moslem with Christians, Buddhists, Taoists, Confucians. *Distribution:* 39% urban.

Language
Bahasa Malaysia (Malay). *English rating:* Excellent.

Economic background
The third richest nation in Asia, after Japan and Singapore, Malaysia is the world's biggest producer of rubber and tin and, after Nigeria, palm oil. Agriculture, forestry, fishing and mining comprise the main parts of the economy, contributing more than 90% of Malaysia's exports. Oil production is becoming more important.

Trade
Gross National Product: M$19,562 million.
Exports: M$7,696 million, chiefly rubber, tin, timber, palm oil, iron ore. *Imports:* M$7,483 million, chiefly transport equipment, machinery, textile yarns, fabrics, iron and steel alloys. *Chief trading partners:* Japan, USA,

UK, Australia, Singapore, W. Germany, Kuwait, Thailand, Netherlands. *Inflation rate:* 4.7%.

Prospects

Under a 20-year plan that ends in 1990, Malaysia is developing its industries, including manufacturing. Overseas investment is encouraged.

Currency

Malaysian dollar (M$), also known as ringgits = 100 cents. £ = M$4.45; $ = M$2.36.

Travel

Visitor's pass is required and is usually obtainable on arrival.

Vaccinations

Smallpox and cholera. Yellow fever recommended.

Airlines

British Airways, MAS, SIA, Cathay Pacific, KLM, Qantas, Sabena.
Flying times: Copenhagen $19\frac{1}{2}$ hrs; London $9\frac{1}{2}$ hrs by Concorde (via Singapore; service suspended at time of going to press), $14\frac{1}{2}$ hrs by 747; New York 23 hrs; Sydney 10 hrs. *Fares:* Copenhagen F Dkr8,435 Y Dkr4,910; London F £656 Y £382; New York F $1,629 Y $1,009; Sydney F A$642 Y A$456.
Airport to city: 22.5 kms (14 mls). *Taxi fare:* M$16.

Duty-free allowances

200 cigarettes *or* $\frac{1}{2}$lb of cigars *or* tobacco; 1 quart of spirits *or* wine.

Local time

West Malaysia: GMT+$7\frac{1}{2}$ hrs.
Sabah, Sarawak: GMT+8 hrs.

Embassy phone numbers

Kuala Lumpur:

Australia 80166	Sweden 26211
Canada 89722	Switzerland 23661
Denmark 25357	W. Germany 208233
Japan 22400	UK 941533
Netherlands 80387	USA 26231

Hotels

Kuala Lumpur: Federal, Fortuna, Hilton, Holiday Inn, Malaysia, Merlin, Miramar. Prices up to M$80 per night.

International banks

Chartered Bank, Hong Kong and Shanghai Banking Corporation, Bank of America, First National City Bank.

Credit cards

All major credit cards.

Office hours

08.30–13.00 and 14.00–16.30 Mon–Fri, 08.30–12.30 Sat.

National holidays

Movable religious holidays plus 1 Jan, Good Friday, 1, 21 May, 7 June, 31 Aug, 25 Dec.

Voltage

230 volts AC.

Communications

Tel: M$33 per 3 mins. *Telex:* M$36 per 3 mins. *Airmail:* 2–5 days. *Cable:* 80 cents per word (7-word minimum).

Social customs

Personal contact is essential in Malaysia and entertainment is an essential part of the business scene. Due to the heat and humidity, there is little formality and the pace of business life tends to be slow.

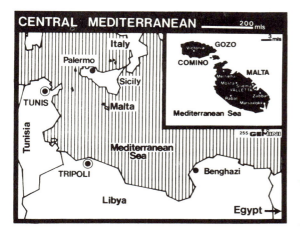

Chief trading partners: UK, Italy, W. Germany, USA, Netherlands, France, Belgium, Japan, Libya, Denmark, Sweden. *Inflation rate:* Not available.

Prospects

Everyone, including Malta's businessmen, is waiting to see what happens when the British leave in 1979.

Currency

Maltese pound = 100 cents = 1,000 mils. £ = £M0.736; $ = £M0.391.

Travel

Visas not required.

Vaccination

Required only if arriving from an infected area.

Airlines

Air Malta, British Airways, Alitalia, Libyan Arab, UTA, Zambia.
Flying times: Copenhagen $5\frac{3}{4}$ hrs; London 4 hrs; New York $9\frac{1}{2}$ hrs; Sydney 30 hrs. *Fares:* Copenhagen F Dkr3,160 Y Dkr2,355; London F £163 Y £108.50; New York F $831 Y $426; Sydney F A$1,391 Y A$888.
Airport to city: 5 kms (3 mls). *Taxi fare:* £M1.

Duty-free allowances

200 cigarettes *or* 225 grammes of cigars *or* tobacco; 1 bottle of spirits *or* wine.

Local time

GMT+1 hr (+2 hrs in summer).

Embassy phone numbers

UK Central 21285.

Hotels

Phoenicia, Grand Hotel Excelsior, Corinthia Palace, Cavalier, Dragonara, Malta Hilton, Preluna. Prices about £M8 per night.

International banks

Bank of Valletta, Mid-Med Bank, Lombard Bank (Malta) Ltd.

Credit cards

All major credit cards.

Area and population

316 sq kms (122 sq mls). Pop. 318,000.
Capital: Valletta (15,200).
Chief cities: None, but towns include Sliema (21,000), Hamrun, Birkirkara, Msida, Gzira, Paola, Cospicua, Mdina. *Port:* Valletta. *Airport:* Luqa.

Climate

Pleasant but healthy. Temperatures range from 10°C (50°F) in Jan to 31°C (88°F) in Aug, sometimes much higher. *Clothing:* Medium-weight for winter, tropical in summer.

People

Mediterranean. *Religion:* Roman Catholic.

Language

English.

Economic background

Malta's economy has depended upon British Service establishments, a presence worth about £28 million a year. Now the British are withdrawing completely, and Malta is trying to build up industry and tourism to replace the lost income. Malta's development corporation provides incentives to assist in the establishment of new industries.

Trade

Gross National Product: £M139.4 million.
Exports: £M63.8 million, chiefly textiles, potatoes, flowers and seed, scrap metal.
Imports: £M144.5 million, chiefly machinery, chemicals, meat, mineral fuels, lubricants, vehicles.

Office hours
08.30–12.45 and 14.30–17.30 Mon-Fri; 08.30–13.00 Sat. Some office hours are 07.30–13.30 June–Sept.

National holidays
1 Jan, Good Friday, 1 May, Carnival (usually in May), 15 Aug, 13, 25 Dec.

Voltage
240 volts AC.

Communications
Tel: £M1.50 per 3 mins. *Telex:* 90 cents per 3 mins. *Airmail:* 3 days. *Cable:* 3 cents 3 mils per word.

Social customs
European business customs prevail. Maltese are excellent businessmen and good hosts. Accommodation and food and drink are comparatively cheap, but summer visits should be planned well in advance because hotels are packed with tourists.

Mauritius

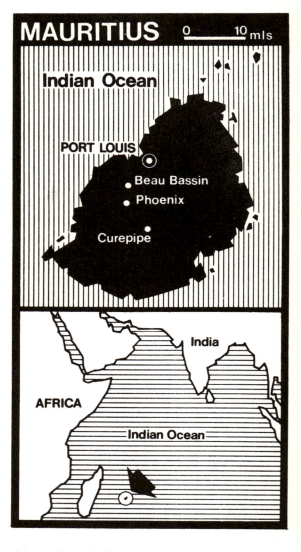

Area and population
1,865 sq kms (720 sq mls). Pop. 863,000.
Capital: Port Louis (138,000).
Chief cities: None but sizeable suburbs of Port Louis include Curepipe and Vacoas (with a combined population of more than 100,000), Beau Bassin (40,000), Rose Hill (40,000), Quatre Bornes (40,000). *Port:* Port Louis. *Airport:* Plaisance.

Climate
Tropical maritime with no extremes. Average temperature 20°C (68°F) the year round. Much rain but rarely in Sept–Nov. Expect cyclones in summer.

Clothing: Tropical clothing is worn throughout the year; lightweight lounge suits for evening. Women need cotton or linen dresses, and evening dresses for formal occasions.

People

68% Indian, 30% mixed African and European descent, 2% Chinese. *Religion:* 50% Hindu, 10% Moslem, 40% Christian. *Distribution:* 50% urban.

Language

English, but French, Hindi and Creole are used in everyday life.

Economic background

Sugar, growing industrial development and tourism form the basis of the economy. Once almost totally dependent upon sugar for its revenue, Mauritius in recent years has introduced some small industries, including clothing and electronic components.

Trade

Gross National Product: US$3,000 million. *Exports:* 2,000 million rupees, chiefly sugar, tea, ores and metal scrap. *Imports:* 2,000 million rupees, chiefly rice, chemicals, petroleum products, textile yarns, fabrics, meal and flour, machinery. *Chief trading partners:* UK, South Africa, China, Iran, France, W. Germany, Japan, Canada, USA, Sudan, Somalia. *Inflation rate:* 8.9%.

Prospects

Further small-scale industrial projects are planned.

Currency

Rupee = 100 cents. £ = 11.64 rupees; $ = 6.19 rupees.

Travel

Visas not required by visitors from UK, Europe and Commonwealth countries.

Vaccinations

Smallpox. Yellow fever and cholera certificates may be required; check before departure.

Airlines

Air France, Lufthansa, Air India, British Airways, Alitalia, SAS, South African Airways. *Flying times:* Copenhagen $24\frac{1}{4}$ hrs; London $15\frac{1}{2}$ hrs; New York 22 hrs; Sydney 12 hrs. *Fares:* Copenhagen F Dkr8,435 Y Dkr5,620; London F £626.50 Y £417.50; New York F $1,491 Y $992; Sydney F A$897 Y A$683. *Airport to city:* 29 kms (18 mls). *Taxi fare:* 85 rupees.

Duty-free allowances

200 cigarettes *or* 250 grammes of tobacco; 750 ccs of spirits and two litres of wine.

Local time

GMT+4 hrs.

Embassy phone numbers

Port Louis: UK 2.0201.

Hotels

Port Louis: Ambassador, Hotel des Touristes, National, Golden Tourist. Prices 30–60 rupees per night.

International banks

Bank of Mauritius (Central Bank), Barclays Bank International, Mauritius Commercial Bank, Mercantile Bank, Habib Bank, Bank of Baroda, Banque Nationale pour le Commerce et l'Industrie, State Commercial Bank, First National City Bank, Bank of Credit and Commerce International SA.

Credit cards

American Express, Barclaycard, Diners Club.

Office hours

Mainly 08.30–16.00. Banks open 10.00–14.00 Mon–Fri, 09.30–11.30 Sat. Shops tend to open 08.00–18.00 every day except European ones in Port Louis, which close Sat.

National holidays

Because of the mixture of religions, holidays are many and varied, so best check before departure. Fixed dates: 1, 2, 27 Jan, 11, 12 Mar, 1 May, 15 Aug, 24 Oct, 1 Nov, 25, 26 Dec.

Voltage

220 volts AC 50 cycles. The standard 13 amp three-pin plug is used in most hotels.

Communications

Telex: 50 rupees per 3 mins. *Airmail:* 5–6 days. *Cable:* 1.20 rupees per word (7-word minimum).

Social customs

A free and easy atmosphere prevails in this island of many cultures. No particular social taboos, although many business contacts will be Chinese or Indian. Much entertaining is done in local restaurants. *Best buys:* Sea shells—very beautiful and very cheap. But don't buy them in the tourist shops. The best bargains are found among beach pedlars.

Area and population
1,969,366 sq kms (760,377 sq mls). Pop. 60 million.
Capital: Mexico City (12 million).
Chief cities: Guadalajara (1.9 m), Monterrey (1.6 m),
Ciudad Juarez (522,000), Puebla (400,000),
Leon (347,000). *Ports:* Veracruz, Tampico,
Coatzacoalcos, Guaymas, Mazatlan, Salina Cruz.
Airport: Central (Mexico City).

Climate
Varies with altitude. Mexico City temperatures range
from 12°C (54°F) Dec–Mar to 18°C (65°F) in May and
June. It is always cold at night, even in summer.
Clothing: European clothing in winter, lightweight in
summer.

People
66% mixed Indian and Spanish, 33% Indian.
Religion: 95% Roman Catholic. *Distribution:* 53% urban.

Language
Spanish. *English rating:* Good.

Economic background
The second most populous country in Latin America
and the largest Spanish-speaking nation, Mexico has
boomed economically during the past 12 years,
transforming itself from an agricultural to an industrial
society. This has been achieved largely through a
balanced mixture of state and private investment. While
heavy industry has increased in capacity each year,
agriculture is still a most important sector, employing

nearly half of the population. Main crops include coffee
and cotton. Mexico is also a major mining nation, being
the world's largest producer of silver.

Trade
Gross National Product: 812,000 million pesos.
Exports: 35,635 million pesos, chiefly metals, minerals,
textile fibres, sugar, fruit, vegetables, cocoa, coffee,
chemicals. *Imports:* 75,709 million pesos, chiefly
machinery, chemicals, vehicles, electrical machinery, iron
and steel, paper. *Chief trading partners:* USA,
W. Germany, Japan, Canada, France, Netherlands, UK,
Venezuela, Italy, Sweden, Switzerland, Spain, Brazil,
Argentina. *Inflation rate:* 17.5%.

Prospects
Further growth of the economy is confidently expected,
particularly in industry and mining.

Currency
Peso = 100 centavos. £ = 43.00 pesos; $ = 22.87 pesos.

Travel
All travellers require a tourist or business card, obtainable
free of charge from Mexican embassies. Check
regulations that are in force concerning travellers arriving
from Cuba.

Vaccinations
Smallpox.

Airlines
Aeromexico, British Airways, Braniff, Iberia, KLM,
Lufthansa, Air France, Sabena, Eastern Airlines, Varig.
Flying times: Copenhagen 16 hrs; London 11½ hrs;
New York 4 hrs; Sydney 25 hrs. *Fares:* Copenhagen
F Dkr5,450 Y Dkr3,380; London F £433.50 Y £264;
New York F $249 Y $190; Sydney F A$2,172 Y A$1,371.
Airport to city: 13 kms (8 mls). *Taxi fare:* 35 pesos.
(shared limousine).

Duty-free allowances
400 cigarettes *or* 1 kilo of cigars *or* tobacco;
2 bottles of spirits *or* wine.

Local time
Central Time (including Mexico City): GMT−6 hrs.
Mountain Time: GMT−7 hrs.
Pacific Time: GMT−8 hrs (GMT−7 hrs May–Oct).

Mexico

Embassy phone numbers
Mexico City:

Australia 566.30.50	Sweden 531.75.40
Canada 533.06.10	Switzerland 533.07.35
Denmark 531.30.60	W. Germany 545.66.55
Japan 574.72.66	UK 511.48.80
Netherlands 511.60.90	USA 525.91.00
Norway 540.34.86	

Hotels
Mexico City: Alameda, Aristos, Camino Real, Chateau Royal, Del Paseo, Del Prado, Gran Hotel, Ciudad Mexico, Maria Isabel-Sheraton, El Presidente, Reforma, Suites Bamer, Suites Embassy.
Prices up to US$45 per night.

International banks
Banco de Comercio.

Office hours
09.00 or 10.00–13.00 or 14.00 and 14.00 or 15.00–19.00 Mon–Fri. There are many variations; government offices, for instance, open 08.00–19.00 on a staggered hours basis.

National holidays
1 Jan, 5 Feb, 21 Mar, Maundy Thursday, Good Friday, 1, 5 May, 15, 16 Sept, 12 Oct, 1, 2, 20 Nov, 25 Dec.

Voltage
110–117 volts.

Communications
Tel: 208.5 pesos per 3 mins. *Telex:* 219 pesos per 3 mins. *Airmail:* 4 or more days. *Cable:* 11.30 pesos per word.

Social customs
Take special care to address businessmen by their correct titles. Mexicans eat their main meal in the early afternoon and take only light food in the evening.

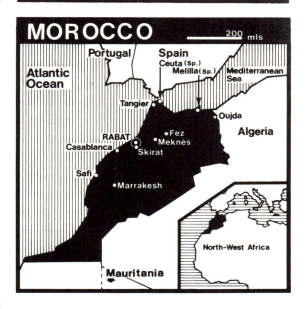

Area and population
458,730 sq kms (177,116 sq mls). Pop. 17.3 million. *Capital:* Rabat-Salé (900,000).
Chief cities: Casablanca (1.9 million), Marrakesh (407,000), Tangier (189,000), Fez (399,000), Meknès (376,000), Tetouan (285,000). *Ports:* Agadir, Casablanca, Kenitra, Safi, Tangier. *Airports:* Nouasseur (Casablanca), Salé (Rabat), Boukhalef (Tangier).

Climate
Temperate on the coast, desert inland. Tangier's average temperature is 12°C (54°F) in January and 24°C (75°F) in August. Casablanca is similar.
Clothing: Medium-weight in winter (Nov–May), lightweight in summer. Sunglasses needed in summer.

People
Arab and Berber. *Religion:* Moslem.
Distribution: 34% urban.

Language
Moroccan Arabic. French and Spanish are used commercially. *English rating:* Poor.

Economic background
With about 40% of the world's known phosphates reserves, Morocco has important mineral deposits that are still being exploited. Most of its people remain poor, but the government, through a series of plans, is developing agriculture, dams, industry and tourism.

Industry is expanding, particularly textiles, construction materials and chemicals.

Trade
Gross National Product: 31,070 million dirhams.
Exports: 5,579 million dirhams, chiefly phosphates, vegetables, fruit, wine, canned fish.
Imports: 11,555 million dirhams, chiefly wheat, industrial machinery, cotton and synthetic textile yarn, iron and steel products. *Chief trading partners:* France, USA, W. Germany, Spain, Italy, Iraq, UK, Poland.
Inflation rate: 8.1%.

Prospects
Morocco is now engaged in a new development plan that stresses agricultural and social development rather than large industrial prospects.

Currency
Dirham = 100 francs. £ = DH7.76; $ = DH4.12.

Travel
Visas not required.

Vaccinations
Required only if travelling from an infected area.

Airlines
Royal Air Maroc, British Airways, British Caledonian, Air France, Iberia, Sabena, Lufthansa, KLM, Swissair, Saudia, Balkan, TWA.
Flying times (to Casablanca): Copenhagen $5\frac{1}{4}$ hrs; London $3\frac{1}{4}$ hrs; New York 8 hrs; Sydney 34 hrs.
Fares: Copenhagen F Dkr3,235 Y Dkr2,310; London F £188.50 Y £125.50; New York F $684 Y $325; Sydney F A$1,493 Y A$956.
Airport to city (Casablanca): 30 kms (19 mls).
Bus fare: 5 dirhams.

Duty-free allowances
200 cigarettes *or* 50 cigars *or* 500 grammes of tobacco; 1 bottle of spirits.

Local time
GMT.

Embassy phone numbers
Casablanca: UK 26.14.40.

Hotels
Casablanca: Asfa-Plages, El Mansour, Marhaba, Casablanca. *Rabat:* Hilton, Tour Hassan.
Tangier: Les Almohades, Inter-Continental, Malabata. Prices up to DH150 per night.

International banks
Banque Marocaine pour l'Afrique et l'Orient, Banque Marocaine du Commerce.

Credit cards
All major credit cards.

Office hours
Tangier: 09.00–12.00 and 16.00–20.00 Mon–Fri, 09.00–12.00 Sat. *Rest of country:* 09.00–12.00 and 15.00–18.00 Mon–Fri, 09.00–12.00 Sat.

National holidays
Moslem holidays, plus 1 Jan, 3 Mar, 1 May, 18 Nov.

Voltage
110–127 volts AC.

Communications
Tel: DH16.62 per 3 mins. *Telex:* DH11.64 per 3 mins. *Airmail:* 5 days. *Cables:* DH1.45 per word (7-word minimum).

Social customs
French customs prevail in most business circles, Moroccan hospitality is extensive. Offer to take your shoes off before entering a Moroccan home.

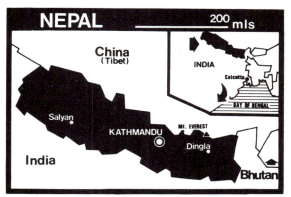

Area and population
140,798 sq kms (54,362 sq mls). Pop. 12 million.
Capital: Kathmandu (160,000).
Chief cities: None, but towns include Biratnagar (45,000), Nepalganj (36,000), Birganj (20,000).
Airport: Tribhuyan (Kathmandu).

Climate
Ranges from sub-tropical monsoon to Alpine climate in the mountains. Temperatures in Kathmandu generally range from −3°C (27°F) in Jan to 26°C (78°F) in July.
Clothing: Medium-weight in winter to lightweight in summer if visiting Kathmandu.

People
Indian, Tibetan and Central Asian stock.
Religion: Hinduism and Mahayana Buddhism.
Distribution: 5% urban.

Language
Nepali. *English rating:* Good.

Economic background
One of the least developed countries in the world, Nepal is almost totally an agricultural country, although industry, particularly that connected with jute and sugar, is growing slowly. Transport difficulties mean that nearly all of Nepal's trade is with India.

Trade
Gross National Product: US$1,300 million (1971).
Exports: US$1,000 million, chiefly rice, jute, ghee, oilseeds, timber, herbs.
Imports: US$1,800 million, chiefly textiles, foodstuffs, petroleum products, machinery and equipment, vehicles and parts. *Chief trading partners:* India, Pakistan, USA, USSR, China. *Inflation rate:* Not available.

Prospects
Nepal's immediate economic future depends upon the further expansion and modernisation of its agriculture. Tourism is growing slowly as a source of revenue.

Currency
Rupee = 100 paisa. £ = R22.56; $ = R12.00.

Travel
Visas required.

Vaccinations
Smallpox.

Airlines
Air India, PIA, Royal Nepalese.
Flying times: Copenhagen $13\frac{1}{4}$ hrs; London $14\frac{1}{2}$ hrs; New York 21 hrs; Sydney 12 hrs. *Fares:* Copenhagen F Dkr6,680 Y Dkr4,455; London F £515 Y £343; New York F $1,502 Y $939; Sydney F A$912 Y A$662.
Airport to city: 6.5 kms (4 mls). *Taxi fare:* R15.

Duty-free allowances
A reasonable quantity of tobacco products, and alcoholic beverages.

Local time
GMT+5 hrs 40 mins.

Embassy phone numbers
Kathmandu: UK 11081.

Hotels
Kathmandu: De l'Annapurna, Crystal, Shanker, Soaltee-Oberoi. Prices up to US$25 per night.

International banks
None.

Credit cards
All major credit cards.

Office hours
09.00–17.00 Mon–Fri.

National holidays
Many and varied and frequently declared at short notice. Check before leaving.

Voltage
230–400 volts AC.

Communications

Tel: R100 per 3 mins. *Telex:* R100 per 3 mins.
Airmail: 5–7 days. *Cable:* R2 per word.

Social customs

Dealings with Nepalese businessmen are marked by friendliness and courtesy. Many contacts are likely to be Indian. Travel within Kathmandu is good, but elsewhere the roads are poor.

Netherlands

Area and population

41,160 sq kms (15,892 sq mls). Pop. 13.7 million.
Capital: Amsterdam (990,000); seat of government
The Hague (Den Haag, 's-Gravenhage) (678,000).
Chief cities: Rotterdam (620,000), Utrecht (274,000),
Eindhoven (189,000), Haarlem (168,000).
Ports: Amsterdam, Rotterdam. *Airports:* Schiphol
(Amsterdam), Rotterdam.

Climate

Similar to Britain, with average temperatures of
2°C (35°F) in Jan and 17°C (63°F) in July.
Clothing: Similar to Britain.

People
Chiefly Germanic stock, with French mixture.
Religion: 41% Protestant, 40% Roman Catholic.
Distribution: 52.7% urban.

Language
Dutch. *English rating:* Excellent.

Economic background
Holland, with the magnificent ports of Amsterdam and Rotterdam and one of Europe's finest airports at Schiphol, can rightly claim to be the transport centre of the Continent. Added to this, rapid industrialisation since the war and highly efficient agriculture have taken Holland to the front rank of industrial powers. Major industries are shipbuilding, engineering, food processing, cotton textiles, electric and electronic goods, nuclear plant, oil refining, petrochemicals, pharmaceuticals and plastics, synthetic fibres and steel. The discovery and exploitation of natural gas boosted prosperity.

Trade
Gross National Product: 186,000 million guilders.
Exports: 76,375 million guilders, chiefly meats, bulbs, petroleum products, natural gas, chemicals, textiles, machinery and electrical equipment.
Imports: 76,506 million guilders, chiefly grains, petroleum, chemicals, textiles, iron and steel products, machinery and electrical equipment.
Chief trading partners: W. Germany, USA, France, UK, Saudi Arabia, Iran, Italy, Nigeria, Sweden, Egypt, Kuwait, Japan, Switzerland, Denmark, Norway, Spain, Austria, Greece, Finland. *Inflation rate:* 4.6%.

Prospects
In spite of inflation and unemployment, the Netherlands is looking for an annual growth rate of 3.75% until 1980.

Currency
Guilder (or florin) = 100 cents. £ = 4.19 guilders; $ = 2.22 guilders.

Travel
Visas not required.

Vaccinations
Not required.

Airlines
All major international airlines.
Flying times (to Amsterdam): Copenhagen $1\frac{1}{4}$ hrs; London 1 hr; New York 8 hrs; Sydney 26 hrs.
Fares: Copenhagen F Dkr1,315 Y Dkr940; London

F £61.50 Y £41; New York F $684 Y $325; Sydney F A$1,466 Y A$937.
Airport to city (Amsterdam): 15 kms (9.3 mls).
Taxi fare: 45 guilders. *Bus fare:* 4.50 guilders.

Duty-free allowances
200 cigarettes *or* 50 cigars *or* 250 grammes of tobacco; 1 litre of spirits and 2 litres of wine.

Local time
GMT+1 hr (+2 hrs Apr–Sept).

Embassy phone numbers
Amsterdam:

Denmark 23.41.45	W. Germany 73.62.45
Norway 24.23.31	UK 73.62.45
Sweden 24.41.24	USA 79.83.01
Switzerland 79.76.26	

Hotels
Amsterdam: American, Amstel, Apolo, Caransa, Carlton, De l'Europe, Krasnapolsky, Hilton, Memphis, Okura. Prices range to over 100 guilders per night.

International banks
All international banks plus Amsterdam–Rotterdam Bank, Algemene Bank Nederland, Hollandsche Bank-Unie, Bank Mees & Hope.

Credit cards
All major credit cards.

Office hours
08.30–17.30 Mon–Fri.

National holidays
1 Jan, Good Friday, Easter Monday, 30 Apr, Ascension Day (May), Whit Monday (May *or* June), 25, 26 Dec.

Voltage
220–380 volts AC.

Communications
Tel: STD code to Britain is 09.44. *Telex:* 5 cents for every 4.62 seconds. *Airmail:* 2 days.
Cable: 8 guilders plus 40 cents per word.

Social customs
Very much as elsewhere in Europe except that the Dutch shake hands more frequently. If invited home, send flowers or chocolates to the hostess.

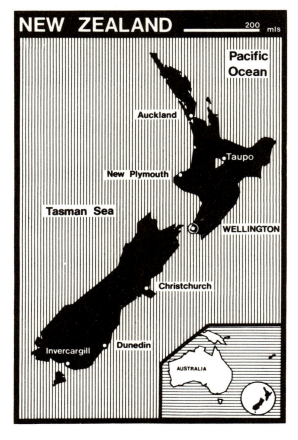

NEW ZEALAND —————— 200 mls

Pacific Ocean

Auckland

Taupo

New Plymouth

Tasman Sea

WELLINGTON

Christchurch

Dunedin

Invercargill

AUSTRALIA

Area and population

268,676 sq kms (103,736 sq mls). Pop. 3.1 million.
Capital: Wellington (349,000).
Chief cities: Auckland (797,000), Christchurch (325,000), Dunedin (120,000), Hamilton (154,000).
Ports: Auckland, Bluff, Dunedin, Lyttleton, Napier, Nelson, New Plymouth, Wellington.
Airports: International (Auckland), International (Christchurch), Wellington.

Climate

Temperate. Temperatures range from 16° to 28°C (60° to 83°F); rarely below 4°C (40°F).
Autumn–winter covers Mar–Aug. Avoid visiting mid-Dec to mid-Feb, when New Zealanders take holidays.
Clothing: Similar to Britain, although top coats seldom needed.

People

90% British stock, 8% Maori. *Religion:* 22% Presbyterian, 35% Church of England, 16% Roman Catholic.
Distribution: 77.3% urban.

Language

English

Economic background

While chiefly an agricultural country—its farming is one of the most efficient in the world—manufacturing, particularly in food and beverages and the processing of primary products, has grown rapidly since the war, a trend that is likely to continue. Nearly 85% of New Zealand's export earnings come from primary products. This proportion will be harder to maintain now that Britain—New Zealand's main market—has joined the European Economic Community. In the meantime, New Zealand is looking to the development of its mining, energy and manufacturing industry.

Trade

Gross National Product: NZ$10,791 million.
Exports: NZ$2,246 million, chiefly meat, dairy products, wool. *Imports:* NZ$2,927 million, chiefly machinery and equipment, industrial raw materials, oil.
Chief trading partners: Australia, UK, Japan, USA, W. Germany, Iran, Kuwait, USSR, Canada, France.
Inflation rate: 15.4%.

Prospects

New Zealand has embarked on a series of major projects aimed at making use of natural resources, such as paper and pulp, iron and steel, plastics, oil and aluminium.

Currency

Dollar (NZ$) = 100 cents. £ = NZ$1.81; $ = NZ$0.96.

Travel

Entry permits required.

Vaccinations

Smallpox.

Airlines

Air New Zealand, British Airways, Qantas, UTA, Pan Am.
Flying times (to Auckland): Copenhagen 31 hrs; London 29 hrs; New York 20 hrs; Sydney 11 hrs.
Fares: Copenhagen F Dkr10,595 Y Dkr6,810; London F £816.50 Y £524.50; New York F $2,498 Y $1,536; Sydney F A$204 Y A$145.
Airport to city (Auckland): 22.5 kms (14 mls).
Taxi fare: NZ$7–8. *Bus fare:* NZ$2.50.

New Zealand

Duty-free allowances
200 cigarettes *or* 50 cigars *or* ½ lb of tobacco;
1 quart of spirits and 1 quart of wine.

Local time
GMT+12 hrs (+13 hrs last Sunday in Oct—first Sunday the following Mar).

Embassy phone numbers
Auckland:

Australia 32.429	Sweden 662.129
Denmark 374.563	W. Germany 31.413
Japan 34.106	UK 32.973
Netherlands 73.530	USA 30.992

Hotels
Auckland: Travelodge, Grafton Oaks Courtesy Inn, Great Northern, Inter-Continental, Royal International, South Pacific. *Christchurch:* Avon Motor Lodge, Clarendon, Ramada Inn, United Service.
Wellington: Abel Tasman, James Cook, Sharella Motor Inn, Wellington Travelodge, White Heron Lodge. Prices up to NZ$35 per night.

International banks
National Bank of New Zealand, Bank of New Zealand, Australia and New Zealand Banking Group, Bank of New South Wales, Commercial Bank of Australia.

Credit cards
All major credit cards.

Office hours
08.30 or 09.00–17.00 Mon–Fri.

National holidays
1 Jan, 6 Feb, Good Friday, Easter Monday, 25 Apr, 5 June, 23 Oct, 25, 26 Dec.

Voltage
230–250 volts AC.

Communications
Tel: NZ$6 per 3 mins. *Telex:* NZ$2.70 per min. *Airmail:* 4–5 days. *Cable:* 20 cents per word (7-word minimum).

Social customs
Very similar to Britain's, only friendlier. Bear in mind, however, that much of New Zealand closes over the weekend, even shops, and transport services are limited.

Nicaragua

Area and population
148,000 sq kms (57,143 sq mls). Pop. 2.2 million.
Capital: Managua (450,000).
Chief cities: Leon (76,000), Granada (45,000), Masaya (46,000), Chinandega (45,000), Matagalpa (65,000). *Ports:* Corinto (Pacific), Bluefields (Atlantic).
Airport: Las Mercedes (Managua).

Climate
One of the very hot Latin American countries, with temperatures ranging from 30° to 36°C (86° to 97°F). Sometimes it reaches 42°C (107°F). Rainy season May–Nov when humidity is up to 100%.
Clothing: Lightest possible; dress is informal because of the heat. While shorts are never worn, sports shirts are common. The best time to visit is Dec–Jan.

People
70% mixed blood, 17% European, 9% Negro, 4% Indian.
Religion: Chiefly Roman Catholic. *Distribution:* 54% urban.

Language
Spanish. *English rating:* Good.

Economic background
70% of Nicaragua's population is engaged in agriculture, chiefly cotton, sugar and coffee. Less well developed than in other Central American republics, industry is growing, particularly food processing.

Trade
Gross National Product: US$900 million.
Exports: US$400 million, chiefly cotton, meat, coffee, sugar, shrimps, lobsters, copper, gold.
Imports: US$500 million, chiefly machinery, chemicals, pharmaceutical products, manufactures, iron and steel.
Chief trading partners: USA, Guatemala, Costa Rica, Japan, W. Germany. *Inflation rate:* Not available.

Prospects
Nicaragua's economy hinges on the discovery of offshore oil.

Currency
Cordoba (C$) = 100 centavos. £ = C$13.26; $ = C$7.05.

Travel
Visas required (except for UK citizens).

Vaccinations
Smallpox.

Airlines
Pan Am, Lanica, Iberia.
Flying times: Copenhagen (no direct flights) 21 hrs; London (no direct flights) 16 hrs; New York 6 hrs; Sydney 30 hrs. *Fares:* Copenhagen F Dkr6,520 Y Dkr4,175; London F £465.50 Y £302; New York F $386 Y $267; Sydney F A$2,063 YA$1,344. *Airport to city:* 9 kms (5.5 mls). *Taxi fare:* C$45.

Duty-free allowances
200 cigarettes; 3 litres of spirits.

Local time
GMT−6 hrs.

Embassy phone numbers
Managua: UK 25301.

Hotels
Managua: Inter-Continental, Motel Las Mercedes. Embassy, King's Palace. Price up to C$200 per night.

International banks
Bank of London and South America, Bank of America, First National City Bank.

Credit cards
American Express, Diners Club.

Office hours
08.00–12.00 and 14.30–17.30 Mon–Sat.

National holidays
1 Jan, Holy Week, 1, 27 May, 14 July, 10 Aug, 14, 15 Sept, 12 Oct, 3, 25–26 Dec.

Voltage
110 volts 60 cycles AC.

Communications
Tel: C$84 per 3 min. *Telex:* C$84 per 3 min. *Airmail:* 4–8 days. *Cable:* C$4.20 per word. *Phone rating:* Poor.

Social customs
Take the usual tropical precautions about food and drink. Avoid uncooked vegetables and fresh fruit.

Niger

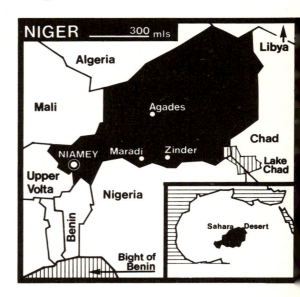

Area and population
1,186,408 sq kms (458,075 sq mls). Pop. 4.2 million. *Capital:* Niamey (90,000). *Chief cities:* None, but towns include Zinder (30,000), Tahoua (20,000), Maradi (30,000). *Airport:* Niamey.

Climate
Dry tropical, one of the hottest regions of the world. Temperatures in Niamey range from 8°C (47°F) to 46°C (114°F). Coolest months: Nov–Jan. *Clothing:* Tropical.

People
50% Hausa, 20% Djerma-Songha, remainder nomads. *Religion:* Moslem. *Distribution:* 66% rural.

Language
French. *English rating:* Poor.

Economic background

One of the poorest countries in the former French West Africa, Niger earns its revenue from the export of groundnuts and cattle. Average *per capita* income is around US$152. Industry plays only a small part, providing less than 7% of gross national product.

Trade

Gross National Product: US$700 million.
Exports: CFAfrancs252.4 million, chiefly groundnuts, livestock. *Imports:* CFAfrancs462.9 million, chiefly cotton textiles, vehicles and parts, food, beverages, oil. *Chief trading partners:* France, USA, Nigeria, W. Germany, UK, Ivory Coast, Algeria, Netherlands, Cameroon, Italy, Mali. *Inflation rate:* Not available.

Prospects

Niger's economy is being developed with the help of aid from France, the European Development Fund and Canada. The government plays a major role in expanding the economy.

Currency

CFAfranc = 100 centimes. £ = CFAfrs421;
$ = CFAfrs223.

Travel

Visas required but not for UK passport holders.

Vaccinations

Smallpox. Yellow fever and cholera recommended.

Airlines

UTA, Air Afrique, Air Algérie.
Flying times: Copenhagen $10\frac{1}{2}$ hrs; London 8 hrs; New York $21\frac{1}{2}$ hrs; Sydney 30 hrs. *Fares:* Copenhagen F Dkr5,815 Y Dkr3,940; London F £404.50 Y £267; New York F $966 Y $596; Sydney F A$1,506 Y A$992. *Airport to city:* 12 kms (7.5 mls). *Taxi fare:* No taxis allowed but hotels meet their guests with free transport.

Duty-free allowances

200 cigarettes *or* 25 cigars *or* 250 grammes tobacco; 1 bottle of spirits.

Local time

GMT+1 hr.

Hotels

Niamey: Grand Hotel de Niger, Hotel Sahel.
Prices about CFAfrs6,000 per night.

International banks

None.

Credit cards

All major credit cards.

Office hours

08.00–12.00 and 15.00–18.30 Mon–Sat.

National holidays

Moslem holidays plus 1 Jan, 1 May, 3 Aug, 18, 25 Dec.

Voltage

220–380 volts AC.

Communications

Tel: CFAfrs1,620 per 3 mins. *Telex:* None.
Airmail: 7 days. *Cable:* CFAfrs129.31 per word.

Social customs

French influences are still apparent in Niger business dealings. Hotels and restaurants serve good French food —but drink only boiled water. Anti-malarial drugs should be taken. There is little in the way of entertainment.

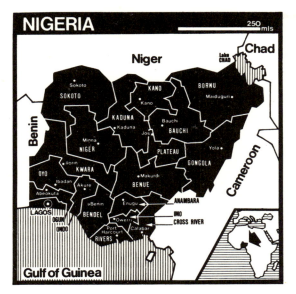

Area and population
923,768 sq kms (356,668 sq mls). Pop. 79.7 million.
Capital: Lagos (2 million).
Chief cities: Ibadan (2 million), Kano (295,000),
Ilorin (208,000), Port Harcourt (180,000), Abeokuta
(187,000), Kaduna (150,000), Maiduguri (140,000),
Enugu (138,000), Benin City (100,000), Warri
(100,000). *Ports:* Lagos/Apapa, Port Harcourt, Warri,
Sapele, Calabar. *Airports:* Murtala Muhammed (Lagos),
Kano.

Climate
Hot and humid. Lagos shares the weather of Southern
Nigeria, where the average temperature is 29°C (84.2°F)
with a high humidity content. In the North daytime
temperatures can reach 43°C (110°F) and can drop below
5°C (41°F) at night in Dec and Jan.
Clothing: Lightweight suits but pullover and slightly
heavier-weight suit are needed in the North during
harmattan, the wind that blows from the Sahara carrying
a fine dust. Women need plenty of lightweight washable
dresses.

People
250 tribal groups, chiefly Yoruba, Ibo and Hausa.
Religion: 44% Moslem, 22% Christian, 33% animist.
Distribution: 16% urban.

Language
English.

Economic background
Petroleum has emerged as Nigeria's main source of
revenue and it now accounts for more than 90% of total
exports. Mining and quarrying are also important to the
economy, but agriculture, which provides under 25% of
gross national product, employs the majority of
Nigerians. The government's task is to use the vast
income from petroleum to establish a wide-based
industrial economy spread throughout the country. As a
result, industrial products are flooding into the country
bound for development sites, jamming Nigeria's ports
and airports.

Trade
Gross National Product: 20,000 million naira.
Exports: 6,249 million naira, chiefly oil, cocoa,
agricultural manufactures, tin, rubber, palm kernels,
timber. *Imports:* 1,447 million naira, chiefly machinery
and transport equipment, manufactured goods,
chemicals, food, mineral fuels, crude materials.
Chief trading partners: UK, W. Germany, USA, Japan,
France, Netherlands. *Inflation rate:* 31.3%.

Prospects
Nigeria's long-term future as the biggest market in
Africa is assured, but in the meantime, foreign exchange
problems remain. The government is giving priority to
developing roads, ports and airports in order to facilitate
Nigeria's rapid growth.

Currency
Naira = 100 kobo. £ = N1.20; $ = N0.63.

Travel
Visas required.

Vaccinations
Smallpox, yellow fever, cholera.

Airlines
Air Afrique, Alitalia, British Caledonian, Cameroon,
Ethiopian, KLM, Nigeria, Pan Am, SAS, Swissair, UTA.
Flying times: Copenhagen 8½ hrs; London 6 hrs;
New York 14 hrs; Sydney 30 hrs. *Fares:* Copenhagen
F Dkr6,600 Y Dkr4,320; London F £403 Y £284;
New York F $976 Y $604; Sydney F A$1,433 Y A$915.
Airport to city (Lagos): 22 kms (13.6 mls). *Taxi fare:* N10.

Duty-free allowances
200 cigarettes *or* 50 cigars *or* 200 grammes of tobacco;
1 litre of spirits and 1 litre of wine. If more is imported,

duty is due on the whole quantity. Champagne and sparkling wine is prohibited on penalty of heavy fine or imprisonment of at least six months.

Local time
GMT+1 hr.

Embassy phone numbers
Lagos:

Australia 25981	Sweden 20381
Canada 53630	Switzerland 25277
Denmark 51540	W. Germany 58430
Japan 23707	UK 51630
Norway 25966	USA 57320

Hotels
Lagos: Bristol, Excelsior, Federal Palace, Ikoyi, Mainland, Regent. *Kano:* Central.

International banks
Standard Bank of Nigeria, Barclays Bank of Nigeria, Arab Bank, Bank of America, Citibank, National Bank of Nigeria.

Credit cards
All major credit cards.

Office hours
Variable from state to state, but usually 08.00–12.30 and 14.00–16.30 Mon–Fri. 08.00–12.30 Sat (Northern states only).

National holidays
All Moslem holidays plus 1 Jan, Good Friday, Easter Monday, 25, 26 Dec.

Voltage
230–400 volts AC.

Communications
Tel: N5.40 per 3 mins. *Telex:* N2 per min. *Airmail:* 7 days. *Cable:* 18K per word (N1.26 minimum charge).

Social customs
The climate makes for much informality. Night life is lively and cocktail parties, dinners and dances are very popular. Avoid tap water and uncooked fruit and vegetables. Anti-malarial drugs are advisable. Allow plenty of time between appointments in Lagos—the traffic jams are horrendous. Take care in walking streets at night.

Area and population
323,886 sq kms (125,182 sq mls). Pop. 4 million.
Capital: Oslo (465,000).
Chief cities: Bergen (214,000), Trondheim (134,000), Stavanger (85,000), Drammen (50,000), Kristiansand (59,000), Haugesund (27,000), Narvik (19,000), Tromsoe (42,000). *Ports:* Aalesund, Bergen, Bodo, Drammen, Haugesund, Kristiansand, Oslo, Stavanger, Trondheim. *Airports:* Fornebu (Oslo), Flesland (Bergen).

Climate
Despite its northerly location, Norway has a favourable climate due to the Gulf Stream. Oslo temperatures range from −18°C (0°F) in winter to 29°C (84°F) in summer.
Clothing: Warm clothing, including strong shoes, needed for winter, but bear in mind that Norwegian central heating is very effective, even in buses and taxis.

People
Nordic. *Religion:* 96% Evangelical Lutheran.
Distribution: 57% urban.

Language
Norwegian. *English rating:* Excellent.

Economic background

A stable, industrious country, Norway has benefited enormously from the discovery of North Sea oil and is already self-sufficient in oil. While it must still import much of its raw material needs and manufactured goods, Norway's industry and agriculture are strong, and the economy is further backed by one of the biggest merchant marines in the world.

Trade

Gross National Product: 128,000 million kroner.
Exports: 37,778 million kroner, chiefly paper and board, pulp, fishery products, petro-chemicals, iron ore, ships, machinery, fertilisers. *Imports:* 50,541 million kroner, chiefly industrial machinery, iron and steel, textiles, chemicals, transport equipment, foodstuffs, grains. *Chief trading partners:* Sweden, W. Germany, UK, USA, Japan, Denmark, Netherlands, France, Belgium/Luxembourg, Canada, Liberia, Finland, Italy. *Inflation rate:* 8.2%.

Prospects

Norway is undertaking ambitious plans, and industry, split into large numbers of small enterprises, is beginning to encourage mergers.

Currency

Krone = 100 ore. £ = Kr10.18; $ = Kr5.41.

Travel

Visas not required.

Vaccination

Not normally required.

Airlines

SAS, British Airways, all major European airlines, Pan Am.
Flying times: Copenhagen 1 hr; London 2 hrs; New York $10\frac{1}{2}$ hrs; Sydney 28 hrs. *Fares:* Copenhagen F Dkr855 Y Dkr655; London F £167.50 Y £111.50; New York F $717 Y $347; Sydney F A$1,512 Y A$978. *Airport to city:* Oslo 8 kms (5 mls); Bergen 19 kms (12 mls). *Taxi fares:* Oslo Kr30; Bergen Kr95. *Bus fares:* Oslo Kr6; Bergen Kr9.

Duty-free allowances

Visitors living in Europe: 200 cigarettes *or* 250 grammes of cigars *or* tobacco; 0.75 litre of spirits and 2 litres of wine. *Visitors living outside Europe:* 400 cigarettes *or* 500 grammes of cigars *or* tobacco; 2 litres of spirits and 2 litres of wine.

Local time

GMT+1 hr.

Embassy phone numbers

Oslo:

Canada 46.69.55	Switzerland 41.70.17
Denmark 44.18.46	W. Germany 56.32.90
Japan 56.48.94	UK 56.38.90
Netherlands 60.21.93	USA 56.68.80
Sweden 44.38.15	

Hotels

Oslo: Astoria, Bristol, Carlton, Continental, Grand, Kna-Hotellet, Savoy, Scandinavia, Viking.
Bergen: Neptun, Norge, Orion, Rosenkrantz, Terminus. Toms. Up to Kr250–300 per night.

International banks

Den Norske Creditbank, Christiana Bank of Kreditkasse, Bergen Bank, Fellesbanken, Andresens Bank, A/S Forretningsbanken, Bergens Skillingsbank.

Credit cards

All major credit cards.

Office hours

08.00 or 09.00–16.00 Mon–Fri.

National holidays

1 Jan, Maundy Thursday, Good Friday, Easter Monday, 1, 17 May, Ascension Day (May), Whit Monday (May *or* June), 25, 26 Dec.

Voltage

220–230 volts AC.

Communications

Tel: Kr12.60 per 3 mins. *Telex:* Kr6.30 per 3 mins. *Airmail:* 2–3 days. *Cable:* Kr1.20 per word plus Kr5 (7-word minimum).

Social customs

Most Norwegians have a light lunch and an early dinner, perhaps at 16.00, with an evening snack at 21.00. Norwegian fish dishes are excellent, particularly fried trout in sour cream. As businessmen, Norwegians are punctual. If invited home, take flowers for the hostess. *Best buys:* Pottery, furs, ceramics, glassware, enamelled silverware, jewellery, sports equipment.

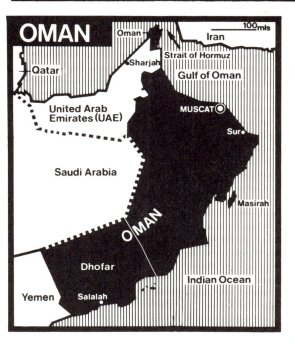

Area and population

300,000 sq kms (130,000 sq mls). Pop. 800,000.
Capital: Muscat (50,000).
Chief cities: Mutrah, Salalah, Sur, Nizwa, Sohar.
Port: Mina Qaboos. *Airports:* Seeb (Muscat), Salalah.

Climate

Extremely hot and humid in summer, mild in winter,
with temperatures ranging from 22°C (71.6°F) in Jan
to 34°C (93°F) in June, but sometimes reaching
45°C (113°F). Humidity 85%. Best time to visit is
Dec–Mar. *Clothing:* Lightweight.

People

Mostly Arab, with minorities of Iranians, Baluchis,
Indians and Negroes. *Religion:* Moslem.
Distribution: 10% urban.

Language

Arabic. *English rating:* Good.

Economic background

Were it not for oil, Oman (Muscat and Oman until 1970)
would be an extremely poor country. Today 98% of its
revenue comes from oil, which permits the government
to carry out an ambitious development plan, which
includes roads, ports, airports, power stations, schools,
hospitals and public services. Oman is expanding its
economy on the basis of copper, cement and flour,
as well as oil.

Trade

Gross National Product: Not available.
Exports: £1,000 million (approx.), almost totally oil.
Imports: £250 million (approx.), including rice, flour,
building materials, clothing, machinery, vehicles.
Chief trading partners: UK, United Arab Emirates,
W. Germany, USA, Japan, Netherlands.
Inflation rate: Not available.

Prospects

Now recovering from a liquidity problem, caused by
sanctioning too many contracts for big projects, Oman is
a good market for consumer goods, building materials
and vehicles.

Currency

Rial Omani (RO) = 1,000 baizas. £ = RO0.651;
$ = RO0.346.

Travel

Visas required.

Vaccinations

Smallpox and cholera.

Airlines

British Airways, Gulf Air, MEA, UTA, Royal Jordanian,
PIA, Air India, Saudia, Iran Air, Somali.
Flying times: Copenhagen 12½ hrs; London 7 hrs;
New York 13 hrs; Sydney 16 hrs. *Fares:* Copenhagen
F Dkr5,960 Y Dkr4,300; London F £446.50 Y £314.50;
New York F $1,295 Y $799; Sydney F A$970 Y A$659.
Airport to city: 40 kms (25 mls). *Taxi fare:* RO3,500.

Duty-free allowances

Unlimited cigarettes. No alcohol permitted.

Local time

GMT+4 hrs.

Embassy phone numbers

Muscat: UK 722411.

Hotels

Muscat: Inter-Continental, Al-Falaj, Mutrah, Ruwi, Gulf.
All US$27–29 per night.

International banks
Arab Bank, Banque de Paris et des Pays-Bas,
British Bank of the Middle East, Chartered First National
City Bank.

Credit cards
American Express, Diners Club.

Office hours
08.30–13.00 and 16.00–18.00 Sat–Thurs.

National holidays
All Moslem holidays, plus 1 Jan, 18, 19 Nov.

Voltage
220–240 volts.

Communications
Tel: RO3 per 3 mins. *Telex:* Not available.
Airmail: 3–4 days. *Cable:* RO0.115 per word.

Social customs
Personal touch is essential in business. Politeness and
patience are vital and business approach should be
low-key. Coffee houses take the place of bars for social
and business meetings. Smoking in public is regarded as
bad taste. Always dress conservatively.
Best buys: Metalware, rush baskets, leather.

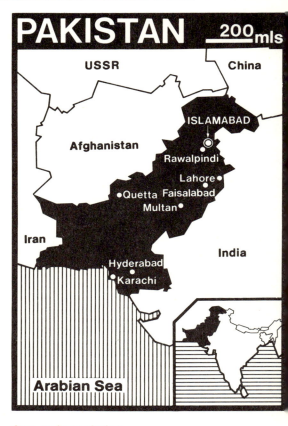

Area and population
803,944 sq kms (310,403 sq mls). Pop. 71 million.
Capital: Islamabad (300,000).
Chief cities: Karachi (3.5 million), Lahore (2.1 million),
Faisalabad (500,000). *Port:* Karachi. *Airports:* Karachi
Civil, Chakiala (Rawalpindi/Islamabad).

Climate
Little rain and very dry conditions, with temperatures up
to 51°C (125°F) in the Indus Valley. Violent monsoon
storms July–Sept. Best time to visit is Nov–Mar, when
temperatures in Karachi range from 19° to 24°C
(67° to 75°F). *Clothing:* Apart from Nov–Mar when
warm clothing is needed, lightweight suits and cotton
dresses.

People
Pathans, Punjabis, Sindhis, Baluchis.
Religion: 88% Moslem. *Distribution:* 13% urban.

Language
Urdu. *English rating:* Excellent.

Economic background

While 30% of revenue still comes from agriculture, providing a living for 70% of its people, Pakistan has considerable resources of natural gas, some minerals, coal and oil. It is turning more and more to industry. Many basic industries have been nationalised and state corporations have emerged. Foreign aid finances most of Pakistan's development plans.

Trade

Gross National Product: 85,700 million rupees.
Exports: US$1,250 million, chiefly jute, textile fabrics, textile yarn, leather. *Imports:* US$2,250 million, chiefly edible oil, wheat, fertilisers, iron and steel, chemicals, petroleum. *Chief trading partners:* China, Japan, Kuwait, Saudi Arabia, Sri Lanka, UK, USA, W. Germany, Hong Kong, Iran, USSR. *Inflation rate:* 6.2%.

Prospects

Pakistan's development hinges upon the River Indus and its tributaries to provide water and power; alternating floods and droughts seriously affect its future.

Currency

Rupee = 100 paisa. £ = 18.61 rupees;
$ = 9.89 rupees.

Travel

No visas required.

Vaccinations

Smallpox. Typhoid, paratyphoid and cholera inoculations strongly recommended.

Airlines

Gulf, JAL, PIA, British Airways, Air France, KLM, Kuwait, Lufthansa, MEA, Pan Am, SAS, Swissair, UTA.
Flying times: Copenhagen $7\frac{1}{4}$ hrs; London $11\frac{1}{2}$ hrs; New York $18\frac{1}{2}$ hrs; Sydney 11 hrs. *Fares:* Copenhagen F Dkr5,975 Y Dkr3,890; London F £460.50 Y £299.50; New York F $1,420 Y $885; Sydney F A$1,002 Y A$716.
Airport to city (Karachi): 19 kms (12 mls).
Taxi fare: 15 rupees.

Duty-free allowances

Travellers from India: 50 cigarettes *or* 50 cigars *or* 4 oz tobacco; $\frac{1}{2}$ pint wine, $\frac{1}{2}$ pint spirits.
Travellers from elsewhere: 200 cigarettes *or* 50 cigars or $\frac{1}{2}$ lb tobacco; 1 bottle of spirits, 1 bottle of wine.
Tourists visiting Pakistan for more than 24 hours but not engaged in any gainful employment or profession: 200 cigarettes *or* 50 cigars *or* $\frac{1}{2}$ lb tobacco; 2 bottles ($\frac{1}{3}$ gallon) of spirits *or* wine.

Local time

GMT+5 hrs.

Embassy phone numbers

Karachi:

Australia 531086	Sweden 515840
Denmark 228562	Switzerland 532038
Japan 511331	W. Germany 531031
Netherlands 515037	UK 532041
Norway 233695	USA 515081

Hotels

Karachi: Beach Luxury, Central, Imperial, Inter-Continental, Mehran, Metropole. Prices 120–400 rupees per night. *Lahore:* Ambassador, International, Inter-Continental. *Islamabad:* Flashman's.

International banks

Grindlay Brandts, Chartered, Habib, Allied Bank of Pakistan, United Bank, First National City Bank, American Express International, Bank of America.

Credit cards

American Express, Diners Club.

Office hours

Variable, although all close Sun. Most offices close Sat afternoon and some Fri afternoon. Government offices 07.30–14.30 Mon–Thurs and Sat, 07.30–12.30 Fri.

National holidays

All Moslem religious holidays plus 1 Jan, 23 Mar, 14 Aug, 6, 11 Sept, 9 Nov, 25 Dec.

Voltage

220–240 volts AC.

Communications

Tel: 85 rupees per 3 mins. *Telex:* 93 rupees per 3 mins.
Airmail: 4 days. *Cable:* 1.95 rupees per word (7-word minimum).

Social customs

A country of strong religious feelings, Pakistan moved in 1977 towards stricter observance of Moslem rules. Officially, only visitors are allowed to drink alcohol. Extra care should be taken during the month-long fast of Ramzan (Ramadan) (season varies), during which Moslems are not allowed to drink, eat or smoke between sunrise and sunset. Moslems do not eat pork and many women are in purdah. Do not photograph Moslem women unless you are sure no objection will be made.

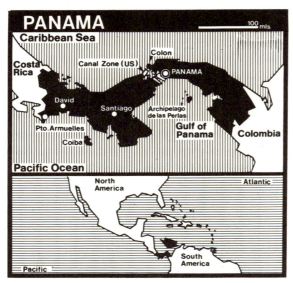

Area and population
75,630 sq kms (29,201 sq mls). Pop. 1.4 million.
Capital: Panama City (418,000).
Chief city: Colon (68,000). *Ports:* Balboa, Cristobal.
Airport: Tocumen (Panama City).

Climate
Tropical, with temperatures from 21°C (70°F) at night to
32°C (90°F) by day throughout the year. Heavy rainfall
Oct–Nov. Jan–Apr the most pleasant months.
Clothing: Lightweight tropical suits and dresses; cotton
or linen are better than man-made fabrics.

People
Mostly mixed blood, with communities of Indians,
Negroes and Asians. *Religion:* Roman Catholic.
Distribution: 47% urban.

Language
Spanish. *English rating:* Good.

Economic background
Panama depends upon the Canal Zone for its revenue,
registration fees paid by merchant ships registered under
Panama's flag of convenience, also, increasingly, on
agriculture and industry. Nearly 40% of its people are
engaged in agriculture, so land reform, including the
clearing of forests, is likely in the future.
Industry, which accounts for 16% of the gross national
product, is expanding significantly. Apart from sugar
mills and cement works, the main industries are food
processing, textiles and clothing, chemicals and plastics.

Trade
Gross National Product: US$900 million.
Exports: US$205 million, chiefly bananas, refined
petroleum, shrimps. *Imports:* US$800 million, chiefly oil,
machinery, vehicles and parts, chemicals, sugar.
Chief trading partners: USA, Colon Free Zone, Ecuador,
Venezuela, Japan, Costa Rica, Spain, UK, W. Germany,
Italy, Netherlands, Norway.
Inflation rate: Not available.

Prospects
With the promise of the return of the Canal Zone from
the USA, plus its industrial and mining prospects,
Panama's economy should grow appreciably.

Currency
Balboa = 100 cents. £ = 1.88 balboas;
$ = 1.00 balboas. US currency is also legal tender.

Travel
Visas or tourists cards required by most nationalities.

Vaccinations
Smallpox. Cholera (for travellers coming from infected
areas), yellow fever (for travellers intending to visit
jungle areas).

Airlines
British Airways, Aeromexico, Pan Am, Iberia, KLM,
Braniff.
Flying times: Copenhagen 19 hrs; London 15 hrs;
New York 7 hrs; Sydney 28 hrs. *Fares:* Copenhagen
F Dkr6,595 Y Dkr4,320; London F £465.50 Y £310;
New York F $394 Y $273; Sydney F A$2,063 Y A$1,344.
Airport to city: 27 kms (17 mls). *Taxi fare:* 12 balboas.

Duty-free allowances
300 cigarettes *or* 50 cigars *or* 3 tins of tobacco;
3 bottles of spirits *or* wine.

Embassy phone numbers
Panama City: UK 23.0451.

Hotels
Panama City: El Continental, Executive, Granada,
El Panama Skyline. All about US$30 per night.

Panama

International banks
Bank of London and South America, First National City Bank, Chase Manhattan, Bank of America, First National Bank of Chicago, Banco de Bogota, Bank of Colombia, Bank of Tokyo.

Credit cards
American Express, Diners Club.

Office hours
08.00–12.00 and 14.00–17.00 Mon–Fri, 08.00–12.00 Sat.

National holidays
1, 19 Jan, Shrove Tuesday, Good Friday, 1 May, 15 Aug, 11, 12 Oct, 3, 4, 5, 28 Nov, 8, 25 Dec.

Voltage
110 volts 3-phase 60 cycles AC (domestic); 220 volts 60 cycles AC (industrial).

Communications
Tel: US$13 plus $1 tax per 3 mins: *Telex:* US$4.80 per min. *Airmail:* 5–10 days. *Cable:* 51 cents per word.

Social customs
Panamanian businessmen observe punctuality—and expect visitors to, as well. There is much handshaking. It is safe to drink water in Panama City and Colon.

Paraguay

Area and population
406,750 sq kms (157,047 sq mls). Pop. 2.5 million. *Capital:* Asuncion (500,000). *Chief cities:* Coronel Oviedo (55,000), Encarnacion (46,000). *Airport:* Presidente Gen. Stroessner (Asuncion).

Climate
Sub-tropical but with great winter–summer differences. Temperatures in summer (Dec–Mar) range up to 43°C (112°F). Autumn falls Mar–June; sweaters, coats and raincoats are needed. Winter (June–Sept) is cold but temperature rarely falls below freezing. Best time to visit is May–Sept. *Clothing:* Clothes should be made of cotton. Shirts are never worn without a jacket. Sunglasses and an umbrella are needed.

People
98% mestizos, 2% Amerindians. *Religion:* Predominantly Roman Catholic. *Distribution:* 36% urban.

Language
Spanish, but most people are bilingual in the Indian Guarani. *English rating:* Poor.

Economic background
A landlocked country, hampered by poor

communications. Paraguay lacks raw materials, industrial skills, and a large enough home market to encourage investment, and has high freight rates. The country is excessively dependent upon imports, chiefly from Argentina. Nevertheless, the economy is growing, much improved by a steady growth in industrial investment. Agriculture still accounts for more than one-third of revenue. Paraguay is looking for more exporting of its manufactured goods, and towards this end the government is trying to improve navigability of the Paraguay River, the main channel for trade to the River Plate, 1,450 kms (900 mls) away.

Trade

Gross National Product: US$734.3 million.
Exports: $130 million, chiefly meat, vegetable oils, cotton fibre, timber, essential oils, tobacco, hides, coffee.
Imports: $108 million, chiefly machinery, transport equipment, iron and steel products, beverages and tobacco, fuels and lubricants, chemicals, agricultural equipment, wheat and flour.
Chief trading partners: W. Germany, USA, Netherlands, UK, Belgium, Uruguay, Argentina, France, Spain, Italy, Sweden. *Inflation rate:* Not available.

Prospects

In spite of its problems, Paraguay's economy is growing steadily, and should be improved by plans for new hydro-electric projects.

Currency

Guarani (₲) = 100 centimos. £ = 235.56 guaranies; $ = 125.29 guaranies.

Travel

Visas required, although UK, USA, Australian, Canadian and German visitors are exempt.

Vaccinations

Smallpox. Inoculations against tetanus, typhoid and paratyphoid recommended.

Airlines

Iberia, Braniff, Varig, Aerolineas Argentinas, LAP.
Flying times: Copenhagen 22¾ hrs; London 14 hrs; New York 12 hrs; Sydney 24 hrs. *Fares:* Copenhagen F Dkr9,320 Y Dkr6,210; London F £721.50 Y £479.50; New York F $858 Y $547; Sydney F A$1,893 Y A$1,376.
Airport to city: 15 kms (9.5 mls).
Bus fare: 300 guaranies.

Duty-free allowances

Reasonable quantities of tobacco and spirits.

Local time

GMT−4 hrs (−3 hrs Oct–Feb).

Embassy phone numbers

Asuncion: UK 4.9146.

Hotels

Asuncion: Guarani, Gran Hotel del Paraguay, Gran Hotel Parana, Presidente. Prices up to US$30 per night.

International Banks

Bank of London and South America, Banco do Brasil, First National City Bank, Bank of America.

Credit cards

American Express, Diners Club.

Office hours

07.00–11.00 and 14.30–15.30 Mon–Fri, 07.00–11.00 Sat. Government offices: 07.00–12.00 Mon–Fri, 07.00–11.00 Sat. Banks 07.30–11.30 Mon–Fri.
Siesta hours 12.00–15.00 are well observed.

National holidays

1 Jan, 3 Feb, 1 Mar, Maundy Thursday, Good Friday, 1, 14, 15 May, Corpus Christi (May *or* June), 12 June, 15, 25 Aug, 29 Sept, 12 Oct, 1 Nov, 8, 25 Dec.

Voltage

220 volts AC.

Communications

Tel: ₲2,025 per 3 mins. *Telex:* ₲1,652 per 3 mins.
Airmail: 6–7 days. *Phone rating:* Poor.

Social customs

Most business is transacted in Asuncion and rarely will the business visitor have to leave the capital. Care should be taken not to drink unboiled water.

PERU

600 mls

Colombia

Ecuador

Iquitos

South America

Chiclayo
Trujillo
Chimbote

Brazil

Cerro de Pasco

LIMA

Bolivia

Arequipa

LAKE TITICACA

Pacific Ocean

Chile

Area and population
1,285,215 sq kms (496,093 sq mls). Pop. 15 million.
Capital: Lima (3.3 million).
Chief cities: Arequipa (110,000), Chimbote (130,000),
Chiclayo (170,000), Iquitos (141,000),
Trujillo (250,000). *Ports:* Callao, Mollendo, Matarani.
Airport: Jorge Chavez International (Lima).

Climate
Temperatures range from 11° to 32°C (51° to 89°F). In
Lima there is up to 98% humidity, but little rain
June–Nov, and not much sunshine, because of the mist
coming in from the sea.
Clothing: Lightweight suits and cotton or linen dresses
Jan–Apr, medium-weight clothes suitable June–Nov.
Women need long dresses for evening parties.

People
46% Amerindians, 42% mestizos, 12% European.
Religion: Roman Catholic. *Distribution:* 54.6% urban.

Languages
Spanish, Quechua and Aymara. *English rating:* Fair.

Economic background
Rich in natural resources, particularly copper, zinc,
lead, wool, coffee and cotton, Peru is now moving

ahead industrially while breaking much of the control of
foreign companies. The military government has
nationalised some industries, and is instituting a
development plan so that Peru can take advantage of the
Andean Pact's regional industrial programmes. Industry
is concentrated in Greater Lima, but two other cities,
Chimbote, centre of the steel industry, and Arequipa, are
important and are growing at a faster rate than Lima.

Trade
Gross National Product: US$8,000 million.
Exports: US$1,400 million, chiefly copper, fish meal, zinc,
sugar, coffee, silver, cotton, iron, lead.
Imports: US$1,100 million, chiefly plant and equipment,
food, chemicals, transport equipment, minerals, paper,
metals, textiles, plastics, rubber.
Chief trading partners: Japan, China, UK, France, Chile,
Canada, Brazil, W. Germany, Belgium/Luxembourg,
Argentina, USA, Italy, Spain, Poland, Yugoslavia,
Mexico, Netherlands, New Zealand, Colombia,
Switzerland, Venezuela. *Inflation rate:* 42.1%.

Prospects
Membership of the Andean Pact should give a boost to
industry.

Currency
Sol = 100 centavos. £ = 291.10 soles; $ = 154.84 soles.

Travel
Tourists entering Peru do not need a visa but must obtain
a tourist card from Peruvian consular offices or airlines.
Businessmen, other than those travelling as tourists,
must obtain from the Peruvian Ministry of Finance a
certificate affirming that they have not taken up paid
employment in Peru. This entails a visit to the Ministry's
office in Lima before departure.

Vaccinations
Smallpox.

Airlines
Air France, British Caledonian, Braniff, Iberia, KLM,
Lufthansa, Alitalia, Avianca.
Flying times: Copenhagen (no direct flights) 20½ hrs;
London 16 hrs; New York 10 hrs; Sydney 36 hrs.
Fares: Copenhagen F Dkr8,025 Y Dkr5,200; London
F £551.50 Y £354; New York F $642 Y $414;
Sydney F A$2,172 Y A$1,423.
Airport to city: 16 kms (9.9 mls). *Taxi fare:* 400 soles.

Philippines

Peru

Duty-free allowances
400 cigarettes *or* 50 cigars; 2 litres of spirits.

Local time
GMT−5 hrs.

Embassy phone numbers
Lima:

Australia 28.8315	Sweden 32.2890
Canada 28.7420	Switzerland 22.7066
Denmark 40.7512	W. Germany 45.9997
Japan 61.4041	UK 28.3830
Netherlands 22.8302	USA 28.6000

Hotels
Lima: Crillon, Gran Hotel Bolivar, Riviera, Sheraton. Prices up to US$27 per night.

International banks
Bank of London and South America, Bank of America, First National City Bank of New York, Bank of Tokyo, Lloyds Bank.

Credit cards
American Express, Diners Club.

Office hours
Government offices: 08.00–13.00 (Jan–Mar) 08.00–16.00 (Apr–Dec). Banks: 08.30–11.30 (Jan–Mar), 08.00–12.00 (Apr–Dec). Commercial offices: 08.30–12.30 and 15.00–19.30 (Apr–Dec), most offices closed Sat. Shops open 09.30–12.45 and 16.15–19.00.

National holidays
1 Jan, Maundy Thursday, Good Friday, 1 May, 29 June, 28, 29 July, 30, Aug, 9 Oct, 1 Nov, 8, 25, 31 Dec.

Voltage
220 volts AC.

Communications
Tel: 400 soles per 3 min. *Telex:* 461.20 soles per 3 min. *Airmail:* 4 days. *Cable:* 334.90 soles for a 7-word minimum.

Social customs
Peruvians, who like good manners and dignity, are not punctual for social engagements. Women are not generally present at business entertainments, which tend to be luncheon rather than dinner engagements. Hospitality is generous.

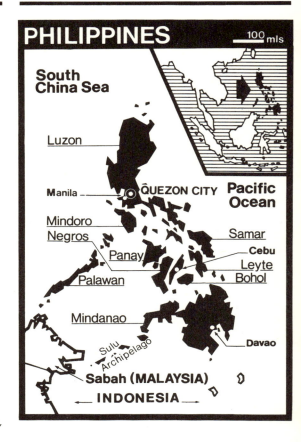

Area and population
300,000 sq kms (115,830 sq mls). Pop. 42.5 million. *Capital:* Quezon City (850,000). *Chief cities:* Manila (4.9 million), Cebu (1.8 m), Davao (1.7 m), Iloilo (1.2 m), Iligan (104,000). *Ports:* Cebu, Davao, Iloilo, Manila. *Airport:* International (Manila).

Climate
Tropical, with dry season (Nov–June) and rainy season (June–Oct). Days are pleasant and nights are cool. Temperatures average 27°C (80°F). Weather is best late Nov–early Mar. *Clothing:* Tropical. Best materials are washable drill, cotton, sharkskin and similar fabrics. Coat and tie required for evening wear.

People
Chiefly Malay, with Mongoloid and aboriginal strains. *Religion:* 80% Roman Catholic, 10% Protestant, 5% Moslem. *Distribution:* 30% urban.

Language
Pilipino. *English rating:* Excellent.

Economic background
Rich in mineral resources, the Philippines has not attained the same growth as other Asian nations, although better progress is now being made. Basically agricultural, the Philippines is encouraging the establishment of new industries through tax and other incentives. Sugar, coconut products, pineapples, bananas and timber are the main sectors in agriculture. Industry now covers food processing, textiles, vehicle assembly, furniture and footwear.

Trade
Gross National Product: US$15,609 million.
Exports: US$2,294.5 million, chiefly timber, sugar, copra, copper, animal and vegetable oils, coconut oil, pineapples. *Imports:* US$3,459.2 million, chiefly oil, chemicals, capital machinery, transport equipment, textiles, clothing, dairy products, grains.
Chief trading partners: Japan, USA, Saudi Arabia, Kuwait, W. Germany, Australia, UK, Netherlands, Iran.
Inflation rate: 7.9%.

Prospects
There is little doubt that the Philippines will continue to develop industrially.

Currency
Peso (P) = 100 centavos. £ = P13.83; $ = P7.35.

Travel
Visas required.

Vaccinations
Smallpox.

Airlines
Cathay Pacific, Philippine Airlines, Air France, JAL, Sabena, SIA, Swissair, Qantas, MAS, Pan Am, KLM, SAS, Thai, Northwest.
Flying times: Copenhagen $20\frac{1}{4}$ hrs; London 22 hrs; New York 25 hrs; Sydney 8 hrs. *Fares:* Copenhagen F Dkr9,030 Y Dkr5,400; London F £701.50 Y £419.50; New York F $1,726 Y $1,079; Sydney F A$708 Y A$506.
Airport to city: 12 kms (7.5 mls). *Taxi fare:* P7.00.

Duty-free allowances
300 cigarettes *or* 50 cigars *or* 1 kilo of tobacco; 1 quart of spirits *or* wine.

Local time
GMT+8 hrs (+9 hrs late Mar–late Sept).

Embassy phone numbers
Manila:

Australia 87.49.61	Norway 49.31.11
Canada 87.65.36	Switzerland 86.55.91
Denmark 86.69.26	W. Germany 59.20.91
Japan 88.23.91	UK 89.10.51
Netherlands 88.77.53	USA 5.80.11

Hotels
Manila: Ambassador, Enrico, Filipinas, Inter-Continental. Hyatt Regency, Hilton, Manila Royal, Tower, Holiday Inn, Mandarin, Plaza.
Prices up to US$35 per night.

International banks
First National City Bank of New York, Bank of America, Chartered Bank, Hong Kong and Shanghai Banking Corporation, Midland Bank.

Credit cards
All major credit cards.

Office hours
08.00–12.00 and 14.00–17.00 Mon–Fri, 08.30–12.00 Sat.

National holidays
1 Jan, Maundy Thursday, Good Friday, 9 Apr, 1 May, 12 June, 4 July, 30 Nov, 25, 30 Dec.

Voltage
110–220 volts AC.

Communications
Tel: P90.20 per 3 mins. *Telex:* P35.42 per min. *Airmail:* 4–10 days. *Cable:* P3.07 per word (7-word minimum).

Social customs
Doing business in the Philippines is sometimes very much like doing business in the USA. Entertainment, too, is very much American-style. Night life is hampered by a 01.00–04.00 curfew. *Best buys:* Imported goods tend to be more expensive here than in other parts of the Far East. Best to buy local products—cloth and wooden carvings.

POLAND
200 mls
Baltic Sea
Gdynia
Gdansk
Szczecin
Bydgoszcz
East Germany
Poznan
WARSAW
Lodz
Lublin
Wroclaw
Katowice
Krakow
EUROPE
Czechoslovakia
USSR

Area and population

312,698 sq kms (120,733 sq mls). Pop. 33 million.
Capital: Warsaw (Warszawa) (1.4 million).
Chief cities: Lodz (787,000), Krakow (668,000),
Wroclaw (568,000), Poznan (506,000), Gdansk
(406,000), Szczecin (363,000), Katowice (321,000),
Bydgoszcz (313,000). *Ports:* Gdansk, Gdynia, Szczecin.
Airport: Okecie (Warsaw).

Climate

Temperate with warm summers and cold winters.
Jan–Feb coldest time of the year, with temperatures
down to −4°C (25°F). July temperatures average
18°C (64°F). *Clothing:* Warm overcoat is essential in
winter, lightweight clothing in summer.

People

Slav. *Religion:* 95% Roman Catholic.
Distribution: 55% urban.

Language

Polish. *English rating:* Good.

Economic background

Eastern Europe's biggest producer of food and one of the
world's top producers of potatoes, rye and sugar beet,
Poland is industrially advanced and is ranked as among
the world's top 15 industrial countries. It has huge
deposits of coal and zinc ores, and its leading
industries include vehicles, petro-chemicals, electrical
engineering, electronics, iron and steel, agriculture,
machinery and machine tools. Industry is grouped in
state combines, each of which controls factories in its
particular sphere.

Trade

Gross National Product: 1,209,300 million zlotys.
Exports: 34,061 million zlotys, chiefly coal, meat, ships
and boats, metallurgical products, clothing,
pharmaceuticals, copper, sulphur, textiles, steel.
Imports: 41,423 million zlotys, chiefly metallurgical
products, iron ores, crude oil, cotton, wheat,
metal-working equipment, petroleum.
Chief trading partners: USSR, W. and E. Germany, UK,
Czechoslovakia, France, USA, Switzerland, Austria,
Sweden, Italy, Netherlands, Belgium, Japan.
Inflation rate: Not available.

Prospects

Poland is developing its industry and agriculture through
a series of state plans. Investment for each industry is
decided by the state.

Currency

Zloty (ZL) = 100 groszy. Fluctuating exchange rates
with three rates of exchange: official rate, one for
resident foreigners, and a third for visitors.
Current tourist rate: £ = ZL60.20; $ = ZL32.02.

Travel

Visa required.

Vaccinations

None.

Airlines

British Airways, LOT, Pan Am, Interflug, Lufthansa,
SAS, Aeroflot, Iberia, KLM, Malev.
Flying times: Copenhagen $2\frac{1}{4}$ hrs; London $3\frac{1}{2}$ hrs;
New York 10 hrs; Sydney 31 hrs. *Fares:* Copenhagen
F Dkr1,255 Y Dkr865; London F £172 Y £114.50;
New York F $796 Y $386; Sydney F A$1,466 Y A$937.
Airport to city: 10 kms (6 mls). *Taxi fare:* ZL30.
Bus fare: ZL5.

Duty-free allowances

250 cigarettes *or* 50 cigars *or* 250 grammes of tobacco;
1 litre of spirits and 1 litre of wine.

Local time

GMT+1 hr (+2 hrs Apr–Sept).

Poland

Embassy phone numbers
Warsaw:

Australia 17.60.81	Sweden 00.00.00
Canada 00.00.00	Switzerland 28.04.81
Denmark 49.00.56	W. Germany 17.30.11
Japan 45.16.71	UK 28.10.01
Norway 00.00.00	USA 28.30.41

Hotels
Warsaw: Bristol, Forum, Grand, Europejski, Metropol, Solec, Victoria. Prices up to ZL900 per night.

International banks
Bank Handlowy w Warszawie.

Credit cards
All major credit cards.

Office hours
08.00–15.00 or 09.00–16.00.

National holidays
1 Jan, Easter Monday, 1, 9 May, Corpus Christi (May *or* June), 22 July, 1 Nov, 25, 26 Dec.

Voltage
220–380 volts AC.

Communications
Tel: ZL100.20 per 3 mins. *Telex:* ZL49.80 per 3 mins. *Airmail:* 2–10 days. *Cable:* ZL6.60 per word.

Social customs
Doing business with Polish state organisations requires patience. The Poles have a reputation of sticking to a contract—and paying on time. Restaurants are excellent and prices are moderate. Offices do not close for lunch and the main meal of the day is taken at 15.00 or shortly afterwards. Shops tend to open 11.00–19.00. *Best buys:* Amber jewellery, cut glass, embroidery, rugs, carved wooden ornaments, silver and metal-ware.

Area and population
92,082 sq kms (35,543 sq mls). Pop. 8.3 million.
Capital: Lisbon (1 million).
Chief cities: Oporto (320,000), Coimbra (110,000), Braga (94,500), Matozinhos (90,500), Leira (83,000).
Ports: Lisbon, Oporto, Leixoes, Setubal.
Airport: Portela de Sacavem (Lisbon).

Climate
One of the most pleasant in Europe. Temperatures in Lisbon range from 8° to 37° C (46° to 98°F). Humidity 60–90%. *Clothing:* Medium-weight clothing for winter, lightweight for summer.

People
Southern European. *Religion:* Roman Catholic.
Distribution: 25% urban.

Language
Portuguese. *English rating:* Good.

Economic background
Economic and financial problems have beset Portugal since the comparatively bloodless coup of 25 April 1974. Inflation, coupled with widespread demands for higher

wages, now plagues the country. Still essentially an agricultural country, Portugal has been slow to industrialise, although this aspect of the economy is now receiving greater priority from the government. Overseas investment is being held up by Portugal's political and economic uncertainties.

Trade
Gross National Product: 338,300 million escudos.
Exports: 60,000 million escudos, chiefly cork, sardines, wines, textiles, minerals, machinery.
Imports: 120,000 million escudos, chiefly machinery and industrial equipment, petroleum products, optical equipment, cotton, steel, wheat, maize.
Chief trading partners: W. Germany, USA, UK, France, Italy, Spain, Netherlands, Switzerland, Sweden, Japan.
Inflation rate: 11.7%.

Prospects
Much depends upon the government's success in overcoming internal dissension.

Currency
Escudo ($) = 100 centavos. £ = 86$10;
$ = 45$79.

Travel
No visas required.

Vaccinations
None.

Airlines
TAP, British Airways, British Caledonian, Pan Am, Air France, Iberia, Swissair, KLM, Sabena, SAS, TWA, Varig, Lufthansa, Alitalia, South African Airways.
Flying times: Copenhagen 3½ hrs; London 2¼ hrs; New York 7½ hrs; Sydney 30 hrs. *Fares:* Copenhagen F Dkr2,645 Y Dkr2,035; London F £143 Y £94; New York F $656 Y $313; Sydney F A$1,493 Y A$956.
Airport to city: 7 kms (4.5 mls). *Taxi fare:* 60 escudos.

Duty-free allowances
200 cigarettes *or* 50 cigars; 1 bottle of spirits, 1 bottle of wine.

Local time
GMT (+1 hr Apr–Sept).

Embassy phone numbers
Lisbon:

Australia 53.91.00	Sweden 67.60.96
Canada 56.25.47	Switzerland 67.31.21
Denmark 53.94.27	W. Germany 56.30.50
Netherlands 66.11.63	UK 66.11.91
Norway 68.31.13	USA 55.51.41

Hotels
Lisbon: Ritz, Sheraton, Avenida Palace, Mundial, Florida, Lutecia, Fenix, Embaixador, Diplomatico, Penta. Prices approx. 300–800 escudos per night.

International banks
Bank of London and South America, Lloyds, Crédit Franco–Portugais, Banco do Brasil.

Credit cards
American Express, Barclaycard, Diners Club.

Office hours
10.00–12.30 and 14.30–18.00 Mon–Fri.

National holidays
1 Jan, Carnival (two days before Ash Wednesday), Good Friday, Easter Monday, 25 Apr, 1 May, Corpus Christi (May *or* June), 10 June, 15 Aug, 5 Oct, 1 Nov, 1, 8, 25 Dec.

Voltage
220 volts 50 cycles AC.

Communications
Tel: 78$00 per 3 mins. *Telex:* 13$00 per min.
Airmail: 1–2 days. *Cable:* 2$50 per word plus 60$00.

Social customs
The Portuguese are invariably polite and gracious, with formal manners and customs. Conservative business suits are worn. Business approach must be low-key. The food and wines are some of the best in Europe—as are the hotels.

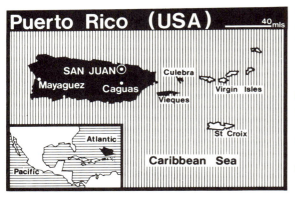

Area and population

8,897 sq kms (3,435 sq mls). Pop. 3.2 million.
Capital: San Juan (852,000).
Chief cities: Ponce (174,000), Mayaguez (95,000).
Port: San Juan. *Airport:* Isla Verde (San Juan).

Climate

Tropical. Temperatures rarely fall below 16°C (60°F),
and never above 32°C (89°F).
Clothing: Lightweight throughout the year.

People

Mixture of ethnic strains, mainly Spanish and African.
Religion: Chiefly Roman Catholic.
Distribution: 60% urban.

Languages

Spanish and English.

Economic background

With one of the fastest economic growth rates in the
world, Puerto Rico has been transformed from an
agricultural to an industrial economy since the 1940s,
a significant achievement since the island lacks mineral
resources. Puerto Rico (a self-governing commonwealth
associated with the USA—its people are US citizens)
has been greatly helped in manufacturing by many US
companies that have set up subsidiaries. Tourism has
also become an important source of revenue. Apart
from any light industry, Puerto Rico has petrochemical
complexes and steel works.

Trade

Gross National Product: US$7,466 million.
Exports: US$6,678 million, chiefly manufactured goods,
coffee, tobacco, sugar, rum.

Imports: US$8,522 million, chiefly consumer goods,
foodstuffs, animal products, fuel, chemicals, machinery.
Chief trading partners: USA, Venezuela, Netherlands,
Spain, Canada, Dominican Republic.
Inflation rate: Not available.

Prospects

In spite of high unemployment, unofficially estimated at
30%, Puerto Rico is expected to continue to expand
industrially, largely through aid.

Currency

US dollar = 100 cents. £ = $1.88.

Travel

US visa required.

Vaccinations

Smallpox.

Airlines

Iberia, Air France, Eastern, American, Avianca, Mexicana,
Pan Am.
Flying times: Copenhagen $14\frac{1}{2}$ hrs; London (no direct
flight) 12 hrs; New York 4 hrs; Sydney 28 hrs.
Fares: Copenhagen F Dkr5,545 Y Dkr3,460; London
F £387 Y £229.50; New York F $203 Y $107;
Sydney F A$1,853 Y A$1,189.
Airport to city: 14.5 kms (9 mls). *Bus fare:* $2.00.

Duty-free allowances

300 cigarettes *or* 50 cigars *or* 3 lbs tobacco;
1 US quart of alcoholic beverages.

Local time

GMT−4 hrs.

Embassy phone numbers

San Juan:

Canada 764.2011	Sweden 785.3571
Denmark 725.3885	Switzerland 724.1200
Netherlands 723.1442	W. Germany 724.2495
Norway 723.0769	UK 767.4435

Hotels

San Juan: Atlantic Beach, Caribe Hilton, El Covento,
Holiday Inn, Puerto Rico Sheraton. In winter season
prices rise to $85 per day, but half that out of season.

International banks

All US banks.

Puerto Rico

Credit cards
All major credit cards.

Office hours
08.30–17.00 Mon–Fri.

National holidays
1, 6, 11 Jan, Third Monday in Feb, Good Friday,
16 Apr, Last Monday in May, 4, 17, 25, 17 July,
First Monday in Sept, 12 Oct, Fourth Thursday in Nov,
19 Nov, 25 Dec.

Voltage
110 volts AC.

Communications
Tel: $9 per 3 mins. *Airmail:* 3–6 days.
Cable: 25 cents per word.

Social customs
Very much as in the USA, but Puerto Ricans are proud
of their own culture. Best, if possible, to avoid
visiting during winter, when the island is packed
with North American tourists escaping harsh weather
at home. Hotel accommodation is expensive and hard
to find.

Qatar

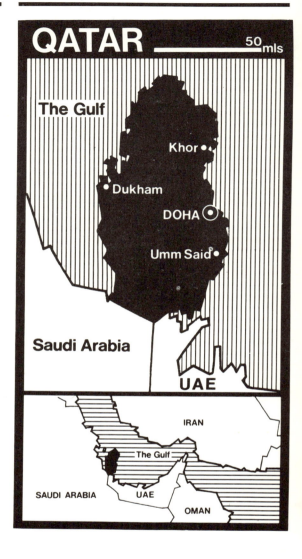

Area and population
11,000 sq kms (4,247 sq mls). Pop. 190,000.
Capital: Doha (140,000).
Chief cities: None, but towns include Umm Said,
Dukhan, Khor, Wakrah. *Port:* Doha. *Airport:* Doha.

Climate
Hot and humid, particularly July–Sept, when noon
temperatures reach 44°C (111°F). Best time to visit is
Dec–Mar, when temperatures range from 10°C (50°F)
to 20°C (68°F). *Clothing:* Lightweight to
medium-weight according to season.

People
Mostly Arab, with Indian, Pakistani, Iranian communities. *Religion:* Moslem.

Language
Arabic. *English rating:* Excellent.

Economic background
Oil provides the overwhelming source of revenue for this Gulf sheikhdom, although the government is trying hard to diversify into non-oil enterprises. Much of the oil revenue has been spent on improving public services, including roads, schools and ports. New industries comprise fertilisers, flour, natural gas liquids, cement, iron and steel, and petrochemicals.

Trade
Gross National Product: Not available.
Exports: US$2,600 million, chiefly oil.
Imports: US$800 million, chiefly capital machinery, foodstuffs, clothing, textiles, transport equipment.
Chief trading partners: Japan, UK, USA, W. Germany, France, Dubai, Italy, Kuwait, Switzerland, Netherlands, India, Lebanon, Bangladesh, Saudi Arabia, China.
Inflation rate: Not available.

Prospects
Huge sums of money are still being spent on industrial and social development, a policy that is likely to continue.

Currency
Qatar riyal (QR) = 100 dirhams. £ = QR7.31; $ = QR3.88.

Travel
Visas required but not by UK citizens.

Vaccinations
Smallpox.

Airlines
British Airways, Gulf, Saudia, Air France, Kuwait, MEA, PIA, Iraqi, Iran Air.
Flying times: Copenhagen (no direct flights) $17\frac{3}{4}$ hrs; London $7\frac{1}{2}$ hrs; New York 14 hrs; Sydney 23 hrs.
Fares: Copenhagen F Dkr5,130; Y Dkr3,710; London F £380.50 Y £267.50; New York F $1,178 Y $716; Sydney F A$1,004 Y A$664.
Airport to city: 8 kms (5 mls). *Taxi fare:* QR20.

Duty-free allowances
No limit on amounts of cigarettes, cigars or tobacco. No alcohol allowed.

Local time
GMT+3 hrs.

Embassy phone numbers
Doha: UK 321991.

Hotels
Doha: Gulf, New Doha Palace, Oasis Alwaha. About QR250 per night.

International banks
Chartered Bank, British Bank of the Middle East, Arab Bank, Qatar National Bank, Citibank, Banque de Paris et des Pays-Bas.

Credit cards
All major credit cards.

Office hours
07.30–12.00 and 14.30–18.00 Sat–Thurs.

National holidays
All Moslem holidays plus 22 Feb, 3 Sept.

Voltage
220–240 volts AC.

Communications
Tel: QR40 per 3 mins. *Telex:* QR43 per 3 mins.
Airmail: 3–7 days. *Cable:* QR1.75 per word.

Social customs
Qatar is a strict Moslem country in which alcohol is forbidden. Eat and drink only with the right hand. Avoid visiting Qatar during the month of Ramadan (season varies), when most businesses are closed.

ROMANIA   200 mls
USSR
Hungary
Iasi
Cluj
Brasov   Galatz
Timisoara
Ploesti
BUCHAREST ⊙ Constanta
Yugoslavia   Black Sea
Bulgaria

Area and population
237,428 sq kms (91,671 sq mls). Pop. 21.5 million.
Capital: Bucharest (Bucuresti) (1.9 million).
Chief cities: Constanta (290,000), Ploiesti (254,000),
Timisoara (282,000), Iasi (284,000), Cluj (262,000).
Ports: Constanta, Galatz.
Airport: Otopeni (Bucharest).

Climate
Continental, with hot summers and cold winters. Average
winter temperature is −2°C (28°F), rising to 21°C (70°F)
and higher in summer. *Clothing:* Warm overcoat and
heavy shoes for winter, lightweight clothes in summer.

People
85% Romanian, with Hungarian, German, Ukrainian,
Serb, Croat, Greek and Turkish minorities.
Religion: 80% Romanian Orthodox Church.
Distribution: 39% urban.

Language
Romanian. *English rating:* Fair.

Economic background
Agriculture is giving way increasingly to industry.
Steel production doubled between 1966 and 1973.
Centrally organised and based on successive five-year
plans, the economy is giving priority to chemicals,
including petrochemicals, power generation, steel and
machinery, and engineering. Agriculture is still the major
sector of the economy, particularly cereals and sugar
beet.

Trade
Gross National Product: US$16,770 million.
Exports: 26,547 million lei, chiefly petroleum, fuel,
chemicals, iron and steel, tractors, drilling equipment,
bearings, agricultural products, timber.
Imports: 26,549 million lei, chiefly electrical equipment,
machine tools, transport equipment, ores, textiles,
clothing. *Chief trading partners:* USSR,
W. and E. Germany, Switzerland, Czechoslovakia,
Italy, China, Poland, France, Iran, UK, Austria, Japan.
Inflation rate: Not available.

Prospects
Substantial investment in heavy industry will continue.

Currency
Leu (plural lei) = 100 bani. Two official rates of
exchange prevail: official and visitor's.
Visitor's £ = 22.79 lei; $ = 12.12 lei.

Travel
Visa required.

Vaccinations
Not required, but smallpox and TAB recommended.

Airlines
British Airways, Tarom, Lufthansa, El Al,
Austrian, SAS, Malev, Pan Am, Alitalia, Air France,
Swissair, Aeroflot.
Flying times: Copenhagen $2\frac{3}{4}$ hrs; London 3 hrs;
New York 10 hrs; Sydney 30 hrs.
Fares: Copenhagen F Dkr2,620 Y Dkr1,750;
London F £239 Y £159; New York F $902
Y $485; Sydney F A$1,397 Y A$893.
Airport to city: 19 kms (12 mls). *Taxi fare:* 50 lei.
Bus fare: 8 lei.

Duty-free allowances
200 cigarettes *or* 50 cigars *or* 250 grammes of tobacco;
1 litre of spirits and 2 litres of wine.

Local time
GMT+2 hrs.

Embassy phone numbers
Bucharest:

Denmark 33.63.80	Switzerland 12.04.18
Japan 12.96.30	W. Germany 12.04.13
Netherlands 33.22.92	UK 11.16.35
Sweden 17.31.84	USA 12.40.40

Romania

Hotels
Bucharest: Inter-Continental, Athenee Palace, Ambassador, Lido, Nord. Prices up to US$44–51 per night.

International banks
None, but there is a joint venture Anglo–Romanian Bank Ltd.

Credit cards
All major credit cards.

Office hours
08.00–11.30 and 12.00–16.00 Mon–Fri, 08.00–12.30 Sat.

National holidays
1 Jan, 1, 2 May, 23, 24 Aug.

Voltage
220 volts AC.

Communications
Tel: 23.60 lei per min (3-min minimum). *Telex:* 30 lei per 3 mins. *Airmail:* 3–10 days. *Cable:* 2.30 lei per word.

Social customs
Much patience and persistence is required in business dealings with Romania. Romanians eat well—usually three good meals each day. Dinner is usually served between 20.00 and 22.00. *Best buy:* Low-priced, good-quality long-playing records purchased at Muzica in Calea Victoriei, Bucharest.

Saudi Arabia

Area and population
2,410,000 sq kms (927,000 sq mls). Pop. 7 million.
Capital: Riyadh (667,000).
Chief cities: Jeddah (561,000), Dammam and Al Khobar (combined pop. 176,000), Dhahran, Mecca (367,000), Medina (198,000).
Ports: Jeddah, Dammam, Ras Tanurah.
Airports: Jeddah, Dhahran, Riyadh.

Climate
Desert. Temperatures in Jeddah rarely rise over 38°C (100°F), but humidity is often over 90%, particularly in Sept. Can be very cold Dec to mid-Feb. Riyadh hotter in summer—up to 49°C (120°F).
Clothing: Lightweight for most of the year, but summerweight clothing in winter. Women need cotton dresses for most of the year.

People
Arab. *Religion:* Moslem.
Distribution: 28% urban.

Language
Arabic. *English rating:* Good.

Economic background
The wealthiest of all the oil nations, Saudi Arabia derives 91% of its income from oil. Agriculture, while accounting for only 3% of the gross national product, employs most of the population. The government is using much of its oil income to improve agricultural

methods and to foster new industries, most of them connected with oil and gas.

Trade
Gross National Product: Not available.
Exports: 40,000 million riyals, chiefly oil.
Imports: 8,000 million riyals, chiefly machinery, cereals, power-generating equipment, industrial goods.
Chief trading partners: Japan, UK, W. Germany, Netherlands, Kuwait, Syria, Italy, Somalia, France, USA, Spain, Brazil. *Inflation rate:* 8.7%.

Prospects
With its huge oil resources, Saudi Arabia is likely to remain the Middle East's richest market for many years to come.

Currency
Riyal (SR) = 100 hallalahs. £ = SR6.46; $ = SR3.43.

Travel
Visas essential but take time and patience to acquire.

Vaccinations
Smallpox. Inoculations against yellow fever and cholera required by visitors from infected areas.

Airlines
Air France, British Airways, Saudia, MEA, KLM, Gulf, Lufthansa, PIA.
Flying times: Copenhagen 11 hrs; London 6 hrs; New York 14 hrs; Sydney 19 hrs.
Fares: Copenhagen F Dkr4,670 Y Dkr3,465; London F £343.50 Y £240.50; New York F $1,060 Y $663; Sydney F A$1,084 Y A$723.
Airport (Jeddah) to city: 2.4 kms (1.5 mls).
Taxi fare: SR20.

Duty-free allowances
Unlimited amount of cigarettes, cigars or tobacco. Alcohol is prohibited, as is the import of pig meat or pig meat products.

Local time
GMT+3 hrs.

Embassy phone numbers
Jeddah:

Australia 51303	W. Germany 53545
Denmark 33044	UK 52544
Japan 52402	USA 2101
Switzerland 51387	

Hotels
Jeddah: Palace, Kandara, Jeddah Airport.
Riyadh: Al Yamama, Inter-Continental. Prices up to SR330 per night.

International banks
British Bank of the Middle East, Riyad Bank, National Commercial Bank.

Credit cards
American Express, Diners Club.

Office hours
No standard hours but roughly:
Jeddah: 09.00–13.30 and 16.30–20.00 Sat–Wed.
Riyadh: 08.30–12.00 and 16.30–19.30 Sat–Wed.
Dhahran: 07.00–11.30 and 13.00–16.30 Sat–Wed.
Offices are closed during the day during Ramadan, but may open 20.00–01.00. Embassies tend to open 08.00–14.00 Sat–Thurs.

National holidays
Id al Fitr (6–8 days) and Id al Adha (5 days). Check dates before departure.

Voltage
100 or 120 volts 60 cycles AC and 220 volts 50 cycles.

Communications
Telex: Limited availability.
Airmail: 3–5 days. *Cable:* SR1.45 per word.

Social customs
Friday is the weekly holiday, although more firms are now closing on Thursday as well. Saudi Arabia is the strictest of Moslem countries. During Ramadan, which ends with Id al Fitr, don't eat, drink or smoke in public. Since electricity standards vary throughout the country, don't rely on being able to use electric razors. In Riyadh all premises close four times a day for prayers.
Best buys: Brass and copperware, jewellery, wooden articles, pottery, baskets, mats, leatherwork, carpets, fabrics and weaving.

Area and population
197,109 sq kms (76,104 sq mls). Pop. 4.5 million.
Capital: Dakar (693,000).
Chief cities: Kaolack (95,000), Thiés (90,000),
Saint Louis (75,000), Ziguinchor (45,000).
Ports: Dakar, Kaolack, Saint Louis.
Airport: Yoff (Dakar).

Climate
Hot and humid and many thunderstorms June–Nov.
Avoid visiting during this period, since many
businessmen take holidays then. Temperatures range
from 24° to 38°C (75° to 100°F). *Clothing:* Tropical
clothing of open-weave material for
May–Nov (not white). Lightweight clothing suitable for
other seasons. Hat and sunglasses are needed.

People
African, mostly Wolof. *Religion:* Moslem, with a few
Roman Catholics. *Distribution:* 30% urban.

Language
French. *English rating:* Poor.

Economic background
Once part of French West Africa, Senegal is a poor
country, deriving its revenue from groundnuts,
phosphates and fishing. It is agricultural and most of the
farms are small and tribally owned. Tourism is growing,
proving to be a useful addition to small industry.

Senegal still receives large amounts of international aid,
as well as help from France.

Trade
Gross National Product: 263,300 million CFAfrancs.
Exports: 90,000 million CFAfrancs, chiefly phosphates,
groundnuts, tinned fish.
Imports: 110,000 million CFAfrancs, chiefly textiles,
machinery, foodstuffs, chemicals, petroleum products.
Chief trading partners: France, W. Germany, USA, China,
Nigeria, Brazil, Italy, Holland, UK, Japan, Spain.
Inflation rate: Not available.

Prospects
The government is following a policy of Africanisation
and development of industry.

Currency
CFAfranc. £ = CFAfrs421; $ = CFAfrs223.

Travel
Visas required.

Vaccinations
Smallpox, yellow fever, cholera.

Airlines
Air Afrique, Air France, British Caledonian,
Royal Air Maroc, Lufthansa, Alitalia, Air Algérie,
Air Zaire, Pan Am, Sabena, Swissair.
Flying times: Copenhagen $12\frac{1}{4}$ hrs; London $5\frac{3}{4}$ hrs;
New York $7\frac{3}{4}$ hrs; Sydney 24 hrs. *Fares:* Copenhagen
F Dkr5,475 Y Dkr3,745; London F £378 Y £251.50;
New York F $832 Y $511; Sydney F A$1,612 Y A$1,083.
Airport to city: 17 kms (10.5 mls). *Bus fare:* CFAfrs200.
Taxi fare: CFAfrs1500.

Duty-free allowances
200 cigarettes *or* 50 cigars *or* 250 grammes tobacco.

Local time
GMT.

Embassy phone numbers
Dakar: UK 22383.

Hotels
Dakar: De la Croix du Sud, Meridien, Teranga.
Prices up to CFAfrs10,000 per night.

Sierra Leone

International banks
None, but local banks include
Banque Internationale pour l'Afrique Occidentale,
Banque Internationale pour le Commerce et l'Industrie,
Union Sénégalaise de Banques pour le Commerce et l'Industrie, Société Générale de Banques au Sénégal.

Credit cards
American Express, Diners Club.

Office hours
08.00–12.00 and 13.00–18.00 Mon–Fri, 08.00–12.00 Sat.

National holidays
Most Moslem holidays plus 1 Jan, Easter Monday, 4 Apr,
1 May, Ascension Day (May),
Whit Monday (May or June), 15 Aug, 1 Nov, 25 Dec.

Voltage
127 volts for lighting, 220 volts for power.

Communications
Tel: CFAfrs2,612 per 3 mins.
Airmail: 3–5 days. *Cable:* CFAfrs130 per word.

Social customs
It is essential to speak French, since English is little spoken. Malaria is prevalent. Avoid unboiled water and uncooked fruit. Doctors are expensive. European customs prevail in business circles.

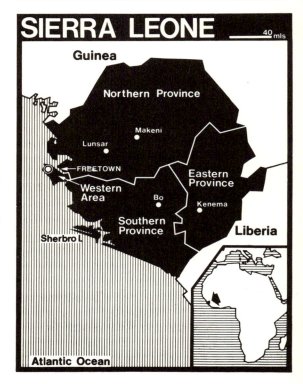

Area and population
72,326 sq kms (27,925 sq mls). Pop. 3 million.
Capital: Freetown (275,000).
Chief cities: Bo (26,000), Kenema (13,000),
Makeni (12,000). *Port:* Freetown.
Airport: Lungi (Freetown).

Climate
Tropical and humid. Heavy rainfall 330 cm (130 ins) per year in Freetown. Wet season lasts mid-Apr to mid-Nov. Average temperature in Freetown is about 26.6°C (80°F). *Clothing:* Lightweight trousers and shirts and washable cotton dresses. Umbrella and lightweight raincoat indispensable May–Oct.

People
32% Mende, 25% Temne, and many others, including 5,000 European expatriates. *Religion:* 33% Moslem, 5% Christian, rest animist. *Distribution:* 10% urban.

Language
English.

Economic background

A small and mountainous country. Sierra Leone is moving gradually from dependence on agriculture and now minerals, chiefly diamonds, iron ore and bauxite, exceed farming as a source of revenue. Industry is also developing, producing principally cigarettes, cement, nails, shoes and knitted goods.

Trade

Gross National Product: US$400 million.
Exports: 125 million leones, chiefly diamonds, iron ore, palm kernels, coffee and cocoa.
Imports: 200 million leones, chiefly manufactured goods, machinery, transport equipment, food.
Chief trading partners: UK, W. Germany, USA, Japan, Netherlands, China, France, Egypt, Nigeria.
Inflation rate: Not available.

Prospects

Still a poor country, but world demand for minerals will aid development.

Currency

Leone (Le) = 100 cents. £ = 2.00 leones; $ = 1.06 leones.

Travel

Entry permits required.

Vaccinations

Smallpox and yellow fever.

Airlines

British Caledonian, Sierra Leone Airways, Interflug, KLM, UTA.
Flying times: Copenhagen 10½ hrs; London 6¼ hrs; New York 10 hrs; Sydney 24 hrs.
Fares: Copenhagen F Dkr6,315 Y Dkr4,210; London F £441.50 Y £289.50; New York F $932 Y $583; Sydney F A$1,576 Y A$1,025.
Airport to city: 29 kms (18 mls). *Taxi:* Negotiable, but journey takes two hours by road and ferry.
Airport bus to Paramount Hotel costs 3.00 leones.

Duty-free allowances

200 cigarettes *or* the equivalent in cigars *or* tobacco; 1 bottle of spirits, 1 bottle of wine.

Local time

GMT.

Embassy phone numbers

Freetown: UK 23961.

Hotels

Freetown: Brookfields, Cape Sierra, Paramount. Up to 20 leones per night.

International banks

Standard Bank of Sierra Leone, Barclays Bank of Sierra Leone, National Commercial Bank.

Credit cards

American Express, Diners Club.

Office hours

08.00–12.00 and 14.00–16.30 Mon–Fri, 08.00–12.30 Sat.

National holidays

Moslem holidays plus 1 Jan, Good Friday, Easter Monday, 19 Apr, 24 Aug, 25, 26 Dec.

Voltage

230–240 volts single phase AC.

Communications

Tel: 8.40 leones per 3 mins. *Telex:* 2.80 leones per 3 mins (minimum charge of 8.40 leones). *Airmail:* 5 days. *Cable:* 26 cents per word.

Social customs

Do not drink unfiltered or unboiled water. Anti-malarial drugs should be taken. It is unnecessary to tip taxi-drivers—but always agree fare before commencing journey.

SINGAPORE

500 mls

15 mls

Malaya

Johore Bahru

Nee
Soon

Choa Chu
Kang

Tuan

Changi

SINGAPORE

South China Sea

Malaysia

Indonesia

Area and population
588 sq kms (226 sq mls). Pop. 2.3 million.
Capital: Singapore (city state).
Cities: None but towns include Bukit Panjana,
Changi, Choa Chu Kang. *Port:* Singapore.
Airport: Paya Lebar International.

Climate
Though only 128 kms (80 mls) north of the Equator,
Singapore's average maximum temperature is
30°C (87°F) and minimum temperature 24°C (75°F),
with humid days and cool, pleasant nights.
Clothing: Informal, with jackets usually worn only in
the evenings. Women should take cotton dresses.
Because of high humidity prepare for frequent changes
of clothing.

People
76% Chinese, 15% Malay, 7% Indian.
Religion: Moslems, Christians, Hindus, and
traditional Chinese religions. *Distribution:* 97% urban.

Languages
English, Mandarin, Malay and Tamil.

Economic background
With few natural resources, Singapore is a prosperous
island republic at the hub of sea and air routes in
South East Asia. Its port is the biggest in the region.
Prosperity is largely due to entrepôt trade, although
industrialisation is playing an increasingly bigger part in

the economy. Industrial estates have sprung up and the
manufacture of electronic products has become
important. Shipbuilding and repair, as well as tourism,
contribute to Singapore's revenue.

Trade
Gross National Product: S$19,400 million.
Exports: S$12,757 million, chiefly tin, rubber, copra,
petroleum, coffee, coconut oil, pineapples, iron,
steel, toys, leather goods, textiles, electronic equipment.
Imports: S$19,270 million, chiefly rice, sugar, cement,
manufactured goods, machinery, transport equipment,
chemicals, fuels, lubricants.
Chief trading partners: Japan, USA, W. Malaysia,
Saudi Arabia, Iran, UK, China, Australia, W. Germany,
Kuwait, Hong Kong, Thailand, Sabah.
Inflation rate: 4.6%.

Prospects
The government, which is still encouraging overseas
investment through incentives, expects manufacturing to
grow in the 1980s. Oil exploration will also give
a firm source of revenue for the foreseeable future.

Currency
Dollar (S$) = 100 cents. £ = S$4.35; $ = s$2.31.

Travel
Visit pass required (normally granted on entry).
The government may refuse entry (even overnight stay)
to visitors who do not comply with their requirements
regarding general appearance and clothing, e.g. 'hippies'
and men with hair reaching below the collar and/or
covering the ears and/or falling across the forehead to
touch the eyebrow.

Vaccinations
Smallpox and cholera.

Airlines
Aeroflot, Air France, Air India, Alitalia, British Airways,
Cathay Pacific, Garuda, Gulf, KLM, Lufthansa, Malaysian,
Olympic, Pan Am, Philippine, Qantas, Sabena, SAS,
SIA, Swissair, Thai, UTA.
Flying times: Copenhagen 15 hrs; London 9 hrs by
Concorde (suspended at time of going to press pending
government talks), 14½ hrs by conventional jet;
New York 27 hrs; Sydney 8½ hrs.
Fares: Copenhagen F Dkr8,435 Y Dkr4,910;
London (Concorde) £754.50, (jet) F £656
Y £382; New York F $1,629 Y $1,009;

Sydney F A$613 Y A$436.
Airport to city: 11 kms (7 mls). *Taxi fare:* S$5.

Duty-free allowances

200 cigarettes *or* 50 cigars *or* 250 grammes of tobacco;
1 bottle of spirits and 1 bottle of wine.

Local time

GMT+7½ hrs.

Embassy phone numbers

Australia 379311	Sweden 550901
Canada 371322	Switzerland 374666
Denmark 362488	W. Germany 371355
Japan 630022	UK 639333
Netherlands 371155	USA 30251
Norway 982266	

Hotels

Singapore: Goodwood Park, Holiday Inn,
Marco Polo, Mandarin, Raffles, Shangri-La,
Singapore Hilton, Hyatt Singapore, Summit.
Prices range US$22–32 per night.

International banks

Singapore is an international banking centre and most
international banks are represented.

Credit cards

All major credit cards.

Office hours

09.00–17.00 Mon–Fri, 09.00–13.00 Sat.

National holidays

Moslem holidays, plus 1 Jan, Chinese New Year
(Jan *or* Feb), Thaipusam (Feb), Good Friday,
1, 21 May, 9 Aug, Deepavali (Oct *or* Nov), 25 Dec.

Voltage

230 volts AC.

Communications

Tel: S$36.30 per 3 mins. *Telex:* S$33 per 3 mins.
Airmail: 3–5 days. *Cable:* 80 cents per word
(7-word minimum).

Social customs

No special business customs but be prepared for
fast pace. Humidity is high but all offices and cars are
air-conditioned. Plenty of lightweight clothes required,
but laundry services are excellent. Singapore hotels and
restaurants are among the best in the region, and
comparatively inexpensive. *Best buys:* As one of the
world's best tax-free markets, Singapore offers Swiss
watches cheaper than in Switzerland and
Japanese cameras cheaper than in Japan. Apart from
duty-free bargains, look out for batik (Malay cotton
fabric), Kelantan silk, and leather goods.

Somalia

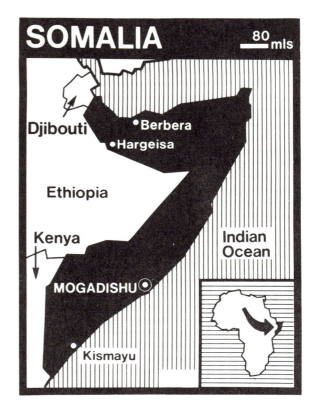

Area and population

637,000 sq kms (246,200 mls). Pop. 3 million.
Capital: Mogadishu (300,000).
Chief cities: Hargeisa (100,000), Berbera (20,000),
Kismayu (18,000). *Ports:* Mogadishu, Berbera.
Airport: International (Mogadishu).

Climate

Tropical, with temperatures ranging from
27° to 32°C (80° to 90°F) and up to 38°C (100°F) in

Berbera. *Clothing:* Light tropical. Coats and ties rarely worn.

People

98% Hamitic plus 35,000 Arabs, 2,000 Italians. 1,000 Indians and Pakistanis. *Religion:* Chiefly Moslem. *Distribution:* No figure available but urbanisation of nomadic people is continuing.

Language

Somali, with a script based on the Latin alphabet (adopted 1972). Before that date the official languages were oral Somali, Arabic, English and Italian.

Economic background

A cattle-and-crop economy, based largely on the acquisition of large individual herds, is augmented by a small industry that serves the internal market. Hence the heavy tariff protection. Half the gross value of industrial production comes from a state-owned sugar factory, and there are plants given over to fish and fruit canning and meat packing. One factory is devoted to the production of textiles.

Trade

Gross National Product: US$254 million.
Exports: So Sh390 million, chiefly live animals, bananas, meat and meat products, fish and fish products, leather, hides and skins, incense and myrrh.
Imports: So Sh898 million, chiefly transport equipment, non-electrical equipment, cereals, yarns and fabrics, metals, pharmaceutical products, paper products.
Chief trading partners: Italy, USSR, China, Kenya, Pakistan, Mauritius, France, Thailand, Japan, UK, Saudi Arabia, Kuwait. *Inflation rate:* Not available.

Prospects

Efforts are being made to develop local industries, but emphasis in present development plans is on livestock and agriculture.

Currency

Somali shilling (So Sh) = 100 cents. £ = So Sh11.83; $ = So Sh6.29.

Travel

Visas required.

Vaccinations

Smallpox, yellow fever and cholera. Vaccination against typhus, typhoid and tetanus recommended.

Airlines

Alitalia, Syrian Arab.
Flying times: Copenhagen 16 hrs; London 12½ hrs; New York 20 hrs; Sydney 24 hrs.
Fares: Copenhagen F Dkr6,580 Y Dkr4,390; London F £498.50 Y £315.50; New York F $1,213 Y $802; Sydney F A$1,390 Y A$975.
Airport to city: 6 kms (4 mls). *Taxi fare:* So Sh10, but drivers tend to charge more.

Duty-free allowances

400 cigarettes *or* 40 cigars *or* 400 grammes of tobacco; 1 bottle of spirits.

Local time

GMT+3 hrs.

Embassy phone numbers

Mogadishu: UK 2288.

Hotels

Mogadishu: Croce del Sud, Arumba, Juba. Prices range up to So Sh120 per day.

International banks

None. All Somali banks are nationalised.

Credit cards

Not generally in use.

Office hours

08.00–12.30 and 16.30–19.00 Sat–Thurs.

National holidays

Moslem holidays plus 1 Jan, 1 May, 26 June, 1 July, 21, 22 Oct.

Voltage

220 volts AC.

Communications

Tel: So Sh88.45 per 3 mins. *Telex:* So Sh77.85 per 3 mins. *Airmail:* 4–14 days. *Cable:* Cost not available.

Social customs

Much of the entertaining, particularly among the expatriate communities, is informal and businessmen should expect to return hospitality in restaurants. Drink bottled water.

Area and population

1,221,042 sq kms (471,445 sq mls). Pop. 24.9 million.
Capitals: Winter: Pretoria (562,000).
Summer: Cape Town (1.1 million).
Chief cities: Johannesburg (1.4 million),
Durban (850,000), Port Elizabeth (475,000),
Bloemfontein (182,000), East London (124,000),
Kimberley (104,000), Pietermaritzburg.
Ports: Cape Town, Durban, Port Elizabeth,
East London. *Airports:* Jan Smuts (Johannesburg),
D.F. Malan (Cape Town). All chief cities have airports,
but international flights land only in Johannesburg and
Cape Town.

Climate

Temperate. Johannesburg temperatures range from
4°C (39°F) June–July to 26°C (78°F) Oct–Feb.
Cape Town tends to be warmer and Durban hotter
still. *Clothing:* European-weight clothing for winter,
lightweight for summer.

People

68% Bantu, 19% European, 10% Cape Coloured,
3% Asian. *Religion:* Predominantly Christian.
Distribution: 47% urban.

Languages

Afrikaans and English.

Economic background

Industrially and agriculturally the most developed nation
in Africa, South Africa derives its prosperity from its
industry and mines. Industries have been growing since
the war, and manufacturing is now the largest

contributor to the national wealth, followed by mining,
trade, gold and diamonds. The country enjoys the
African continent's highest standards of living for all
communities, and growth has continued even during
the world recession. With the worldwide
controversy over apartheid, and the political
uncertainties it has brought, South Africa's
development is now hampered by a steep decline in
the influx of overseas investment funds.

Trade

Gross National Product: 19,855 million rand.
Exports: 5,000 million rand, chiefly precious stones,
wool, copper, iron and steel ores, fruits and nuts,
mineral fuels. *Imports:* 5,000 million rand, chiefly
boilers, machinery, vehicles, mineral fuels, artificial resins,
plastics, man-made fibres. *Chief trading partners:* UK,
W. Germany, Japan, Italy, France, USA, Belgium,
Switzerland, Canada, France. *Inflation rate:* 9.9%.

Prospects

With its vast natural resources, despite lacking oil,
South Africa's economic future is assured. Doubts about
the immediate future remain because the economy is
now being affected by worldwide reaction against
South Africa's domestic racial policies.

Currency

Rand = 100 cents. £ = 1.64 rand; $ = 0.87 rand.

Travel

Visas not normally required, although certain categories
of people, such as journalists and students, must apply
for admission.

Vaccinations

Smallpox. If travelling from infected areas, visitors must
have cholera and yellow fever inoculations.

Airlines

Most major international airlines.
Flying times: Copenhagen $14\frac{3}{4}$ hrs; London 12 hrs
(non-stop); New York $18\frac{1}{4}$ hrs; Sydney 18 hrs.
Fares (to Johannesburg): Copenhagen F Dkr8,080
Y Dkr5,065; London F £585 Y £369;
New York F $1,213 Y $802; Sydney F A$1,030 Y A$788.
Airport to city: Johannesburg 24 kms (15 mls);
Cape Town 14 kms (9 mls).
Taxi fares: Johannesburg 10 rand; Cape Town 8 rand.

Duty-free allowances
400 cigarettes *or* 50 cigars *or* 250 grammes of tobacco;
1 litre of spirits, 1 litre of wine.

Local time
GMT+2 hrs.

Embassy phone numbers
Johannesburg:

Australia 922.5268	Switzerland 838.5102
Canada 834.6521	W. Germany 23.6166
Denmark 838.7167	UK 21.8161
Netherlands 834.8401	USA 834.3051
Norway 834.5721	

Hotels
Johannesburg: Carlton, Landrost, Park Lane,
President, Rand International, Tollman Towers.
Cape Town: Mount Nelson, Herengracht, President,
De Waal. *Durban:* Edward, Elangeni, Beverly Hills,
Blue Waters. Prices vary but about 12–15 rand per night.

International banks
Barclays, Standard Bank of South Africa, Midland Bank,
Nedbank, Trust Bank of Africa, Volkskas Beperk.

Credit cards
All major credit cards.

Office hours
08.00–16.30 or 17.00 Mon–Fri.

National holidays
1 Jan, Good Friday, Easter Monday,
Ascension Day (May), 31 May, 4 Sept, 10 Oct,
16, 25, 26 Dec.

Voltage
380–220 volts, except in Pretoria and Port Elizabeth,
where it is 433–250 volts.

Communications
Tel: 2.40 rand per min. *Telex:* 2.38 rand per min.
Airmail: 4–5 days. *Cable:* 18 cents per word
(7-word minimum).

Social customs
European business customs prevail throughout
South Africa, together with much hospitality. The
working day begins much earlier than in Europe.
Business entertaining is divided equally between the
republic's excellent hotels (among them some of the
cheapest five-star accommodation in the world) and
businessmen's homes. Food is served in more than ample
portions and drinks are poured in large measures.
South African wines are excellent.
Best buys: African drums, zebra skins, masks, spears,
beads.

Spain

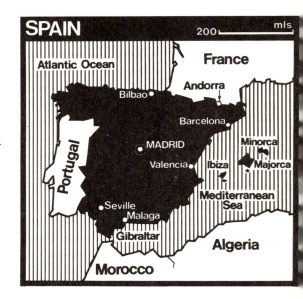

Area and population
474,875 sq kms (189,950 sq mls). Pop. 35 million.
Capital: Madrid (3.5 million).
Chief cities: Barcelona (3.6 m), Bilboa (950,000),
Valencia (1 m), Seville (788,000), Zaragoza (550,000),
Malaga (350,000), Vigo (250,000),
San Sebastian (162,000). *Ports:* Bilbao, Malaga,
Santander, Cadiz, Huelva. *Airports:* Barajas (Madrid),
Barcelona, Malaga.

Climate
Temperate in the north, dry, hot summers in central
and southern areas. Madrid temperatures range from
8° to 39°C (46° to 102°F). Humidity is 63%–90%.
Clothing: Medium-weight clothing in winter, lightweight
in summer.

People
Southern European. *Religion:* Roman Catholic.
Distribution: 48% urban.

Language

Spanish. *English rating:* Good.

Economic background

Big economic changes have occurred in recent years. Local industry has grown, both in consumer and heavy engineering sectors, and the demands of the tourist trade have led to fundamental changes in agriculture, from wheat and cheap wine to meat, vegetables and feed grains. The government assists economic growth through financial incentives in given sectors.

Trade

Gross National Product: US$35,000 million.
Exports: 440,000 million pesetas, chiefly footwear, textiles, clothing, non-electrical machinery, chemicals, furniture. *Imports:* 930,000 million pesetas, chiefly feed grains, machinery, transport equipment, metals, chemicals, tobacco. *Chief trading partners:* USA, Saudi Arabia, W. Germany, France, UK, Italy, Iraq, Netherlands, Japan, Switzerland, Brazil, Iran, Belgium, Sweden, Algeria, Cuba, Portugal, Venezuela. *Inflation rate:* 22%.

Prospects

With tourism improving and industrial development continuing, Spain is expected to expand considerably in coming years, although political stability following the death of Franco has still to be achieved.

Currency

Peseta = 100 centimos. £ = 145.80 pesetas; $ = 77.55 pesetas.

Travel

Visas not required.

Vaccinations

Only if travelling from or via an infected area.

Airlines

British Airways, Iberia, Alitalia, Sabena, Swissair, Aviaco, SAS, South African Airways, LOT, CSA, Pan Am, TAP, Malev, Balkan, Aerolineas Argentinas, Varig, TWA.
Flying times (to Madrid): Copenhagen $3\frac{1}{4}$ hrs; London 3 hrs; New York $6\frac{3}{4}$ hrs; Sydney 26 hrs.
Fares: Copenhagen F Dkr2,220 Y Dkr1,700; London F £126 Y £94; New York F $684 Y $325; Sydney F A$1,473 Y A$940.
Airport to city: 16 kms (10 mls).
Taxi fare: 200 pesetas. *Bus fare:* 35 pesetas.

Duty-free allowances

200 cigarettes *or* 50 cigars *or* 250 grammes of tobacco; 1 bottle of spirits.

Local time

GMT+1 hr (+2 hrs Apr–Sept).

Embassy phone numbers

Madrid:

Australia 458.7200	Sweden 419.7550
Canada 225.9119	Switzerland 225.4461
Denmark 226.8296	W. Germany 419.9100
Japan 270.2205	UK 419.0200
Netherlands 458.2100	USA 276.3400

Hotels

Madrid: Castellana, Eurobuilding, IFA Madrid, Luz Palacio, Melia Castilla, Melia Madrid, Mindanao, Monte Real, Palace, Plaza, Ritz, Villa Magna, Wellington. *Barcelona:* Arycasa, Avenida Palace, Colon, Diplomatic. Prices range from 1,500 to 2,000 pesetas per night.

International banks

Bank of London and South America, Crédit Lyonnais.

Credit cards

American Express, Barclaycard, Diners Club.

Office hours

Considerable variation, but generally 09.00–14.00 and 16.00–18.45 Mon–Fri in winter, 09.00–14.00 in summer.

National holidays

1, 6 Jan, 19 Mar, Maundy Thursday ($\frac{1}{2}$ day), Good Friday, 1 May, Ascension Day (May), Corpus Christi (May *or* June), 24 June, 25 July, 15 Aug, 12 Oct, 1 Nov, 8, 25 Dec.

Voltage

110–125 volts AC 50 cycles, but 220 volts AC 50 cycles in modern hotels.

Communications

Tel: 190 pesetas per 3 mins. *Telex:* 18 pesetas per 3 mins. *Airmail:* 3 days. *Cable:* 11 pesetas per word (7-word minimum).

Social customs

A land of great hospitality—but rarely in the home. A courteous and friendly people. Lunch is usually at 14.30 and dinner at 21.30 or later. *Best buys:* Clothes, ceramics, leather goods, straw-work, fans and Spanish brandy.

Economic background

While basically an agricultural country, Sri Lanka (formerly Ceylon) still needs to import much of its food, causing acute shortages of foreign currency. The government has embarked on a series of development plans, with agriculture, industry and the creation of new jobs as its principal targets.

Trade

Gross National Product: US$2,500 million.
Exports: US$430 million, chiefly tea, coconut, coffee, rubber, animal and vegetable oils, fruits and nuts.
Imports: US$430 million, chiefly cereals, petroleum, fertilisers, machinery, boilers, cotton, vehicles.
Chief trading partners: USA, Japan, France, China, UK, W. Germany, Australia, Pakistan, India, USSR, Canada.
Inflation rate: 1.3%.

Prospects

Much depends upon the success of the government's plans to expand industry and develop agriculture. Sri Lanka is the recipient of foreign aid.

Currency

Rupee = 100 cents. £ = 29.26 rupees; $ = 15.56 rupees.

Travel

Entry visas required.

Vaccinations

Smallpox. If arriving from an infected area, yellow fever and cholera.

Airlines

Air Ceylon, British Airways, UTA, KLM, Swissair, Aeroflot, PIA, SIA, Indian Airlines, Thai,
Flying times: Copenhagen 16 hrs; London 22 hrs; New York 24 hrs; Sydney 14 hrs.
Fares: Copenhagen F Dkr6,830 Y Dkr4,460; London F £526.50 Y £343.50; New York F $1,540 Y $939; Sydney F A$854 Y A$610.
Airport to city: 32.2 kms (20 mls). *Taxi fare:* 85 rupees.

Duty-free allowances

200 cigarettes *or* 50 cigars *or* 12 oz tobacco; 2 bottles of spirits, 2 bottles of wine.

Local time

GMT + $5\frac{1}{2}$ hrs.

Area and population

64,644 sq kms (24,959 sq mls). Pop. 13.2 million.
Capital: Colombo (564,000).
Chief cities: Jaffna (107,000), Kandy (92,000), Galle (71,000), Negombo (56,000), Trincomalee (40,000). *Ports:* Colombo, Galle, Trincomalee. *Airports:* Bandaranaike (Colombo), Ratmalana (Colombo).

Climate

Temperatures in Colombo range from 26° to 28°C (79° to 82°F), with the hottest time Mar–May and coolest time late Nov–early Feb. Best time to visit is Oct–Feb. *Clothing:* Light tropical clothing throughout the year, except in cool hill districts, where warm clothing is needed. Sunglasses needed.

People

70% Sinhalese, 22% Tamil.
Religion: 67% Buddhist, 17% Hindu, 8% Christian, 7% Moslem. *Distribution:* 19% urban.

Languages

Sinhalese and Tamil. *English rating:* Excellent.

Sri Lanka

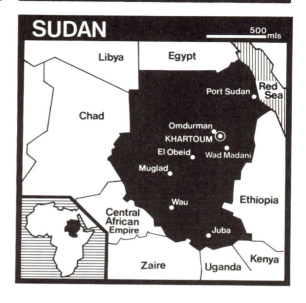

Embassy phone numbers
Colombo: UK 27611.

Hotels
Colombo: Galle Face, Havelock Tourinn, Inter-Continental, Taprobane, Holiday Inn, Mount Lavinia Hyatt. Prices up to 200 rupees per night.

International banks
Bank of Ceylon, Chartered Bank, Hong Kong and Shanghai Banking Corporation, Grindlays, State Bank of India.

Credit cards
American Express, Diners Club.

Office hours
08.30–16.30 Mon–Fri.

National holidays
Many and varied, so check before departure. Fixed holidays include 1 Jan, 1, 22 May, 30 June, 25, 26, 31 Dec.

Voltage
230–240 volts 50 cycles AC.

Communications
Tel: 40 rupees per 3 mins. *Telex:* 50 rupees per 3 mins. *Airmail:* 4–7 days. *Cable:* 1.25 rupees per word.

Social customs
Since Sri Lanka is a multi-religion country, it's best to consult locally before offering entertainment. Water should be boiled or filtered. Anti-malarial drugs should be taken if intending to visit isolated parts.

Area and population
2,505,805 sq kms (967,491 sq mls). Pop. 18.2 million. *Capital:* Khartoum (321,000). *Chief cities:* Omdurman (305,000), Port Sudan (123,000), El Obeid (74,000), Wad Madani (81,000), Juba (75,000). *Port:* Port Sudan. *Airport:* Civil (Khartoum).

Climate
In the northern desert and along the Red Sea coast, dry heat with a temperature of more than 38°C (100°F) prevails the year round. Khartoum temperatures range from 32°C (90°F) in winter to 41°C (106°F) in summer. Best time to visit is Oct–mid-Apr. *Clothing:* Lightweight and usually informal. Suits required only for the most formal calls.

People
40% Arabs, 20% Negroid, 14% black African tribesmen, 6% Beja tribesmen, 5% Nuba, 5% Nilo-Hamitic, 5% Sudanic plus minorities of West Africans, Egyptians, Asians and Europeans. *Religion:* 70% Moslem, 27% animist, 1% Christian and small Jewish and Hindu minorities. *Distribution:* 13% urban.

Language
Arabic. *English rating:* Good.

Economic background
Primarily agricultural and largely dependent on cotton,

Sudan's economy is gradually becoming more industrialised, although only 10% of the population earn their living from industry, mostly in the processing of agricultural and fishing products. Light industries include tanning, cement, brewing, meat-packing, canning, sugar refining, soap, spinning, weaving, hosiery and knitwear. Most industry is located in Khartoum North. New industries are being set up through government investment.

Trade
Gross National Product: £S752 million.
Exports: £S122 million, chiefly raw cotton, foodstuffs and live animals, peanuts, castor oil seed.
Imports: £S247 million, chiefly machinery, transport equipment, chemicals, textiles, sugar, cereals, iron and steel. *Chief trading partners:* Iran, India, UK, China, USA, W. Germany, Japan, Italy, France, Saudi Arabia, Netherlands, Venezuela, Egypt, Hong Kong, Belgium, Thailand. *Inflation rate:* 16.1%.

Prospects
Through development plans, the government is encouraging the modernisation of agriculture and irrigation, together with the expansion of tobacco, coffee, tea, rice and sugar plantations.

Currency
Sudanese pound (£S) = 100 piastres = 1,000 milliemes.
£ = £S0.752; $ = £S0.400.

Travel
Visas required.

Vaccinations
Smallpox and cholera. Travellers intending to visit Southern Sudan should have a yellow fever certificate.

Airlines
British Airways, Sudan Airways, Alitalia, Ethiopian, Saudi, Swissair, Interflug, Lufthansa, Air France, MEA, Egyptair, Kuwait.
Flying times: Copenhagen $11\frac{1}{4}$ hrs; London 8 hrs; New York $15\frac{1}{2}$ hrs; Sydney 24 hrs.
Fares: Copenhagen F Dkr4,765 Y Dkr3,680; London F £351.50 Y £257.50; New York F $1,060 Y $689; Sydney F A$1,128 Y A$746.
Airport to city: 4 kms (2.5 mls). *Taxi fare:* £S0.50.

Duty-free allowances
200 cigarettes *or* 50 cigars *or* 1 lb tobacco; $\frac{1}{2}$ litre of spirits.

Local time
GMT+2 hrs (+3 hrs in summer)

Embassy phone numbers
Khartoum: UK 70760.

Hotels
Khartoum: Sudan, Oasis, Acropole, Metropole, Excelsior, Sahara, Meridien, Canary. Prices range up to £S15 per night.

International banks
None.

Credit cards
None.

Office hours
08.30–13.30 and 17.00–20.00 Sat–Thurs.

National holidays
All Moslem holidays plus 1 Jan, 3 Mar, Easter (Western and Orthodox; Christians only), 25 May, 12 Oct, 25 Dec.

Voltage
240–415 volts AC.

Communications
Tel: £S4.11 per 3 mins. *Telex:* £S3.135 per 3 mins. *Airmail:* 2–3 days. *Cable:* 126 milliemes per word.

Social customs
Nothing of significance to the visitor, but extreme caution needs to be taken with the heat.

Area and population
449,750 sq kms (173,624 sq mls). Pop. 8.2 million.
Capital: Stockholm (1.6 million).
Chief cities: Gothenburg (Goteborg) (692,000),
Malmo (450,000), Uppsala (140,000),
Norrkoping (120,000). *Ports:* Gothenburg, Malmo,
Halsingborg. *Airport:* Arlanda (Stockholm).

Climate
Varied. Temperatures in Stockholm range from
−3°C (27°F) to more than 21°C (70°F). Average
humidity 80%. Winter lasts Nov–Apr; coldest time
Dec–Mar. *Clothing:* Warm outer clothes in winter, but
lightweight suits and dresses as everywhere, even trains,
tends to be over-heated.

People
Northern European. *Religion:* 99% Lutheran.
Distribution: 77% urban.

Language
Swedish. *English rating:* Excellent.

Economic background
Until recent years Sweden's economy was thought to be
a model of the welfare state in operation. It produced
one of the highest living standards in the world, but
strains started to show in 1974 when the government
tried to keep the country in full employment at a time
of world recession. Sweden's production costs rose
dramatically—nearly 30% between 1974 and 1976—as a
result of high wages, and the government is still
committed to a policy of full employment by supporting
home consumption.

Trade
Gross National Product: US$36,350 million.
Exports: 80,217 million kronor, chiefly machinery,
transport equipment, paper, iron and steel, pulp, timber,
ores. *Imports:* 83,264 million kronor, chiefly machinery,
petroleum, transport, equipment, textile yarn, iron and
steel, non-ferrous metals. *Chief trading partners:* EEC and
OPEC countries, USA, Norway, Finland, Japan,
USSR, Poland, Switzerland. *Inflation rate:* 12.9%.

Prospects
Awaiting a world trade boom, Sweden is committed to
sustaining its economy through state subsidies.

Currency
Krona = 100 ore. £ = 8.58 kronor; $ = 4.56 kronor.

Travel
No visas required for visitors staying up to 90 days.

Vaccinations
None.

Airlines
SAS, British Airways, Air Canada, Air France, Austrian,
Iberia, JAT, KLM, Kuwait, Pan Am, Sabena, TWA.
Flying times: Copenhagen 1¼ hrs; London 2½ hrs;
New York 9 hrs; Sydney 24 hrs.
Fares: Copenhagen F Dkr855 Y Dkr655;
London F £204 Y £136; New York F $762 Y $374;
Sydney F A$1,512 Y A$978.
Airport to city: 41 km (25 mls). *Taxi fare:* 100–120 kronor.

Duty-free allowances
Visitors living in Europe: 200 cigarettes *or* 50 cigars;
1 litre wine, ¾ litre spirits.
Visitors living outside Europe: 400 cigarettes *or* 100 cigars;
2 litres wine, 2 litres spirits.

Switzerland

Local time
GMT+1 hr.

Embassy phone numbers
Stockholm:

Australia 24.46.60	Norway 67.06.20
Canada 23.79.20	Switzerland 23.15.50
Denmark 23.18.60	W. Germany 63.13.80
Japan 63.04.40	UK 67.01.40
Netherlands 24.71.80	US 63.05.20

Hotels
Stockholm: Carlton, Diplomat, Grand, Park. All between 150 and 225 kronor per night, plus 15% service and 15% taxes.

International banks
Most banks represented.

Credit cards
American Express, Diners Club.

Office hours
08.30–17.00 Mon–Fri. Many offices open and close 1 hr earlier in summer.

National holidays
1, 6 Jan, Good Friday, Easter Monday, 1 May, Ascension Day (May), Whit Monday (May *or* June), Midsummer Day (June), All Saints (Nov), 25, 26 Dec.

Voltage
220 volts AC and DC (domestic), 220–380 volts 3-phase (industrial).

Communications
Tel: 9.90 kronor per 3 mins. *Telex:* 3.45 kronor per 3 mins. *Airmail:* 2–3 days. *Cable:* 15.95 kronor minimum charge.

Social customs
Punctuality is the norm. There is considerable business entertainment, in restaurants or in the home. It is customary to take flowers to the host's wife. There is much use of titles. Safety excellent.

Area and population
41,287 sq kms (15,941 sq mls). Pop. 6.2 million.
Capital: Berne (Bern) (162,000).
Chief cities: Zurich (422,000), Basle (Basel) (212,000), Geneva (173,000), Lausanne (173,000), Winterthur (91,000), St Gallen (80,000), Lucerne (Luzern) (67,000), Bienne (61,000).
Airports: Kloten (Zurich), Cointrin (Geneva), Basle.

Climate
Varies with altitude. Average Zurich temperatures range from −1°C (30.2°F) in winter to 15°C (59°F) in summer. Geneva temperatures are similar but slightly warmer in summer. *Clothing:* European clothing.

People
65% Swiss-German, 18% French, 12% Italian.
Religion: 52% Roman Catholic, 45% Protestant.
Distribution: 45% urban.

Languages
German, French and Italian. *English rating:* Excellent.

Economic background
Highly industrialised, with one of the highest *per capita* incomes in the world, Switzerland is among the most

prosperous countries. Although its population is small, its industries include heavy engineering, heavy electrical equipment, textiles, footwear, watchmaking, chemicals and pharmaceuticals, as well as a wide range of light industry. Agriculture, which is heavily subsidised, is also important to the economy.

Trade
Gross National Product: 133,800 million Swiss francs.
Exports: 37,045 million francs, chiefly machinery, watches, chemicals, textiles.
Imports: 36,871 million francs, chiefly chemicals, crude oil, clothing, machinery, vehicles.
Chief trading partners: W. Germany, France, Italy, USA, UK, Austria, Netherlands, Belgium/Luxembourg, Japan, Sweden. *Inflation rate:* 1.4%.

Prospects
Switzerland's financial and industrial stability is still regarded as among the firmest in Europe, but in order to protect its currency the government is imposing restrictions on the amount of Swiss francs each visitor may bring into the country.

Currency
Franc = 100 centimes. £ = SFr3.44; $ = SFr1.82.

Travel
Visas not required.

Vaccinations
Not required.

Airlines
All major international airlines.
Flying times: Copenhagen $1\frac{3}{4}$ hrs; London $1\frac{1}{2}$ hrs; New York $8\frac{1}{2}$ hrs; Sydney 30 hrs.
Fares (to Zurich): Copenhagen F Dkr1,700 Y Dkr1,215; London F £104.50 Y £69.50; New York F $717 Y $347; Sydney F A$1,459 Y A$929.
Airport to city: Zurich 12 kms (7.5 mls); Geneva 4 kms (2.5 mls). *Taxi fares:* Zurich SFr25; Geneva SFr12.

Duty-free allowances
Visitors living in Europe: 200 cigarettes *or* 50 cigars *or* 250 grammes of tobacco; 1 litre of spirits, 2 litres of wine.
Visitors living outside Europe: 400 cigarettes *or* 100 cigars *or* 500 grammes of tobacco; 1 litre of spirits, 2 litres of wine.

Local time
GMT+1 hr.

Embassy phone numbers
Zurich:

Denmark 25.05.25	Sweden 25.26.33
Japan 24.08.11	W. Germany 32.69.36
Netherlands 32.18.88	UK 47.15.20
Norway 32.69.90	USA 55.25.66

Hotels
Zurich: Ascot, Astor, Carlton Elite, Continental, Dolder Grand, Eden au Lac, St Gotthard, Zurich.
Geneva: D'Angleterre, Arbalete, Beau-Rivage, Des Bergues, Bristol, Inter-Continental, Mediterranée, De la Paix, President, La Réserve, Du Rhône. Prices to suit all pockets can be found, but a good-class hotel is now charging up to SFr145 per night.

International banks
International banking centre. Leading banks include Swiss Bank Corporation, Union Bank of Switzerland, Swiss Credit Bank, Lloyds Bank International, First National City Bank, British Bank of the Middle East, Handelsbank, Barclays International, Midland.

Credit cards
All major credit cards.

Office hours
08.00–12.00 and 14.00–18.00 Mon–Fri.

National holidays
Many local holidays and holiday periods, plus 1 Jan, Good Friday, Easter Monday, Ascension Day (May), Whit Monday (May *or* June), 1 Aug, 25, 31 Dec.

Voltage
220 volts AC 50 cycles.

Communications
Tel: SFr2 per min. *Telex:* SFr1 per min. *Airmail:* 1–2 days.
Cable: SFr7.50 for 7-word minimum.

Social customs
A more formal approach to business is taken than in most other parts of Europe. Promptness is important. If invited to dinner, it is customary to give the hostess flowers or chocolates. *Best buys:* Watches, chocolate, cheese, sports clothes, embroidered textiles, ceramics and music-boxes.

SYRIA
100 mls
Turkey
Mediterranean Sea
• Aleppo
Hama •
Deir ez Zor •
• Homs
Abu Kemal •
Lebanon
Iran
○ DAMASCUS
Dera •
Jordan
Israeli-occupied
territories
Israel

Area and population
184,434 sq kms (71,210 sq mls). Pop. 6.3 million.
Capital: Damascus (1.6 million).
Chief cities: Aleppo (792,000), Homs (613,000),
Hama (586,000), Latakia (435,000),
Deir-ez-Zor (326,000), Hasakeh (532,000),
Idleb (421,000). *Port:* Latakia.
Airport: International (Damascus).

Climate
Hot summers, cold winters. Spring and autumn
temperatures range from 20°C (70°F) to 27°C (84°F), in
the winter from 5°C (40°F) to 15°C (60°F), and in summer
from 30°C (90°F) to 35°C (100°F). *Clothing:* Lightweight
essential for summer. An overcoat is often useful in
winter. Spring and summer evenings can be chilly.

People
Arab. *Religion:* 87% Moslem, 13% Christian.
Distribution: 40% urban.

Language
Arabic. French and English are also commercial
languages. *English rating:* Fair.

Economic background
With a state-controlled economy, Syria allows private
enterprise to function. But all of Syria's development
programmes remain in the hands of the government.
Industry is concentrated in the Damascus and Aleppo
areas, but Homs is beginning to build up as a

manufacturing centre. Latakia, the main port, is used as a
free trade zone for goods in transit to Iraq, Jordan,
Saudi Arabia and the Gulf.

Trade
Gross National Product: £S9,259 million.
Exports: £S3,440.9 million, chiefly cotton, live animals,
lentils. *Imports:* £S6,235 million, chiefly textiles,
machinery, petroleum, vehicles, food.
Chief trading partners: W. Germany, Italy, France, USA,
Japan, Brazil, UK, Lebanon, Romania, Switzerland,
USSR, Belgium, Yugoslavia, Greece.
Inflation rate: 6.5%.

Prospects
Many developments have been suspended as a result of
Syria's heavy commitment in the Lebanon.

Currency
Syrian pound (£S) = 100 piastres. £ = £S7.37;
$ = £S3.92.

Travel
Visas required.

Vaccinations
Smallpox.

Airlines
British Airways, Syrian, SAS, Air France, KLM, Lufthansa,
Austrian, Alitalia, MEA, Pan Am, Malev.
Flying times: Copenhagen $7\frac{1}{2}$ hrs; London $4\frac{3}{4}$ hrs;
New York 13 hrs; Sydney 27 hrs.
Fares: Copenhagen F Dkr3,560 Y Dkr2,420;
London F £283.50 Y £192.50; New York F $987
Y $665; Sydney F A$1,133 Y A$750.
Airport to city: 30 kms (18 mls). *Taxi:* £S15.
Bus fare: £S1.

Duty-free allowances
200 cigarettes *or* 50 cigars *or* 500 grammes of tobacco;
1 bottle of spirits, 1 bottle of wine.

Local time
GMT+2 hrs (+3 hrs May–Aug).

Embassy phone numbers
Damascus:
Japan 339421   USA 332814
UK 332561

Syria

Hotels
Damascus: New Omayad, New Semiramis,
International Airport, Cattan's Meridien, Sheraton.
Prices about £S85 per night.

International banks
None.

Credit cards
American Express, Diners Club.

Office hours
Government offices: 08.00–14.00 Sat–Thurs.
Private offices: May–Oct: 08.30–13.30 and
17.00–20.00 Sat–Thurs. Oct–May: 09.00–14.00 and
16.00–19.00 Sat–Thurs.

National holidays
All Moslem holidays plus 1 Jan, 8 Mar, Western and
Orthodox Easter, 17 Apr, 23 July, 1 Sept, 25 Dec.

Voltage
115–200 volts or 220–380 volts AC.

Communications
Tel: £S40 per 3 mins. *Airmail:* 3 days. *Cable:* £S1.52 per
word. *Telex:* Available at some hotels.

Social customs
Syria's business atmosphere dictates patience and a
soft-note approach. Much coffee-drinking, sometimes in
coffee houses. Tipping is not prevalent in Syria.
Best buys: Copper and brassware, glass, silk brocades,
mother-of-pearl boxes. While bargaining still continues,
the government is encouraging shops to have fixed
prices.

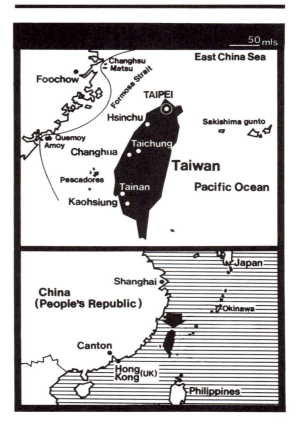

Area and population
35,981 sq kms (13,892 sq mls). Pop. 16.5 million.
Capital: Taipei (2.1 million).
Major cities: Kaohsiung (1.1 m), Tainan, Taichung,
Hsinchu. *Ports:* Kaohsiung, Keelung.
Airport: Sung Shan (Taipei).

Climate
Tropical and sub-tropical, with warm summers and mild
winters. Temperatures range from 15°C (59°F) to
30°C (86°F). Summer is long (Apr–Nov).
Clothing: Lightweight. Conservative business suits are
recommended.

People
Predominantly Chinese plus 1% aborigines of Indonesian
descent. *Religion:* Taoism and Buddhism, with strong
Christian and Moslem minorities.
Distribution: Predominantly urban.

Language
Mandarin. *English rating:* Excellent.

Economic background

For the past 20 years Taiwan has been developing from an agricultural to an industrial economy and has built up a strong export trade, particularly in textiles, machinery and electrical appliances. Food processing, chemicals and chemical products, tobacco, glass, cement, leather and rubber are also important. In agriculture, rice is the single most important crop, and there are important sugar, pineapple, hemp and jute, and fruit and vegetable sectors.

Trade

Gross National Product: US$14,400 million.
Exports: US$5,300 million, chiefly textile yarns and fabrics, clothing, telecommunications equipment, plywood, metals, machinery, sugar, fruit, rice and cement.
Imports: US$5,900 million, chiefly fuel, petroleum, chemicals, lubricants, machine tools, ores, manufactured goods, cotton, wool, transport equipment.
Chief trading partners: USA, Japan, Hong Kong, W. Germany, Australia, Canada, Thailand.
Inflation rate: Not available.

Prospects

In spite of Taiwan's precarious political situation—the island is still claimed by Mainland China—industrial expansion is continuing, based on an ample and relatively cheap supply of labour.

Currency

New Taiwan dollar (NT$) = 100 cents. £ = NT$67.68; $ = NT$36.00.

Travel

Visas required.

Vaccinations

Smallpox, cholera.

Airlines

All Nippon, Cathay Pacific, China Air Lines, Korean, Malaysian, Northwest, Philippine, Singapore, Thai.
Flying times: Copenhagen 22½ hrs; London 24 hrs; New York 26 hrs; Sydney 19 hrs (including overnight stay in Kuala Lumpur or Hong Kong).
Fares: Copenhagen F Dkr9,600 Y Dkr5,800; London F £740 Y £447; New York F $1,825 Y $1,170; Sydney F A$887 Y A$633.
Airport to city: 5 kms (3.1 mls). *Taxi fare:* NT$50.

Duty-free allowances

200 cigarettes *or* 25 cigars *or* ½ lb tobacco; 1 bottle of spirits.

Local time

GMT+8 hrs.

Embassy phone numbers

Taipei: USA 333551.

Hotels

Taipei: Ambassador, Hilton, Olympic, Grand, Imperial, Mandarin, President. Prices up to US$35 per night.

International banks

Most US banks.

Credit cards

All major credit cards.

Office hours

08.00–12.00 and 13.00–17.00 Mon–Fri, 08.00–12.00 Sat.

National holidays

1 Jan, Chinese New Year (Jan *or* Feb), 29 Mar, Dragon Boat Festival (May *or* June), 10, 25, 31 Oct, 13 Nov, 25 Dec.

Voltage

110–220 volts AC.

Communications

Tariffs not available.

Social customs

A warm welcome, with much entertaining, awaits overseas businessmen. Business cards, which should be also be printed in Mandarin, are produced quickly and cheaply in Taipei.

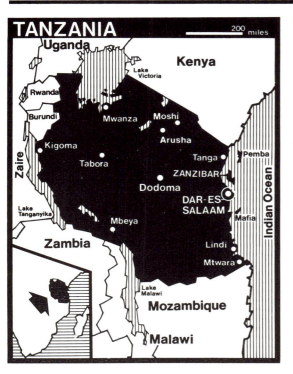

Economic background

One of the 25 poorest nations in the world, according to the United Nations, Tanzania has a widely-based agricultural economy and earns its revenue from cotton, coffee, sisal and tobacco. Textiles, cement, cigarettes and beer are manufactured locally, with the primary aim of saving foreign exchange. The government encourages the establishment of import-substitution industries.

Trade

Gross National Product: 9,850 million shillings.
Exports: 2,500 million shillings, chiefly coffee, cotton, diamonds, sisal, cashew nuts. *Imports:* 3,500 million shillings, chiefly machinery and industrial equipment, manufactured goods, textiles.
Chief trading partners: China, UK, Japan, W. Germany, Iran, India, Hong Kong. *Inflation rate:* 7.2%.

Prospects

Agriculture will remain Tanzania's main source of income for the foreseeable future.

Currency

Shilling (Tshs) = 100 cents. £ = Tshs14.58; $ = Tshs7.75.

Travel

Visitors' passes are required, obtainable either at Tanzanian embassies or at the point of entry.

Vaccinations

Smallpox. Yellow fever inoculation recommended.

Airlines

Air France, Alitalia, Air Zaire, British Airways, Ethiopian, KLM, Lufthansa, Pan Am, Sabena, SAS, Swissair, Zambia.
Flying times: Copenhagen $12\frac{1}{4}$ hrs; London $16\frac{1}{4}$ hrs; New York 20 hrs; Sydney 24 hrs.
Fares: Copenhagen F Dkr7,490 Y Dkr4,780; London F £546.50 Y £345; New York F $1,213 Y $802; Sydney F A$1,128 Y A$746.
Airport to city: 13 kms (8 mls). *Taxi fare:* Tshs50.

Duty-free allowances

250 grammes of cigarettes, cigars *or* tobacco; 1 litre of spirits *or* wine.

Local time

GMT+3 hrs.

Area and population

942,004 sq kms (363,708 sq mls). Pop. 14.8 million.
Capital: Dar es Salaam (460,000).
Chief cities: Zanzibar (81,000), Tanga (84,000), Arusha (73,000), Mwanza (52,000), Dodoma (50,000). Dodoma is destined to be the new capital.
Ports: Dar es Salaam, Zanzibar, Tanga.
Airport: International (Dar es Salaam).

Climate

Hot and humid for much of the year, with temperatures rising to over 32°C (90°F) Dec–Apr. Humidity over 90%. June–Sept temperatures rise to 21°C (70°F); this is the best time to visit. *Clothing:* Much informality and even tropical-weight lounge suits seldom needed. Best to pack plenty of cotton clothing, including underwear.

People

99% African, chiefly Bantu, small minorities of Asians, Arabs and Europeans. *Religion:* 31% Moslem, 25% Christian, the rest animist. *Distribution:* 5% urban.

Language

Swahili. *English rating:* Excellent.

Tanzania

Embassy phone numbers
Dar es Salaam: UK 29601.

Hotels
Dar es Salaam: Kilimanjaro, New Africa, Oyster Bay.
Prices about Tshs200 per night.

International banks
None.

Credit cards
American Express, Diners Club.

Office hours
07.30–14.30 Mon–Fri.

National holidays
Moslem holidays plus 12 Jan, 5 Feb, Good Friday,
Easter Monday, 26 Apr, 1 May, 7 July, 9, 25 Dec.

Voltage
230 volts, 50 cycles AC.

Communications
Tel: Tshs75 per 3 mins. *Telex:* Tshs60 per 3 mins.
Airmail: 3–4 days. *Cable:* Tshs1.85 per word
(7-word minimum).

Social customs
In business circles, European customs prevail, but visitors
should be aware that their contacts may be Hindus or
Moslems. Tanzania is sensitive about visitors
photographing bridges, railways and government
buildings. Visitors should take care not to walk alone in
lonely places, and at night even main streets in
Dar es Salaam are not regarded as safe.

Thailand

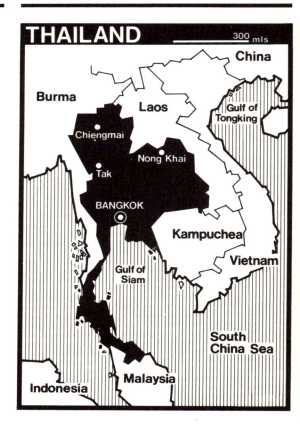

Area and population
514,000 sq kms (198,455 sq mls). Pop. 43 million.
Capital: Bangkok (3.2 million).
Chief city: Chiengmai (500,000). *Port:* Bangkok.
Airport: Don Muang (Bangkok).

Climate
Temperature remains fairly constant around 30°C (86°F),
but humidity varies considerably. Best time to visit is
mid-Nov to early/mid-Jan. Apr and May are very hot.
It rains about two hours a day July–Oct.
Clothing: Tropical. Dark suits are favoured for evening
wear.

People
Primarily Thai stock. *Religion:* Predominantly Buddhist
but with a Moslem minority in the south.
Distribution: 15% urban.

Language
Thai. *English rating:* Good.

Economic background

The Thai economy is still largely based on the production of basic agricultural, mineral, forest and other raw materials. The main crop is rice, followed by sugar, tapioca and maize. Tourism is also increasing in importance. Industrialisation, which has been under way for 20 years, is being encouraged by the government and there are now oil refineries, iron and steel plants, textile plants, vehicle assembly plants and tyre factories. Oil and gas have been found in the Gulf of Thailand.

Trade

Gross National Product: US$14,500 million.
Exports: 31,146 million baht, chiefly rice, rubber, maize, tin, cement, jute. *Imports:* 42,184 million baht, chiefly machinery, transport equipment, iron, steel, fuel, lubricants, chemicals, manufactured goods, raw materials. *Chief trading partners:* Japan, USA, W. Germany, UK, Australia, Taiwan, Kuwait, France, Switzerland, Italy, Singapore, Hong Kong, Malaysia. *Inflation rate:* 8.3%.

Prospects

The Thai economy is very flexible and is changing to meet the new economic circumstances in South East Asia.

Currency

Baht = 100 sarang. £ = 38.09 baht; $ = 20.26 baht.

Travel

Visas required. Most common visas are transit visas, permitting a 7-day stay, or tourist visas, permitting a 30-day stay. The Thai government may refuse entry to visitors (e.g. hippies) who do not comply with their requirements regarding general appearance and clothing.

Vaccinations

Smallpox.

Airlines

Aeroflot, Air France, Air India, Alitalia, British Airways, Burma, Cathay Pacific, Finnair, Garuda, KLM, Lufthansa, Malaysian, PIA, Pan Am, Philippine, Qantas, Sabena, SAS, SIA, Swissair, Thai.
Flying times: Copenhagen 12 hrs; London $13\frac{1}{2}$ hrs; New York 22 hrs; Sydney 8 hrs. *Fares:* Copenhagen F Dkr8,325 Y Dkr4,830; London F £647.50 Y £375.50; New York F $1,612 Y $996; Sydney F A$109 Y A$79.
Airport to city: 25 kms (15.5 mls). *Taxi fare:* 40 baht. Most hotels send limousines or transit vans to meet incoming flights.

Duty-free allowances

200 cigarettes *or* 250 grammes of cigars *or* tobacco; 1 litre of spirits *or* 1 bottle of wine.

Local time

GMT+7 hrs.

Embassy phone numbers

Bangkok: UK 252.7161

Hotels

Bangkok: Many and mainly excellent. Main ones include Amarin, Asia, Dusit Thani, Erawan, First, Indra, Manhattan, Montien, Oriental, President, Rama, Siam Inter-Continental, Sheraton. Prices up to 400–500 baht per night.

International banks

Hong Kong and Shanghai, Chartered, Mercantile, Mitsui, Banque de l'Indochine, Bank of America, Chase Manhattan, Bank of Tokyo.

Credit cards

All major credit cards.

Office hours

08.00–17.00 Mon–Fri, 08.00–12.00 Sat.

National holidays

Buddhist holidays plus 1 Jan, Chinese New Year (Jan *or* Feb), 6, 13 Apr, 1, 5 May, Ploughing Day (May), King's Birthday (Dec), 10, 31 Dec.

Voltage

220–380 volts AC.

Communications

Tel: 285 bahts per 3 mins. *Telex:* 285 bahts per 3 mins. *Airmail:* 3–4 days. *Cable:* 11 bahts per word.

Social customs

Remove shoes before entering a Thai home or a temple. Entertainment is extensive and elaborate. Bangkok's heat can be oppressive, with little or no alleviation at nightfall. Drink only bottled water. Thai food tends to be spicy and peppery, but many restaurants tone down the flavouring to meet European tastes. *Best buys:* Thai silk, wooden carvings, jewellery.

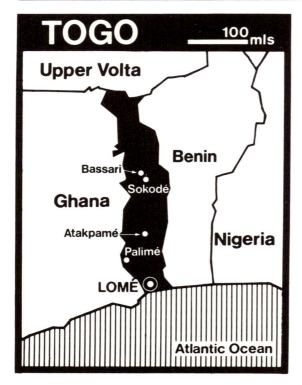

TOGO
100 mls

Upper Volta

Ghana

Bassari

Sokodé

Benin

Atakpamé

Palimé

LOMÉ

Nigeria

Atlantic Ocean

Area and population
56,785 sq kms (21,926 sq mls). Pop. 2.2 million.
Capital: Lomé (170,000).
Chief cities: Sokodé (30,000), Palimé (21,000),
Atakpamé (18,000), Bassari (16,000). *Port:* Lomé.
Airport: Lomé.

Climate
Humid and tropical. Average temperatures range from
22° to 35°C (72° to 95°F). Lomé has an average rainfall of
76.2 cm (30 in) Mar–July and Sept–Nov.
Clothing: Tropical.

People
Three main tribal groups: Ewe, Adja-Watyi and
Kabrai-Losso. *Religion:* 25% Christian, 11% Moslem, rest
animist. *Distribution:* 15% urban.

Language
French. *English rating:* Poor.

Economic background
Agriculture supports most of the population, the chief
crops being manioc, yams, maize, sorghum, millet, beans
and rice. Cash crops include coffee, cocoa and palm
kernels, and cotton production is increasing. Lime
phosphate produces much of Togo's export revenue.
Industry is still very small, with textiles and the processing
of agricultural products accounting for more than half of
all production.

Trade
Gross National Product: CFAfrs86,000 million.
Exports: CFAfrs45,174 million, chiefly phosphate, cocoa,
coffee, palm kernels, cotton, tapioca.
Imports: CFAfrs28,612 million, chiefly manufactured
goods, food, beverages and tobacco, fuels and
lubricants, raw materials. *Chief trading partners:* France
and other EEC countries, Venezuela, Japan, China, USA.
Inflation rate: Not available.

Prospects
With an open-door trade policy, Togo hopes to develop
its economy. Unlike other former French African nations,
it has not given France preferential trade treatment, and
so can count on wider trade contacts.

Currency
CFAfranc = 100 centimes. £ = CFAfrs421; $ = CFAfrs223.

Travel
Visas generally required.

Vaccinations
Smallpox and yellow fever.

Airlines
Air Afrique, Air Zaire, Ghana, Nigeria, UTA.
Flying times: Copenhagen $10\frac{1}{2}$ hrs; London 12 hrs;
New York 17 hrs; Sydney 30 hrs. *Fares:* Copenhagen
F Dkr6,595 Y Dkr4,315; London F £463 Y £297;
New York F $976 Y $604; Sydney F A$1,433 Y A$915.
Airport to city: 4 kms (2.5 mls). *Taxi fare:* About
CFAfrs500.

Duty-free allowances
200 cigarettes *or* 25 cigars *or* 250 grammes of tobacco;
1 bottle of spirits, 1 bottle of wine.

Local time
GMT.

Hotels

Lomé: Hotel de la Paix, Hotel de Bénin, Hotel du Golfe, Miramar, L'Auberge Provençale, Hotel de la Plage. Prices about CFAfrs4,500.

International banks

None.

Credit cards

All major credit cards.

Office hours

07.30–12.00 and 14.30–17.00 Mon–Fri, 07.30–12.00 Sat.

National holidays

1, 13 Jan, Easter Monday, 27 Apr, Ascension Day (May), 1 May, Whit Monday (May *or* June), 15 Aug, 1 Nov, 25 Dec.

Voltage

110–220 volts AC.

Communications

Tel: CFAfrs3,000 per 3 mins. *Telex:* CFAfrs2,500 per 3 mins. *Airmail:* 3–7 days. *Cable:* CFAfrs160 per word.

Social customs

Although Togo has been independent since 1960, many French business customs still prevail. Watch out for stomach upsets, wash all fruit and drink only bottled water. Swimmers, even strong ones, should be cautious of bathing in the sea since the surf is dangerous. Hotels and restaurants tend to be French-orientated.

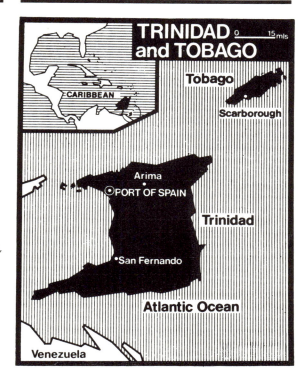

Area and population

5,128 sq kms (1,980 sq mls). Pop. 1.1 million.
Capital: Port of Spain (120,000).
Chief cities: None but towns include
San Fernando (60,000), Arima (20,000). Chief town of Tobago is Scarborough (3,000). *Port:* Port of Spain.
Airport: Piarco (Port of Spain).

Climate

Tropical and high humidity. Coolest months are Jan–Feb, when average temperature is 20°C (68°F). Warmest months are Apr, May and Oct, when average temperature is 32°C (98°F). *Clothing:* Tropical and tends to be informal.

People

43% Negro, 36% East Indian, 16% mixed descent, 2% European. *Religion:* 71% Christian, mainly Roman Catholic and Anglican, 23% Hindu, 6% Moslem. *Distribution:* 18% urban.

Language

English.

Economic background

Petroleum is now Trinidad and Tobago's main source of income, although it employs only about $7\frac{1}{2}$% of the working population. Agriculture, while employing 22%, contributes only 8% to gross national product. Main agricultural crops are sugar, cocoa and coffee. Manufacturing is growing steadily and there are now plants engaged in vehicle assembly, fertilisers, cement, furniture, clothing and agricultural produce.

Trade

Gross National Product: TT$4,103 million (1974).
Exports: TT$3,878 million, chiefly petroleum, lubricants, sugar, chemicals, fertilisers, fruit and vegetables, coffee.
Imports: TT$3,243 million, chiefly machinery, transport equipment, foodstuffs, manufactured goods, chemicals.
Chief trading partners: USA, UK, EEC countries, Japan, Commonwealth Caribbean, Canada.
Inflation rate: 10.2%.

Prospects

Trinidad and Tobago has plans to become the manufacturing centre of the Caribbean. For this reason the government encourages minority overseas investment.

Currency

Trinidad and Tobago dollar (TT$) = 100 cents.
£ = TT$4.51; $ = TT$2.39.

Travel

Visas not required.

Vaccinations

Smallpox.

Airlines

Air Canada, Air France, ALM, British Airways, BWIA, Eastern, KLM, Pan Am, SAS, Viasa.
Flying times: Copenhagen $13\frac{1}{4}$ hrs; London 9 hrs; New York $4\frac{3}{4}$ hrs; Sydney 28 hrs. *Fares:* Copenhagen F Dkr6,565 Y Dkr4,300; London F £450 Y £286; New York F $371 Y $248; Sydney F A$2,011 Y A$1,344.
Airport to city: 25.5 kms (16 mls). *Taxi fare:* TT$15.

Duty-free allowances

200 cigarettes *or* 50 cigars *or* $\frac{1}{2}$ lb tobacco; 40 ounces of spirits *or* 1 quart of wine.

Local time

GMT−4 hrs.

Embassy phone numbers

Port of Spain: UK 52861.

Hotels

Port of Spain: Hilton, Queen's Park, Bretton Hall, Holiday Inn, Chaconia Inn, Kapok, Farrell House, Gulf Coast, Bel Air, Pan American, Scarlet Ibis.
Tobago: Arnos Vale, Mount Irvine Bay, Radisson Crown Reef, Turtle Beach. Prices tend to be high, ranging up to US$50 in winter, but may be 50% cheaper in summer.

International banks

Barclays, Canadian Imperial Bank of Commerce, Bank of Nova Scotia, Chase Manhattan, Citibank.

Credit cards

All major credit cards.

Office hours

08.00–16.00 Mon–Fri.

National holidays

1 Jan, Carnival (Feb), Good Friday, Easter Monday, Whit Monday (May *or* June), Corpus Christi (May *or* June), 19 Jun, Discovery Day (Aug), 31 Aug, 24 Sept, 25, 26 Dec.

Voltage

115–400 volts AC.

Communications

Tel: TT$18.72 per 3 mins. *Telex:* Available in most hotels. *Airmail:* 3–4 days. *Cable:* 44 cents per word.

Social customs

One of the most cosmopolitan societies in the Caribbean. Overseas visitors meet an easy atmosphere and the food is some of the best in the region. Taxis are not marked— and are not cheap. Agree the price beforehand and ascertain whether the driver means US or TT dollars.

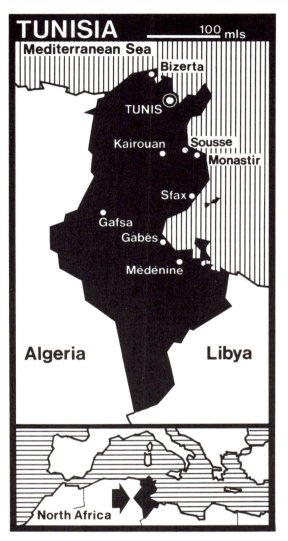

People
97% Arabs and Berbers, 1% European. *Religion:* Moslem. *Distribution:* 42% urban.

Language
Arabic. French is the main commercial language. *English rating:* Poor.

Economic background
Agriculture, phosphate rock, expanding industry and tourism are the mainstays of Tunisia's economy. Chief crops include wheat, barley, olives, citrus fruits, dates and grapes. All mineral deposits, including phosphate rock, are owned and mined by the government. Industry has progressed rapidly since independence, with the food industry accounting for 40% of the total value in manufacturing. European clothing firms have set up factories in Tunisia.

Trade
Gross National Product: 1,377 million dinars.
Exports: 397 million dinars, chiefly mineral fuels, animal and vegetable products, raw materials, food and live animals, chemicals, basic manufactures, beverages and tobacco. *Imports:* 488 million dinars, chiefly machinery and transport equipment, basic manufactures, food and live animals, chemicals, mineral fuels, raw materials, animal and vegetable products.
Chief trading partners: France, Italy, USA, W. Germany, UK, Iraq, Saudi Arabia, Belgium/Luxembourg, Brazil, Netherlands, Libya, Indonesia. *Inflation rate:* 9.6%.

Prospects
Tunisia's prospects are regarded as good, particularly in view of the government's incentive programme to encourage overseas investment.

Currency
Dinar (D) = 1,000 millimes. £ = D0.772; $ = D0.410.

Travel
Visas not required.

Vaccinations
Smallpox. TAB recommended.

Airlines
Aeroflot, Air Algérie, Air France, Balkan, British Caledonian, JAT, KLM, Kuwait, Lufthansa, Royal Air Maroc, Sabena, Saudia, Syrian, Swissair, Tunis Air.
Flying times: Copenhagen $4\frac{1}{2}$ hrs; London $2\frac{3}{4}$ hrs;

Area and population
164,150 sq kms (63,380 sq mls). Pop. 5.6 million.
Capital: Tunis (944,000).
Chief cities: Sfax (475,000), Sousse (255,000), Bizerta (62,000), Kairouan (54,000). *Ports:* Tunis, La Goulette, Sfax, Sousse, Bizerta. *Airport:* Carthage (Tunis).

Climate
Mediterranean and desert. Tunis, on the coast, has temperatures of up to 37°C (100°F) mid-May to Oct, but averages 13°C (55.5°F) for the rest of the year.
Clothing: Lightweight in summer, but warmer European clothes are needed in winter.

New York 12 hrs; Sydney 33 hrs. *Fares:* Copenhagen
F Dkr2,640 Y Dkr2,005; London F £140 Y £103.50;
New York F $797 Y $416; Sydney F A$1,395 Y A$891.
Airport to city: 8 kms (5 mls). *Taxi fare:* D1.

Duty-free allowances
200 cigarettes *or* 50 cigars *or* 14 ounces of tobacco;
1 litre of spirits.

Local time
GMT+1 hr (+2 hrs May–Sept).

Embassy phone numbers
Tunis: UK 245.100.

Hotels
Tunis: Africa, Hilton, Hotel du Lac, Hotel Majestic,
Tunisia Palace. Prices range up to D15 per night.

International banks
Arab Bank.

Credit cards
All major credit cards.

Office hours
Winter: 08.00–12.30 and 14.30–18.00 Mon–Fri,
08.30–13.00 Sat. *Summer:* 07.00–13.00 Mon–Sat.

National holidays
Moslem holidays plus 1, 18 Jan, 20 Mar, 9 Apr, 1 May,
1 June, 25 July, 3, 13 Aug, 15 Oct.

Voltage
220 volts AC.

Communications
Tel: D1.584 per 3 mins. *Telex:* D0.816 per 3 mins.
Airmail: 2–3 days. *Cable:* 99 millimes per word.

Social customs
A fairly informal business community, but a good
knowledge of French is needed in order to do business.
There are a number of good restaurants in Tunis.
Imported spirits are expensive, but local wine and beer
are good.

Area and population
780,372 sq kms (301,302 sq mls). Pop. 40.1 million.
Capital: Ankara (1.9 million).
Chief cities: Istanbul (2.6 m), Izmir (900,500).
Ports: Istanbul, Izmir, Mersin, Iskenderun.
Airports: Yesilkoy (Istanbul), Esenboga (Ankara).

Climate
Varies throughout country, but Ankara and Istanbul tend
to be warm, with temperatures ranging from 4.5°C (40°F)
in winter to 22.5°C (72°F) in summer. Summer humidity
over 80%. Apr–June and end Sept-early Dec are the
best times to visit. *Clothing:* Warm clothing needed in
winter, but lightweight clothing in late spring and
summer.

People
90% Turkish. *Religion:* Mostly Moslems but with
Christian and Jewish minorities. *Distribution:* 38% urban.

Language
Turkish. *English rating:* Good.

Economic background
Turkey is striving hard to find European prosperity
through a major expansion of industry and modernisation
of its agriculture. In recent years it has been beset with
political and international financial problems, but
nevertheless manages to keep up the momentum of
progress. Turkey is the recipient of development credits
from abroad, and from Britain it receives more aid than
any other non-Commonwealth country.

Trade
Gross National Product: 410,000 million lira.
Exports: US$1,600 million, chiefly cotton, fruit and
vegetables, tobacco, copper, live animals, cereals,

chromium ore, building materials.
Imports: US$5,000 million, chiefly machinery and electrical equipment, chemicals, mineral products, oil, base metals, textiles, rubber and plastics, paper-making materials. *Chief trading partners:* W. Germany, Iraq, USA, Italy, UK, Switzerland, France, Japan, Netherlands, Belgium/Luxembourg. *Inflation rate:* 44.6%.

Prospects
Could have some of the best in the area. The government is tackling economic problems with determination.

Currency
Lira = 100 kurus. £ = 45.75 liras; $ = 24.33 liras.

Travel
Visas not required.

Vaccinations
Not required unless coming from an infected area.

Airlines
Alitalia, Austrian, British Airways, SAS, El Al, Lufthansa, MEA, Balkan, Malev, Turkish fly to Istanbul. Pan Am, Lufthansa, MEA, Turkish fly to Ankara.
Flying times: Copenhagen $3\frac{1}{4}$ hrs; London 4 hrs; New York 15 hrs; Sydney 18 hrs. *Fares* (to Istanbul): Copenhagen F Dkr3,145 Y Dkr2,170; London F £224 Y £160; New York F $917 Y $505; Sydney F A$1,310 Y A$835.
Airport to city: Istanbul 24 kms (15 mls); Ankara 35 kms (22 mls). *Taxi fare:* Istanbul 100–125 liras; Ankara 150 liras.

Duty-free allowances
200 cigarettes *or* 50 grammes of tobacco *or* 20 cigars, 1 litre of spirits; 200 grammes of tea.

Local time
GMT+2 hrs (+3 hrs Apr–Sept).

Embassy phone numbers
Istanbul:

Denmark 40.42.17	W. Germany 44.49.47
Japan 45.25.33	UK 44.75.40
Netherlands 49.53.10	USA 45.32.20
Norway 49.97.53	Switzerland 48.50.70
Sweden 45.06.76.	

Hotels
Istanbul: Inter-Continental, Sheraton, Hilton, Park, Divan, Buyuk Tarabya. *Ankara:* Dedeman, Kent, Marmara. Prices up to US$50 per night.

International banks
None, but largest local banks, all with international connections, are Turkiye Is Bankasi, Yapi ve Kredi Bankasi, Akbank, Turk Ticaret Bankasi, Turkiye Granti Bankasi, Ottoman Bank.

Credit cards
American Express, Diners Club.

Office hours
08.30–12.00 and 13.00–17.30 Mon–Fri.

National holidays
Moslem holidays plus 1 Jan, 23 Apr, 1, 19, 27 May, 30 Aug, 29 Oct.

Voltage
110–200 volts AC (domestic), 380 volts AC (industrial).

Communications
Tel: 90 liras per 3 mins. *Telex:* 39 liras per 3 mins. *Airmail:* 3 days. *Cable:* 345 kurus per word (7-word minimum).

Social customs
Nearly all business entertaining is done in restaurants. Food, particularly fish, can be excellent. Turkish businessmen are becoming more westernised, in both business and social life. *Best buys:* Leather, gold, silverware and rugs.

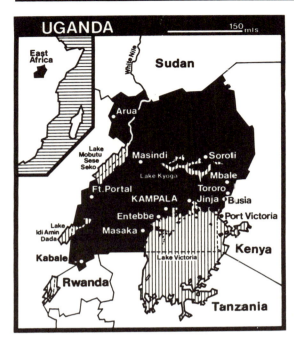

Area and population
236,860 sq kms (91,452 sq mls). Pop. 12 million (estimated).
Capital: Kampala (400,000).
Chief cities: None but towns include Jinja (60,000), Mbale (25,000). *Airport:* Entebbe (Kampala).

Climate
Though near the Equator, Uganda is warm rather than hot. Temperatures vary little throughout the year, with an average of 21.6°C (71°F).
Clothing: Lightweight the year round.

People
Various tribal groups, principally Baganda, Banyoro, Banyankole, Batoro, Iteso, Lango, Achole and Karamojong, plus few Asians and Europeans.
Religion: Basically Christian with Moslem and Hindu minorities. *Distribution:* 8.4% urban.

Languages
English and Kiswahili.

Economic background
Little up-to-date information on Uganda is available, but its economy appears to be running down. Most Ugandans live at subsistence level through agriculture; cotton and coffee provide most of Uganda's foreign currency earnings. Tourism was beginning to develop until the general world antagonism towards the Amin regime. In industry, the production of beer, tobacco and textiles was increasing. The present state of industry is not accurately known.

Trade
Gross National Product: Sh9,725 million (estimated).
Exports: US$325.9 million (1974), chiefly coffee, cotton, copper. *Imports:* US$217.7 million, chiefly machinery, chemicals, textiles and yarns, transport equipment.
Chief trading partners (1973): UK, USA, W. Germany, Japan, Yugoslavia, France, Netherlands.
Inflation rate: Not available.

Prospects
Insufficient information is available.

Currency
Uganda shilling (Sh) = 100 cents. £ = Sh14.20; $ = Sh7.55.

Travel
Visas generally required.

Vaccinations
Smallpox and yellow fever.

Airlines
Western airlines have been withdrawing their air services to Entebbe; check flights and flying times with travel agent. *Fares:* Copenhagen F Dkr6,935 Y Dkr4,495; London F £521 Y £329.50; New York F $1,213 Y $802; Sydney F A$1,128 Y A$746.
Airport to city: 35.5 kms (22 mls). *Taxi fare:* Sh50.

Duty-free allowances
200 cigarettes *or* tobacco equivalent; 1 bottle of spirits.

Local time
GMT+3 hrs.

Embassy phone numbers
Kampala:
Netherlands 54061   Sweden 59011
Norway 63926   USA 54451

Hotels
Kampala: International, Grand, Speke, Nile, Fairway. Current prices not available.

International banks

None.

Credit cards

None.

Voltage

240 volts.

Office hours

08.00–12.30 and 14.00–17.30 Mon–Fri,
08.00–12.30 Sat.

National holidays

Moslem holidays plus 1 Jan, Good Friday, Easter
Monday, 1 May, 9 Oct, 25, 26 Dec.

Communications

No current information available.

Social customs

No current information available.

**(Abu Dhabi, Dubai, Sharjah, Ajman, Ras al
Khaimah, Umm al Qaiwain, Fujairah).**

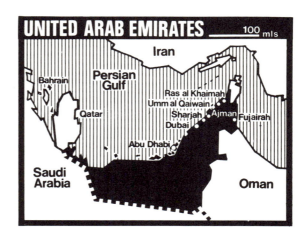

Area and population

123,500 sq kms (32,000 sq mls). Pop. 650,000.
Chief cities: Abu Dhabi Town (150,000), capital of
Abu Dhabi Emirate; Dubai (206,000), Sharjah (85,000),
Ajman (20,000), Ras Al Khaimah (55,000).
Ports: Dubai, Sharjah. *Airports:* International
(Abu Dhabi), Dubai.

Climate

Hot and humid in summer, mild in winter. Temperatures
range up to 48°C (120°F). Best time to visit is
Dec–Mar, when temperatures range up to 20°C (68°F).
Clothing: Lightweight clothing. Sunglasses essential.

People

Arabs, with Indian, Pakistani and Iranian minorities.
Religion: Moslem.

Language

Arabic. *English rating:* Good.

Economic background

The United Arab Emirates' economy is dominated by the
oil of Abu Dhabi and Dubai. The wealthiest of the
emirates is Abu Dhabi, produced from both on- and
off-shore fields. Dubai is the main port and import
centre for the emirates and has a big re-export trade to
Oman, Iran and India. Oil revenue is used to find and
develop major projects.

Trade

Gross National Product: Not available.
Exports: US$8,000 million, almost entirely crude and refined oil. *Imports:* US$3,000 million, chiefly machinery, building materials, consumer goods, clothing. foodstuffs, electrical equipment.
Chief trading partners: UK, USA, W. Germany, Japan, France, Lebanon, Italy, Netherlands.
Inflation rate: Not available.

Prospects

Large-scale economic expansion is envisaged

Currency

Dirham (DH) = 100 fils. £ = 7.31 dirhams;
$ = 3.88 dirhams.

Travel

Transit visas (96 hrs) and visitors' visas are required. Consult local consulate offices.

Vaccinations

Smallpox.

Airlines

Alia, British Airways, Gulf Air, Saudia, Sabena, KLM, Swissair, Kuwait, PIA, MEA, Tunis Air, Lufthansa.
Flying times: Copenhagen 11 hrs (Abu Dhabi);
London $7\frac{1}{2}$ hrs (Abu Dhabi), $8\frac{1}{4}$ hrs (Dubai);
New York $13\frac{1}{2}$ hrs (Abu Dhabi and Dubai);
Sydney 19 hrs (Abu Dhabi and Dubai).
Fares (Abu Dhabi): Copenhagen F Dkr5,570 Y Dkr4,025; London F £415.50 Y £292.50; New York F $1,227 Y $750; Sydney F A$998 Y A$680.
Airports to city: Abu Dhabi 19 kms (12 mls);
Dubai 4 kms (2.5 mls). *Taxi fares:* Abu Dhabi DH20–25; Dubai DH20.

Duty-free allowances

Abu Dhabi: 400 cigarettes *or* 100 cigars.
Dubai: 1,000 cigarettes *or* 200 cigars. Abu Dhabi forbids the import of alcohol, but non-Moslem visitors to Dubai may take in $1\frac{1}{2}$ litres of spirits.

Local time

GMT+4 hrs.

Embassy phone numbers

Abu Dhabi: UK 43033. *Dubai:* UK 31070.

Hotels

Abu Dhabi: Abu Dhabi Hilton, Al Am Hilton, Al Ain Palace, Omar Al Khayyam, Zakker.
Dubai: Ambassador, Bustan, Carlton, Inter-Continental, Oasis. Prices up to 370 dirhams per night.

International banks

Algemene Bank Nederland, Arab Bank, Banque de Paris et des Pays-Bas, Barclays International, British Bank of the Middle East, Chartered Bank, Citibank, Toronto Dominion Bank.

Credit cards

American Express, Diners Club.

Office hours

08.00–13.00 and 16.00–19.30 in summer, 08.00–13.00 and 15.30–19.00 in winter, Sat-Thurs. Hours vary slightly in parts of UAE but everywhere Friday is the weekly holiday. Shops usually close 13.00–16.00.

National holidays

All Moslem holidays (check before arrival).
Fixed holidays: 1 Jan, 6 Aug, 2 Dec.

Voltage

240–415 volts in Abu Dhabi; 220–380 volts in Northern Emirates.

Communications

Tel: 40 dirhams per 3 mins. *Telex:* 14.33 dirhams per min.
Airmail: 3–4 days. *Cable:* 2.20 dirhams per word (7-word minimum).

Social customs

Patience is required in all business dealing in the UAE. A low-key approach, coupled with courteousness, should be adopted at all times. As in many other Middle East countries, coffee houses replace bars as meeting places. *Best buys:* Gold and silver jewellery, pearls, local coffee pots made from brass or copper.

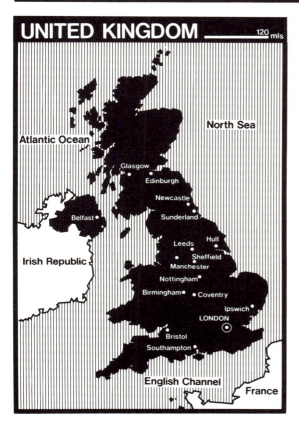

UNITED KINGDOM _____ 120 mls

Atlantic Ocean

North Sea

Glasgow
Edinburgh
Newcastle
Belfast
Sunderland
Irish Republic
Leeds Hull
Sheffield
Manchester
Nottingham
Birmingham Coventry
Ipswich
LONDON
Bristol
Southampton
English Channel
France

Area and population

244,785 sq kms (94,512 sq mls). Pop. 55.9 million.
Capital: London (7.3 million); Cardiff (276,880), capital of Wales; Edinburgh (448,682), capital of Scotland; Belfast (390,700), capital of Northern Ireland.
Chief cities: Birmingham (1,087,000), Glasgow (835,622), Liverpool (574,560), Manchester (530,580), Sheffield (511,860), Leeds (748,070), Bristol (421,800), Coventry (336,000), Nottingham (294,000), Bradford (292,340), Wolverhampton (269,530), Derby (217,930), Hull (281,560), Leicester (287,530), Newcastle-upon-Tyne (212,430), Southampton (212,020), Stoke-on-Trent (260,140), Sunderland (214,820), Dundee (180,674), Aberdeen (179,575), Swansea (173,150), Portsmouth (200,380).
Ports: Bristol, Clydeport, Felixstowe, Grangemouth, Hartlepools, Harwich, Hull, Immingham, Ipswich, Leith, Liverpool, London, Manchester, Middlesbrough, Newcastle, Southampton. *Airports:* Gatwick, Heathrow (London), Ringway (Manchester), Abbotsinch (Glasgow), Aldergrove (Belfast).

Climate

Generally mild but unpredictable. Take a raincoat or purchase one in London, where they are a good buy. Average London temperatures range from 4°C (40°F) in winter to 17°C (63°F) in summer. In London dial 246.8091 for weather forecast. Weather tends to be colder the farther North you travel.
Clothing: Medium-weight but overcoat and umbrella needed in winter.

People

Varied racial stocks that settled before the 11th century plus about 1.5 million Indians, Pakistanis and West Indians. *Religion:* Predominantly Christian plus large Jewish and Moslem minorities. *Distribution:* 77% urban.

Language

English.

Economic background

Once the world's leading industrial power, Britain's position declined in the past 20 years as other nations industrialised and Britain strove to maintain its traditional role of banker to the sterling area. As a result its rate of growth sank to one of the lowest in the industrialised world. Nevertheless, economically Britain is strong and is determined to pursue slow but positive growth policies. While living standards have fallen in comparison with those of North America and industrialised Europe, successive governments have tried, now apparently successfully, to curb raging inflation while at the same time trying to maintain near-full employment.

Trade

Gross National Product: £123,650 million.
Exports: £33,308.2 million, chiefly road vehicles, non-metallic mineral manufactures, machinery for specialised industries, petroleum and petroleum products, general industrial machinery, power generator machinery. *Imports:* £36,996 million, chiefly petroleum and petroleum products, road vehicles, non-metallic mineral manufactures, other transport equipment, textiles and yarn, non-ferrous metals.
Chief trading partners: USA, W. Germany, France, Netherlands, Belgium/Luxembourg, Ireland, Switzerland, Sweden, Nigeria, Italy. *Inflation rate:* 9.1%.

Prospects

In spite of Britain's economic troubles, prospects are generally bright, largely through the exploitation of oil in the North Sea and Britain's improving export performance. As in other nations in Western Europe, unemployment remains a problem and no easy solution is foreseeable in the next few years.

Currency
£ = 100 pence. $ = £0.53.

Travel
Visas not required.

Vaccinations
Not required.

Airlines
Every major international airline.
Flying times: Copenhagen 1½ hrs; New York 6¾ hrs; Sydney 27 hrs. *Fares:* Copenhagen F Dkr2,090 Y Dkr1,395; New York F $656 Y $313; Sydney F A$1,473 Y A$940.
Airport to city: Heathrow 24 kms (15 mls).
Taxi fare: £5–6. *Bus fare:* £1.
Gatwick 43 kms (27 mls). *Taxi fare:* About £10.
Train: £1.50.
Manchester Ringway 16 kms (10 mls). *Bus fare:* 55p.
Glasgow Abbotsinch 14 kms (9 mls). *Bus fare:* 66p.
Belfast Aldergrove 21 kms (13 mls).

Duty-free allowances
Visitors residing within EEC: 200 cigarettes *or* 50 cigars *or* 250 grammes of tobacco; 1 litre of spirits; 2 litres of wine. *Visitors residing outside EEC:* 400 cigarettes *or* 100 cigars *or* 500 grammes of tobacco; 1 litre of spirits, 2 litres of wine.

Local time
GMT (+1 hr Mar–Oct).

Embassy phone numbers
London:

Australia 836.2435	Norway 235.7151
Canada 930.9741	Sweden 499.9500
Denmark 584.0102	Switzerland 723.0701
Japan 493.6030	W. Germany 235.5033
Netherlands 584.5040	USA 499.9000

Hotels
London: Berkeley, Carlton Tower, Claridges, Dorchester, Grosvenor House, Hilton, Inn on the Park, Inter-Continental, Ritz, Royal Garden, Savoy, Montcalm, Browns, Britannia, Cumberland, Duke's, Europa, Hyde Park, Kensington Palace, Mayfair, Mount Royal, Waldorf, Westbury.

Manchester: Grand, Midland, Piccadilly, Portland, Excelsior.
Glasgow: Albany, Central, Glasgow Centre, Grosvenor, Royal Stuart.
Edinburgh: Caledonian, Carlton, Edinburgh Crest, King James, North British, Post House, Roxburghe, Barnton, Royal Scot.
Cardiff: Angel, Cardiff Centre, Post House.
Belfast: Europa, International, Midland, Royal Avenue, Russell Court.
Birmingham: Albany, Birmingham Centre, Grand, Holiday Inn, Metropole, Midland, Royal Angus, Strathallan, Excelsior, Post House.
Liverpool: Adelphi, Atlantic Tower, Liverpool Centre, Holiday Inn.
Hotel prices vary enormously—from £10 per night upwards outside London, and £20 upwards in London.

International banks
All major international banks.

Credit cards
All major credit cards.

Office hours
09.00–17.30 Mon–Fri.

National holidays
1 Jan, 2 Jan (Scotland), 17 Mar (N. Ireland), Good Friday, Easter Monday, 1 May, Whit Monday (May *or* June: not Scotland), 12 July (N. Ireland), Last (Scotland: First) Monday in Aug, 25, 26 Dec.

Voltage
220–240 volts.

Social customs
British businessmen, according to overseas visitors, are frank, friendly and straightforward. Business entertainment is not as lavish as in other European countries, generally confined to lunches and occasional dinners. Prior appointments are usually necessary.
Food and hotel accommodation have improved tremendously in recent years, and it's best to reserve accommodation well in advance, since Britain's tourist season lasts the year round. *Best buys:* London is noted for men's tailoring, ladies' coats and tailored suits, country clothes, sportswear, knitwear, leather goods, fine linen, china, porcelain, crystal, silver and pewter, gin and whisky.

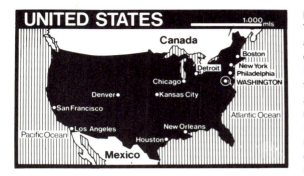

Area and population

9,363,350 sq kms (3.6 million sq mls). Pop. 213 million.
Capital: Washington (3 million).
Chief cities: New York (11.5 m), Los Angeles (7 m),
Chicago (7 m), Philadelphia (4.8 m), Detroit (4.4 m),
Boston (3.4 m), San Francisco (3.1 m),
Pittsburgh (2.3 m), Houston (2.1 m), Baltimore (2.3 m),
Dallas (2.5 m), Cleveland (2 m), Minneapolis-St Paul
(2 m), Atlanta (1.6 m).
Ports: New York, Boston, Baltimore, San Francisco,
Los Angeles, New Orleans, Mobile.
Airports: John F. Kennedy, La Guardia (New York),
Dulles (Washington), Logan (Boston), O'Hare (Chicago),
Metropolitan (Detroit), International (Los Angeles),
International (Philadelphia), International
(San Francisco), Seattle-Tacoma (Seattle),
Intercontinental (Houston), Dallas-Fort Worth (Dallas),
International (Miami).

Climate

Varies with zone. Temperatures in New York range
from 3°C (37°F) to 28°C (82°F); average humidity 73%.
Temperatures in San Francisco range from 7°C (44°F)
to 31°C (87°F); average humidity 85%. Winters are severe
except in South and South-West. *Clothing:* Extensive
use of central hearing dictates lightweight suits and
dresses in winter with heavy overclothes and hats for
outdoors. Lightweight clothing for summer.

People

88% Caucasian, 11% Negro. *Religion:* 66% Protestant,
25% Roman Catholic, 3% Jewish.
Distribution: 74% urban.

Language

English.

Economic background

The United States does not belong to any trade bloc
and its tariff schedule employs a different system of
classification from that of the Brussels Tariff
Nomenclature. Although steps have been taken to adopt
this system, the process could take up to 10 years.
A high standard of marketing technique is essential in a
market as immense and sophisticated as that of the
United States. While the USA does represent a single
market for some goods, for most products, especially
consumer ones, cover of the market should be
regionalised. The USA can be divided roughly into six
regional markets, whose main centres of distribution are:
New York, Boston and Philadelphia for the North-East;
Chicago, Cleveland, Detroit, Minneapolis-St Paul,
Pittsburgh and St Louis for the Mid-West; Los Angeles
and San Francisco for the South-West Coast; Dallas/Fort
Worth and Houston for the South-West; Atlanta and
Miami for the South-East; and Seattle for the
North-West.

Trade

Gross National Product: $1,398,000 million.
Exports: $100,000 million, chiefly machinery and
equipment, food and live animals, raw materials,
chemicals, manufactured goods, scientific instruments,
textiles, rubber, paper, mineral fuels.
Imports: $102,000 million, chiefly machinery and
equipment, manufactured goods, food and live animals,
raw materials, mineral fuels.
Chief trading partners: Canada, Japan, W. Germany,
Venezuela, UK, Mexico, Nigeria, Italy, France, Iran,
Taiwan, Netherlands Antilles, Brazil, Indonesia.
Inflation rate: 6.5%.

Prospects

After the worst recession since the war, the US economy
began to show modest signs of improvement from April
1975, when the recession was generally recognised to
have bottomed out. Even so, recovery has not come as
swiftly as was hoped.

Currency

Dollar = 100 cents. £ = $1.88.

Travel

Visa essential, its type depending on nature of visit.
Check with airline or local US consulate before departure.
For visiting businessmen, issue of visa is usually just a
formality.

Vaccinations
Smallpox certificate if visitor is arriving from an infected area.

Airlines
Virtually every international carrier.
Flying times: New York: Copenhagen 9½ hrs; London (Concorde) 3½ hrs, (conventional jet) 7½ hrs; Sydney 22 hrs. *Chicago:* Copenhagen 10¾ hrs; London 8 hrs; Sydney 24 hrs. *Los Angeles:* Copenhagen 11¼ hrs; London 11 hrs; Sydney 16 hrs.
Fares: Copenhagen–New York F Dkr4,675 Y Dkr2,265; Copenhagen–Los Angeles F Dkr6,865 Y Dkr3,460; London–New York (Concorde) £430.50, (jet) F £356.30 Y £170; London–Los Angeles F £532 Y £269.50; Sydney–New York F A$1,378 Y A$896; Sydney–Los Angeles F A$1,163 Y A$747.
Airport to city: Boston 6.4 kms (4 mls); Chicago 35 kms (21 mls); Houston 40 kms (25 mls); Los Angeles 24 kms (15 mls); Miami 11 kms (7 mls); New York 22 kms (14 mls); Washington 43 kms (27 mls).
Taxi fares: Boston $6; Chicago $10–12; Houston $15–20; Los Angeles $10; Miami $8–10; New York $15–20; Washington $20.

Duty-free allowances
300 cigarettes *or* 50 cigars *or* 3 lbs tobacco: one US quarter of spirits; articles for personal use.

Local time
Eastern Standard Time: GMT−5 hrs.
Central Standard Time: GMT−6 hrs.
Mountain Standard Time: GMT−7 hrs.
Pacific Standard Time: GMT−8 hrs.
(All zones 1 hr earlier end Apr–end Oct.)

Embassy phone numbers
New York:

Australia 245.4000	Norway 944.6920
Canada 586.2400	Sweden 751.5900
Denmark 697.5101	Switzerland 758.2560
Japan 986.1600	W. Germany 688.3523
Netherlands 246.1429	UK 752.8400

Hotels
Prices to suit everybody, but count on $30–35 per night plus sales tax of up to 8% per night.

International banks
All major international banks are represented.

Credit cards
American Express, Barclaycard, Diners Club.

Office hours
08.00 or 09.00–17.00 or 18.00 Mon–Fri.

National holidays
In addition to local state holidays, which should be checked before departure, 1 Jan, Third Monday in Feb, 4 July, First Monday in Sept, 11 Nov, Fourth Thursday in Nov, 25 Dec.

Voltage
110–120 volts AC.

Communications
Tel: $5.40 per 3 mins. *Telex:* $2.55 per min.
Airmail: 2–3 days. *Cable:* 23 cents per word.
Phone rating: Excellent.

Social customs
Expect a straightforward welcome and frankness in business conversation. Hospitality can be lavish by European standards, and can usually be accepted without fear of ulterior motive. Arrival hint: unless you know exactly where you are going, it is best to take a taxi rather than an airport bus, which tends to call at a number of hotels. Safety varies enormously, but few big cities feel safe after dark.

URUGUAY 200 mls

Brazil

Rivera
Salto
Paysandu
Durazno
Fray Bentos
S.Jose Minas
R.Plate
BUENOS AIRES MONTEVIDEO

Argentina

South America

Atlantic

Wealth is more evenly distributed than in many other South American republics and living standards are high. While there is no heavy industry, light industries such as textiles, plastics, rubber goods, glass, domestic hardware, sanitary ware, aluminium, cement and electrical appliances are well established.

Trade
Gross National Product: US$2,421.9 million.
Exports: US$321.5 million, chiefly meat and meat preparations, wool, textiles, agricultural products, hides.
Imports: US$284.8 million, chiefly machinery, fuels and lubricants, motor vehicles, drugs and chemicals, building materials. *Chief trading partners:* Argentina, Brazil, USA, W. Germany, Nigeria, Kuwait, UK, Spain, Italy, Netherlands, France, Belgium/Luxembourg, Poland, USSR, Japan. *Inflation rate:* 59.9%.

Prospects
Further industrial expansion may have to wait until there is more monetary stability.

Currency
New Peso (N$) = 100 centesimos. £ = N$11.52; $ = N$6.12.

Travel
No visas required.

Vaccinations
Smallpox.

Airlines
Aerolineas Argentinas, Lufthansa, Alitalia, SAS, Iberia, Air France, Pan Am, Varig, KLM.
Flying times: Copenhagen $19\frac{1}{4}$ hrs; London (no direct flights) 21 hrs; New York 15 hrs; Sydney 37 hrs.
Fares: Copenhagen F Dkr9,320 Y Dkr6,210; London F £721.50 Y £474.50; New York F $876 Y $596; Sydney F A$1,873 Y A$1,376.
Airport to city: 19 kms (12.5 mls).
Taxi fare: Approx. N$30.

Duty-free allowances
Reasonable quantities of tobacco and spirits.

Local time
GMT−3 hrs (−2 hrs Oct–Mar).

Embassy phone numbers
Montevideo: UK 912501.

Area and population
186,926 sq kms (72,172 sq mls). Pop. 2.7 million.
Capital: Montevideo (1.23 million).
Chief city: Paysandu (60,000). *Port:* Montevideo.
Airport: Carrasco (Montevideo).

Climate
Temperate. Winter temperatures (June–Sept) average 15°C (59°F), with prolonged rain July and Aug. Summer temperatures average 21°C (70°F). Jan and Feb are holiday periods. *Clothing:* Lightweight or tropical in summer, medium-weight clothes in winter.

People
90% European stock, mostly Spanish and Italian, 10% mestizo. *Religion:* Roman Catholic.
Distribution: 84% urban.

Language
Spanish. *English rating:* Fair.

Economic background
Uruguay is a pastoral country, relying on wool and meat for its revenue. 90% of its income comes from agriculture.

Hotels
Montevideo: Columbia Palace, Lancaster, Victoria Plaza. Prices up to US$30 per night.

International banks
Bank of London and South America, First National City Bank, Bank of America.

Credit cards
All major credit cards.

Office hours
08.30–12.00 and 14.30–19.00 Mon–Fri.

National holidays
1, 6 Jan, Carnival (most businesses closed for the week containing Ash Wednesday), Holy Week, 19 Apr, 1, 18 May, 19 June, 18 July, 25 Aug, 12 Oct, 2 Nov, 8, 25 Dec.

Voltage
220 volts AC 50 cycles.

Communications
Tel: N$56.55 per 3 mins. *Telex:* N$35.64 per 3 mins. *Airmail:* 3–5 days. *Cable:* N$2.60 per word (7-word minimum).

Social customs
Business customs are similar to Spain and Italy, but there are large expatriate communities of Britons, Americans and Germans. People eat late, usually 21.00 or 22.00. *Best buys:* Woollen goods, suede and leather, jackets and belts.

Area and population
22.4 million sq kms (8.65 million sq mls). Pop. 255 million. *Capital:* Moscow (Moskva) (7.6 million). *Chief cities:* Leningrad (4.3 m), Kiev (1.9 m), Baku (1.5 m), Gorky (1.5 m), Tashkent (1.7 m), Odessa (900,000). *Ports:* Leningrad, Odessa, Vladivostok. *Airport:* Sheremetyevo (Moscow).

Climate
Temperatures in Moscow and Leningrad range from −9°C (15°F) to 30°C (86°F) in summer. Colder in Siberia but warmer in Southern Russia and Ukraine. *Clothing:* Very warm clothing and rubber overshoes needed in winter, but summer can be surprisingly hot, so take lightweight clothes.

People
55% Russians, 18% Ukrainians, 4% Byelorussians, 3% Uzbeks, 1.5% Armenians, 1.5% Georgians, many other national minorities. *Religion:* Where practised, chiefly Russian Orthodox, with Moslems in Central Asia. *Distribution:* 55% urban.

Language
Russian. *English rating:* Fair.

Economic background
All economic activity is state-controlled and all foreign trade is conducted through Foreign Trade Corporations, each specialising in a particular range of goods and commodities, and most dealing with both import and export. Though foreign trade forms only a small part of total Soviet economic activity, the USSR is anxious to import the latest technology from the West despite a chronic shortage of hard currency.

Trade
Gross National Product: 353,700 million roubles. *Exports:* 20,737.8 million roubles, chiefly equipment and

materials for complete factories, crude petroleum, rolled ferrous products, oil, raw cotton. *Imports:* 18,834 million roubles, chiefly clothing and linen, equipment for ships, and for chemical industry, footwear, rolling stock, vegetables, fruit, raw sugar.
Chief trading partners: E. Germany, Poland, Czechoslovakia, Bulgaria, W. Germany, Hungary, Japan, Cuba, Romania, Finland, USA, Yugoslavia, UK.
Inflation rate: Not available.

Prospects

Prospects of more trade with the West are always dependent upon availability of hard currency and USSR's political considerations.

Currency

Rouble = 100 kopeks. £ = 1.29 roubles; $ = 0.68 roubles.

Travel

Visas are essential, even for tourists, and should be correct in every detail in order to avoid entry delays. Before a visa can be issued, Soviet embassies require a completed application form, three passport photos on white background with owner's signature on the front left edge, valid passport, letter outlining purpose of visit, itinerary, period of stay, exact dates of journey to and from USSR, and name of organisation to be visited with clearly stated acceptance of visit.

Vaccinations

None for most visitors, although smallpox certificate required if arriving from Asia, South America or Africa.

Airlines

British Airways, Aeroflot, most other international airlines.
Flying times (to Moscow): Copenhagen $2\frac{1}{2}$ hrs; London $4\frac{1}{2}$ hrs; New York 10 hrs; Sydney 24 hrs.
Fares: Copenhagen F Dkr2,525 Y Dkr1,885; London F £267 Y £188.50; New York F $913 Y $487; Sydney F A$1,566 Y A$1,070.
Airport to city: 30 kms (18 mls). *Taxi fare:* 5 roubles.

Duty-free allowances

200 cigarettes; 1 litre of spirits, 2 litres of wine.

Local time

GMT+3 hrs (Moscow); other time zones to eastward range from GMT+4 hrs to GMT+13 hrs.

Embassy phone numbers

Moscow:

Australia 241.2035	Sweden 147.9009
Canada 241.9034	Switzerland 295.5322
Denmark 202.7866	W. Germany 255.0013
Japan 291.8500	UK 231.9555
Netherlands 291.2999	US 252.0011
Norway 290.3872	

Hotels

Moscow: Intourist, Metropol, National, Rossiya, Ukraine. Prices are about 40 roubles per night.

International banks

Moscow Narodny Bank is USSR's chief foreign trade bank. Some Western banks, including Barclays, National Westminster and Lloyds Bank International, have representatives in Moscow.

Credit cards

American Express, Diners Club.

Office hours

09.00–18.00 Mon–Fri.

National holidays

1 Jan, 8 Mar, 1, 2, 9 May, 7 Oct, 7 Nov, 5 Dec.

Voltage

127 and 220 volts AC.

Communications

Tel: 4.28 roubles per 3 mins. *Telex:* 2.40 roubles per 3 mins. *Airmail.* 10 days. *Cable:* 22 kopeks per word. *Phone rating:* Poor.

Social customs

Virtually all entertaining is done in hotels and restaurants; a Western visitor is rarely invited to a home. Safety excellent. In business dealings with government officials, be prepared for Soviet contacts to be non-Russians.

Area and population

921,417 sq kms (355,759 sq mls). Pop. 13 million.
Capital: Caracas (2.5 million).
Chief cities: Maracaibo (800,000), Valencia (366.000),
Barquisimeto (334,000), Ciudad Guayana (100,C00),
Puerto La Cruz (100,000). *Ports:* Carupano, Guanta,
La Guaira, Maracaibo, Puerto Cabello.
Airport: Simon Bolivar (Caracas).

Climate

Tropical, with little seasonal change. Caracas
temperatures range from 9°C (48°F) in Jan and Feb to
32°C (90°F) in July. *Clothing:* Dark tropical suits.

People

65% mestizo, 21% European, 7% Negro, 2% Indian.
Religion: Roman Catholic. *Distribution:* 75% urban.

Language

Spanish. *English rating:* Fair.

Economic background

Petroleum has emerged as the mainstay of Venezuela's
economy and has brought wealth that has enabled it to
build up its industry, including petrochemicals, steel and
hydro-electric power. Agriculture is extensive; main
crops comprise meat, milk, maize, bananas, eggs, coffee,
sugar and sesame. Industry is concentrated mainly in the
Caracas area, but the government is encouraging fresh
industrial development in other parts of the country.

Trade

Gross National Product: US$28,000 million.
Exports: 13,711 million bolivars, chiefly petroleum, fuel,
iron ore, crude materials, tobacco, cocoa.
Imports: 9,593 million bolivars, chiefly machinery,
transport equipment, chemicals, metals, manufactured
goods, raw materials, foodstuffs.
Chief trading partners: USA, W. Germany, Japan, Italy,
UK, France, Canada, Switzerland, Belgium/Luxembourg,
Spain, Mexico, Netherlands, Aruba Islands, Curacao,
Puerto Rico, Panama, Brazil, Trinidad and Tobago.
Inflation rate: 7.3%.

Prospects

Vigorous growth is anticipated.

Currency

Bolivar (B) = 100 centimos. £ = B8.10; $ = B4.30.

Travel

Visas required. Before departure, holders of ordinary
visas must obtain clearance from income tax authority.

Vaccinations

Smallpox.

Airlines

Aeromexico, Air Canada, Air France, Alitalia, Avianca,
Delta, Iberia, KLM, Lufthansa, Pan Am, TAP, Viasa.
Flying times: Copenhagen (no direct flights) $28\frac{1}{4}$ hrs;
London $9\frac{1}{2}$ hrs; New York $4\frac{1}{2}$ hrs; Sydney 29 hrs.
Fares: Copenhagen F Dkr6,455 Y Dkr4,300; London
F £450.50 Y £310; New York F $383 Y $256;
Sydney F A$2,011 Y A$1,344.
Airport to city: 20 kms (13 mls). *Taxi fare:* B35.

Duty-free allowances

200 cigarettes *or* 25 cigars; 2 litres of spirits.

Local time

GMT−4 hrs.

Embassy phone numbers

Caracas:

Canada 91.32.77	Sweden 32.39.11
Denmark 32.30.08	Switzerland 32.01.55
Japan 32.18.21	W. Germany 33.47.44
Netherlands 91.14.22	UK 91.10.91
Norway 32.57.03	USA 33.86.61

Venezuela

Hotels
Caracas: Avila, Everest, Hilton, Las Americas, Tamanaco. Prices about US$30 per night.

International banks
First National City Bank, Lloyds.

Credit cards
All major credit cards.

Office hours
08.00–18.00 Mon–Fri.

National holidays
1, 6 Jan, Carnival (Feb), 19 Mar, Maundy Thursday to Easter Monday, 19 Apr, 1 May, Ascension Day (May), 24, 29 June, 5, 14 July, 15 Aug, 12 Oct, 1 Nov, 8, 17, 24, 25, 31 Dec.

Voltage
110 volts AC.

Communications
Tel: B54 per 3 mins. *Telex:* B40.50 per 3 mins. *Airmail:* 3–7 days. *Cable:* B2.75 per word (5-word minimum).

Social customs
Informality marks business life in Caracas. Dining is late. Newly-arrived visitors are advised not to hurry in the high altitude. Special attention should be paid in passing any statue of Simon Bolivar, who is greatly respected throughout Venezuela; people have been known to be fined for showing 'disrespect'.

West Indies

(see also Jamaica; Trinidad and Tobago)

Area and population
Barbados: 430 sq kms (166 sq mls). Pop. 250,000.
Grenada: 311 sq kms (120 sq mls). Pop. 103,000.
Antigua: 208 sq kms (108 sq mls). Pop. 70,000.
Dominica: 751 sq kms (290 sq mls). Pop. 70,000.
St Kitts, Nevis (Anguilla): 176 sq kms (68 sq mls), 130 sq kms (50 sq mls), 91 sq kms (35 sq mls), respectively. Pop. 53,000.
St Lucia: 616 sq kms (238 sq mls). Pop. 100,000.
St Vincent: 388 sq kms (150 sq mls). Pop. 90,000.
Montserrat: 98 sq kms (38 sq mls). Pop. 12,500.
Capitals: Barbados: Bridgetown (95,000). Grenada: St George's (12,000). Antigua: St John's (15,000). Dominica: Roseau (11,000). St Kitts-Nevis: Basseterre (15,800). St Lucia: Castries (40,000). St Vincent: Kingstown (20,000). Montserrat: Plymouth (20,000).
Ports: Bridgetown, St George's, St John's, Roseau, Basseterre, Castries, Kingstown.
Airports: Grantley Adams (Barbados), Pearls (Grenada), Coolidge Field (Antigua), Melville Hall (Dominica), Hewanorra (St Lucia), Arnos Vale (St Vincent), Blackburne (Montserrat).

Climate
Tropical, high humidity, with rain May–Nov. Average daily temperature 28°C (83°F). Best time to visit is Dec–Apr. *Clothing:* Lightweight clothing throughout the year. Take an umbrella and sunglasses.

People
90% African stock, remainder mostly European origin. *Religion:* Christian, mostly Anglican. *Distribution:* 45% urban.

Language
English.

Economic background

The economy of all the islands is based on agriculture and tourism, although Barbados has made a determined effort to introduce industry. All the islands hope to attract overseas investment in order to foster job-creating industries to take the place of crop economies which are at the mercy of world price trends.

Trade

Gross National Product: BDS$500 million (estimate). *Exports:* EC$170 million, chiefly sugar, fish, rum, fruit. *Imports:* EC$600 million, chiefly machinery, transport equipment, manufactured goods, mineral fuels, chemicals, meat, cereals. *Chief trading partners:* UK, USA, Canada, Venezuela, Trinidad and Tobago. *Inflation rate:* Not available.

Prospects

Industry is growing, particularly in Barbados, but agriculture and tourism are expected to be the mainstays for many years to come.

Currency

Barbados: Barbados Dollar (BDS$) = 100 cents. £ = BDS$3.76; $ = BDS$2.00. *Other islands:* Dollar (EC$) = 100 cents (issued by the East Caribbean Currency Authority). £ = EC$5.08; $ = EC$2.70.

Travel

Visas not required.

Vaccinations

Smallpox (issued not less than eight days before arrival).

Airlines

British Airways, Caribbean, BWIA, Air Canada, American, LIAT, SAS. *Flying times* (to Barbados): Copenhagen 8¾ hrs; London 8½ hrs; New York 4 hrs; Sydney 30 hrs. *Fares:* Copenhagen F Dkr6,375 Y Dkr4,220; London F £450.50 Y £271; New York F $349 Y $233; Sydney F A$2,073 Y A$1,393. *Airport to capital:* Barbados 18 kms (11 mls); Grenada 19.3 kms (12 mls); Antigua 9.5 kms (6 m s); St Lucia 64 kms (40 mls). *Taxi fares:* Barbados BDS$13; Antigua EC$9.

Duty-free allowances

200 cigarettes *or* 50 cigars *or* 8 oz of tobacco; 40 oz bottle of alcoholic beverage.

Local time

GMT−4 hrs.

Embassy phone numbers

Barbados: UK 63525.

Hotels

Barbados: Hilton, Holiday Inn, Sandy Lane. *Antigua:* Holiday Inn. Prices range from US$30 out of season to US$80 in season (mid-Dec to Apr) per night.

International Banks

Barclays Bank International, Royal Bank of Canada, Canadian Imperial Bank of Commerce, Bank of Nova Scotia, Bank of America, First National City Bank, Chase Manhattan Bank.

Credit cards

American Express, Barclaycard, Diners Club.

Office hours

Vary, but generally 08.00–16.00 Mon–Fri, 08.00–12.00 Sat.

National holidays

Varied and best to check before departure, but main holidays are 1 Jan, Easter, 1 May, Whit Monday (May *or* June), August Bank Holiday, First Monday in Oct, Christmas. In addition, some islands celebrate Carnival and other local holidays.

Voltage

100 volts AC (Barbados), 220 volts AC (Grenada), 230 volts AC (Dominica, St Kitts, Nevis, Anguilla, St Lucia, St Vincent), 220–230 volts AC (Montserrat), 230 volts AC (Antigua).

Communications

Tel: EC$20.16 per 3 mins. *Telex:* EC$20.16 per 3 mins. *Airmail:* 3–4 days. *Cable:* 46 cents per word.

Social customs

All the islands present an informal business and social scene, and there are no social customs of significance. Cheerful and friendly, the islands' chief drawback is the cost of visiting, particularly during the tourist season, which runs from mid-Dec to mid-Apr, when prices are prohibitive. Best to visit out of season, when hotel prices halve.

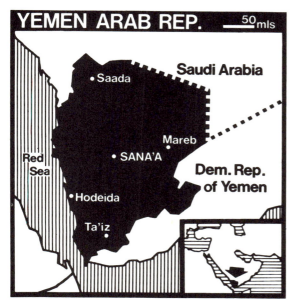

Area and population

189,847 sq kms (73,300 sq mls). Pop. 6.25 million.
Capital: Sana'a (150,000).
Chief cities: Ta'iz (100,000), Hodeida (100,000).
Ports: Hodeida, Mocha. *Airport:* El-Rahaba (Sana'a).

Climate

Temperatures can be high throughout the year, with an annual average of 30°C (86°F). Rain falls July–Dec, and temperatures can fall sharply at night.
Clothing: Lightweight May–Oct in Sana'a, warmer clothing Nov–Apr.

People

Arab. *Religion:* Moslem. *Distribution:* Not available.

Language

Arabic. *English rating:* Fair.

Economic background

More than 1 million Yemenis, about a quarter of the population, have emigrated, but the Yemen's economy benefits from their remittances. The country is basically agricultural, with many peasants still working with ox-drawn ploughs. Vegetables and fruit, coffee, cereals and cotton are grown. Industry accounts for only 1% of the Yemen's revenue, but its handicraft industry is renowned for its skill and artistry. The Yemen, after centuries of isolation, is now opening up to the outside world, and industrial development is being encouraged.

Trade

Gross National Product: 3,710 million riyals.
Exports: 45.1 million riyals, chiefly coffee, hides and skins, cotton and qat. *Imports:* 876.1 million riyals, chiefly machinery, textiles, sugar, glass, iron and steel, petroleum, vehicles and consumer goods.
Chief trading partners: Japan, China, People's Democratic Republic of Yemen (Aden), W. Germany, Saudi Arabia, UK, USSR. *Inflation rate:* 17%.

Prospects

Large-scale aid is coming into the country to help finance its development.

Currency

Riyal = 100 fils. £ = 8.40 riyals; $ = 4.46 riyals.

Travel

Visas required.

Vaccinations

Smallpox. Cholera inoculation strongly recommended.

Airlines

Saudia, Ethiopian, Kuwait, Air Djibouti, Syrian.
Flying times: Copenhagen (no direct flights) 18¾ hrs; London 11 hrs; New York 16 hrs; Sydney 24 hrs.
Fares: Copenhagen F Dkr5,395 Y Dkr4,045; London F £402 Y £286.50; New York F $1,103 Y $701; Sydney F A$1,218 Y A$816.
Airport to city: 3 kms (2 mls). *Taxi fare:* 20 riyals.

Duty-free allowances

A reasonable amount of cigarettes and tobacco. Strictly no alcohol.

Local time

GMT+3 hrs.

Embassy phone numbers

Sana'a: UK 2684 and 5714.

Hotels

Sana'a: Hamd Palace, Mocha. *Ta'iz:* Plaza.
Hodeida: Borg, Ikhwa, Red Sea.
Prices up to 100 riyals per night.

International banks

Arab Bank, British Bank of the Middle East, First National City Bank.

Yemen Arab Republic

Yugoslavia

Credit cards
None.

Office hours
08.00–12.30 and 16.00–19.00 Sat–Thurs.

National holidays
All Moslem holidays plus 13 June, Revolution Anniversary (usually 5 days in Sept), 14 Oct.

Voltage
220 volts AC.

Communications
Tel: 51 riyals per 3 mins. *Telex:* 53 riyals per 3 mins. *Airmail:* 3–4 days. *Cable:* 1.75 riyals per word.

Social customs
The drinking of alcohol is strictly forbidden for all Moslems, although the foreign community is allowed a ration. It is not uncommon for Western businessmen to be invited to private Yemeni functions, where Yemenis chew a mild narcotic called qat. Westerners will not give offence if they decline qat. Do not drink untreated water. Stomach upsets among Western visitors are fairly common.

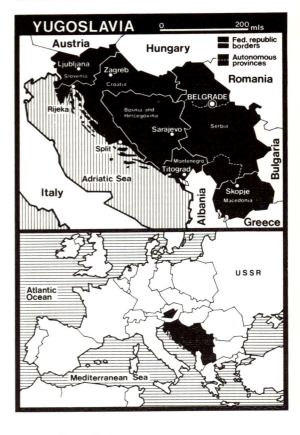

Area and population
255,804 sq kms (98,766 sq mls). Pop. 21.3 million.
Capital: Belgrade (Beograd) (1.2 million).
Chief cities: Zagreb (602,000), Sarajevo (292,000), Skopje (388,000), Ljubljana (258,000), Titograd (98,000). *Ports:* Rijeka (Fiume), Split. *Airports:* Surcin (Belgrade), Zagreb.

Climate
With a mild continental climate, Belgrade is never too warm or too cold. Average temperatures 18° to 20°C (65° to 68°F) in the spring, 25° to 31°C (77° to 86°F) in the summer and 15° to 20°C (60° to 68°F) in the autumn. Temperatures fall to −1°C (30°F) in winter. The Adriatic coast has a Mediterranean climate. *Clothing:* European-weight except in summer, when lightweight clothing is required.

People
Serbs, Croats, Slovenes, Macedonians, Bosnians, with Albanian and Hungarian minorities.

Religion: 42% Orthodox Christians, 25% Roman Catholic, 10% Moslem. *Distribution:* 41% urban.

Languages

Serbo-Croat, Slovene and Macedonian.
English rating: Good.

Economic background

Economically, perhaps the most successful communist country, Yugoslavia has been transformed from a backward agricultural to an industrial-agrarian nation in the years since the war. A wide range of industrial products is manufactured, including ships, railway stock, heavy vehicles, cars, electrical machinery, electronic equipment, textiles, chemicals, petrochemicals, plastics, fertilisers and consumer goods. Beef and pig meat are important in the agricultural sector. Yugoslavia is also well endowed with natural resources, including timber and coal.

Trade

Gross National Product: 503,000 million new dinars.
Exports: 82,927 million dinars, chiefly transport equipment, non-ferrous metals, meat and meat preparations, electrical machinery, chemicals, clothing.
Imports: 125,325 million dinars, chiefly non-electrical machinery, transport equipment, chemicals, iron and steel. *Chief trading partners:* W. Germany, USSR, Italy, Iraq, USA, Czechoslovakia, France, UK, Austria, E. Germany, Switzerland, Poland, India, Romania. *Inflation rate:* 11.6%.

Prospects

Yugoslavia is continuing to develop as an industrial state, with fast-growing industries such as tourism, food processing, mineral extraction and processing, construction, transport and telecommunications.

Currency

New Dinar (ND) = 100 para. £ = ND35.53; $ = ND18.89.

Travel

Visas not required by UK citizens.

Vaccinations

Not required unless entering from an infected area.

Airlines

JAT, British Airways, Air France, Lufthansa, Austrian, CSA, Interflug, KLM, Qantas, Swissair, SAS, Alitalia, Air Algérie, Pan Am, Zambia.

Flying times: Copenhagen $3\frac{1}{4}$ hrs; London $3\frac{3}{4}$ hrs; New York $10\frac{1}{4}$ hrs; Sydney 24 hrs. *Fares:* Copenhagen F Dkr2,120 Y Dkr1,430; London F £179 Y £119; New York F $828 Y $429; Sydney F A$1,395 Y A$891.
Airport to city (Belgrade): 20 kms (12 mls).
Taxi fare: ND170.

Duty-free allowances

200 cigarettes *or* 50 cigars *or* 250 grammes of tobacco; $\frac{1}{4}$ litre of spirits, 2 litres of wine.

Local time

GMT+1 hr.

Embassy phone numbers

Belgrade:

Australia 624.655	Sweden 626.422
Canada 434.524	Switzerland 646.899
Denmark 647.826	W. Germany 645.755
Japan 768.255	UK 645.055
Netherlands 626.699	USA 645.655
Norway 343.933	

Hotels

Belgrade: Jugoslavija, Majestic, Metropol, Moskva, Slavija. Prices for a good-class hotel up to US$20 per night.

International banks

None.

Credit cards

All major credit cards.

Office hours

Government offices: 07.00–15.00 Mon–Fri but 07.00–17.00 Wed. Commercial offices 07.00–14.30 Mon–Fri.

National holidays

1, 2 Jan, 1, 2 May, 4 July, 7 (Serbia only), 13 (Montenegro only), 22 (Slovenia only), 27 (Bosnia, Croatia, Hercegovina only) July, 2 Aug (Macedonia only), 11 Oct (Macedonia only), 29, 30 Nov.

Voltage

220 volts AC.

Communications

Tel: ND36.00 per min. *Telex:* ND30 per 3 mins.
Airmail: 7 days. *Cable:* ND3.44 per word.

Social customs

A friendly country in which visitors are free to go where they like, although the police are very strict about motoring offences. Western businessmen are warmly welcomed, usually with brandy, coffee or fruit juice. *Best buys:* Traditional craft products, leather goods, handwoven rugs, ceramics, lace, dolls and woodcarvings. If paid in foreign currency or travellers' cheques, many shops will give a discount.

Zaire

Area and population

2,334,885 sq kms (905,365 sq mls). Pop. 24.4 million. *Capital:* Kinshasa (2 million). *Chief cities:* Kananga (596,000), Lubumbashi (401,000), Kisangani (297,000). *Ports:* Boma, Matadi. *Airports:* N'Djili (Kinshasa).

Climate

Hot and humid. Average temperatures year round 25° to 26°C (77° to 79°F). Zaire experiences heavy rains, and in Kinshasa the rainy season extends from late Oct to late May, with an average annual rainfall of 164 cm (65 in). *Clothing:* Lightweight year round.

People

Chiefly Bantu, with 2–3 million people of Sudanese descent in North and North-East. *Religion:* 60% animist, 40% Christian. *Distribution:* 30% urban.

Languages

French plus Bantu languages. *English rating:* Poor.

Economic background

Based primarily on mining and agriculture, the economy in recent years has turned more towards industry, particularly for local consumption. Zaire's most important mineral is copper, and there are important deposits of diamonds, uranium and cobalt. These comprise Zaire's main exports, and as a result the country is at the mercy of fluctuating world prices. About 75% of the people are engaged in agriculture, most of them at subsistence level, and there are few exports other than coffee.

Trade

Gross National Product: US$1,920 million. *Exports:* 211 million zaires, chiefly copper, cobalt, diamonds, tin and other minerals, coffee, vegetable oils, rubber, manufactured goods. *Imports:* 281 million zaires, chiefly foodstuffs, manufactured goods, mineral products, machines and tools, transport equipment, chemical products. *Chief trading partners:* Belgium/Luxembourg, France, W. Germany, USA, Canada, UK, Italy, Netherlands. *Inflation rate:* 85.1%.

Prospects

Zaire's economy has been hard hit by the declining price of copper, the growing dependence on food imports and the high cost of petroleum. Zaire suffers from a chronic lack of foreign exchange.

Currency

Zaire (Z) = 100 makuta (K). £ = Z1.51; $ = Z0.80.

Travel

Visas required.

Vaccinations

Smallpox and yellow fever. Typhoid and paratyphoid vaccinations recommended.

Airlines

Aeroflot, Air Afrique, Air Zaire, Alitalia, Iberia, Lufthansa, Pan Am, Sabena, Swissair, TAP, UTA. *Flying times:* Copenhagen 15¾ hrs; London 12 hrs;

New York 17 hrs; Sydney 27 hrs. *Fares:* Copenhagen
F Dkr6,635 Y Dkr4,920; London F £494 Y £356.50;
New York F $1,084 Y $688; Sydney F A$1,236; Y A$860.
Airport to city: 25 kms (15 mls). *Taxi fare:* Z10.

Duty-free allowances
100 cigarettes *or* 50 cigars *or* ½ lb of tobacco;
1 bottle of spirits.

Local time
GMT+ 1 hr (Equateur and Bas Zaire provinces);
+2 hrs elsewhere.

Embassy phone numbers
Kinshasa: UK 23483.

Hotels
Kinshasa: Okapi, Memling, Inter-Continental, Regina.
Prices up to Z40 per night.

International banks
Barclays, Citibank, Grindlays.

Credit cards
All major credit cards.

Office hours
07.30–13.30 Mon–Fri, 07.30–12.00 Sat.

National holidays
1, 4 Jan, 1, 20 May, 24, 30 June, 1 Aug, 14, 27 Oct,
17, 24 Nov.

Voltage
220 volts AC.

Communications
Tel: Z2.50 per min. *Telex:* Z9.89 per 3 mins.
Airmail: 4–10 days. *Cable:* K48.40 for 7-word minimum.

Social customs
With one of the highest costs of living in Africa, visitors
should be prepared to spend Z50 per day on hotel and
food. The cost of entertaining is correspondingly high.
Kinshasa has a reputation for violence and care should
be taken when walking at night.

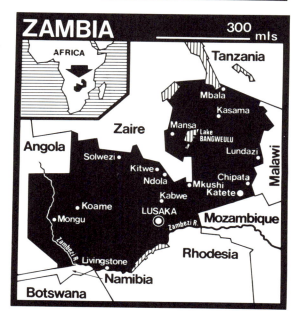

Area and population
752,614 sq kms (290,586 sq mls). Pop. 5 million.
Capital: Lusaka (400,000).
Chief cities: Kitwe/Nkana (270,000), Ndola (216,000),
Chingola/Nchanga (140,000), Mufulira (130,000),
Luanshya/Roan (116,000). *Airport:* Lusaka.

Climate
Tropical but pleasant because of high altitude. Lusaka
temperatures range from 4°C (39°F) to 39°C (100°F).
Clothing: Lightweight but sweaters needed in all but the
hot months, Sept–Nov.

People
98% Bantu, plus European and Asian minorities.
Religion: 45% Christian, 40% animist, plus a Moslem
minority. *Distribution:* Not available.

Language
English.

Economic background
Rapid post-war expansion has faltered many times
largely through fluctuations in the world price of copper,
Zambia's principal source of revenue, and the cost to
Zambia of supporting African nationalist movements.
Industrialisation has been slow and the agriculture does
not yet meet domestic requirements.

Trade
Gross National Product: 1,115 million kwacha.
Exports: 741 million kwacha, chiefly copper and other minerals. *Imports:* 346 million kwacha, chiefly machinery, transport equipment, chemicals, petroleum, food and live animals, textiles, iron and steel.
Chief trading partners: UK, South Africa, USA, Japan, W. Germany, Iran, Italy, France, Brazil, India.
Inflation rate: 21.3%.

Prospects
Zambia's economic future is still dependent upon copper, although the government is trying to diversify and has acquired 51% interest in most industrial undertakings.

Currency
Kwacha (K) = 100 ngwee. £ = K1.54; $ = K1.40 (fixed).

Travel
Visas not required.

Vaccinations
Smallpox.

Airlines
Alitalia, British Caledonian, Lufthansa, Zambia.
Flying times: Copenhagen (no direct flights) 14½ hrs; London 10 hrs; New York 20 hrs; Sydney 24 hrs.
Fares: Copenhagen F Dkr7,595 Y Dkr4,905; London F £561 Y £356.50; New York F $1,213 Y $802; Sydney F A$1,080 Y A$788.
Airport to city: 26 kms (16 mls). *Taxi fare:* K7.

Duty free allowances
200 cigarettes *or* 450 grammes of tobacco; 1 bottle of spirits.

Local time
GMT+2 hrs.

Embassy phone numbers
Lusaka: UK 51122.

Hotels
Lusaka: Inter-Continental, Ridgeway, Lusaka, Andrews. Prices up to K30 per night.

International banks
Barclays, Standard, Grindlays.

Credit cards
Not generally accepted.

Office hours
08.00–12.30 and 14.00–16.30 Mon–Fri.

National holidays
1 Jan, 15 Mar, Good Friday, 1, 25 May, 3, 4 July, 24 Oct, 25 Dec.

Voltage
220–380 volts AC.

Communications
Tel: K4.50 per 3 mins. *Telex:* K6.00 per 3 mins.
Airmail: 5–7 days. *Cable:* K3.00 per 15 words.

Social customs
Most entertaining is carried out in restaurants or hotels and in expatriate clubs.